New Actors and Alliances in Development

This collection brings together an interdisciplinary group of scholars exploring how development financing and interventions are being shaped by a wider and more complex platform of actors than usually considered in the existing literature. The contributors also trace a changing set of key relations and alliances in development – those between business and consumers; NGOs and celebrities; philanthropic organisations and the state; diaspora groups and transnational advocacy networks; ruling elites and productive capitalists; and between 'new donors' and developing country governments. Despite the diversity of these actors and alliances, several commonalities arise: they are often based on hybrid transnationalism and diffuse notions of development responsibility; rather than being new per se, they are newly being studied as engaging in practices that are now coming to be understood as 'development'; and they are limited in their ability to act as agents of development by their lack of accountability or pro-poor commitment. The articles in this collection point to images and representations as increasingly important in development 'branding' and suggest fruitful new ground for critical development studies.

This book was originally published as a special issue of *Third World Quarterly*.

Lisa Ann Richey is Professor of International Development Studies at the Department of Society and Globalisation, Roskilde University, Denmark. She is the author of *Brand Aid: Shopping Well to Save the World* with Stefano Ponte (2011), *Population Politics and Development: From the Policies to the Clinics* (2008), and the co-editor of "Women and Development: Rethinking Policy and Reconceptualizing Practice" (special issue of *Women's Studies Quarterly*, 2003). She works on new actors in international aid, citizenship and body politics, and gender and the global South.

Stefano Ponte is Professor of International Political Economy at the Department of Business and Politics, Copenhagen Business School, Denmark. He is interested in how the global economy is governed and in how developing countries and emerging economies fare in it. His work examines how standards, labels and certifications on social and environmental conditions of production shape agro-food value chains. In recent research, he has been examining the increasing importance of celebrities and branding in mobilising 'compassionate consumption' and new forms of corporate social responsibility that are 'distant and disengaged'. His most recent books are *Brand Aid: Shopping Well to Save the World* (co-author with Lisa Ann Richey, 2011) and *Governing through Standards: Origins, Drivers and Limitations* (co-editor with Peter Gibbon and Jakob Vestergaard, 2011).

Thirdworlds
Edited by Shahid Qadir, *University of London*

THIRDWORLDS will focus on the political economy, development and cultures of those parts of the world that have experienced the most political, social, and economic upheaval, and which have faced the greatest challenges of the postcolonial world under globalisation: poverty, displacement and diaspora, environmental degradation, human and civil rights abuses, war, hunger, and disease.

THIRDWORLDS serves as a signifier of oppositional emerging economies and cultures ranging from Africa, Asia, Latin America, Middle East, and even those 'Souths' within a larger perceived North, such as the U.S. South and Mediterranean Europe. The study of these otherwise disparate and discontinuous areas, known collectively as the Global South, demonstrates that as globalisation pervades the planet, the south, as a synonym for subalterity, also transcends geographical and ideological frontiers.

Terrorism and the Politics of Naming
Edited by Michael Bhatia

Reconstructing Post-Saddam Iraq
Edited by Sultan Barakat

From Nation-Building to State-Building
Edited by Mark T. Berger

Connecting Cultures
Edited by Emma Bainbridge

The Politics of Rights
Dilemmas for feminist praxis
Edited by Andrea Cornwall and Maxine Molyneux

The Long War – Insurgency, Counterinsurgency and Collapsing States
Edited by Mark T. Berger and Douglas A. Borer

Market-led Agrarian Reform
Edited by Saturnino M. Borras, Jr.

After the Third World?
Edited by Mark T. Berger

Developmental and Cultural Nationalisms
Edited by Radhika Desai

Globalisation and Migration
New issues, new politics
Edited by Ronaldo Munck

Domestic and International Perspectives on Kyrgyzstan's 'Tulip Revolution'
Motives, mobilizations and meanings
Edited by Sarah Cummings

War and Revolution in the Caucasus
Georgia Ablaze
Edited by Stephen F. Jones

War, Peace and Progress in the 21st Century
Development, Violence and Insecurities
Edited by Mark T. Berger and Heloise Weber

Renewing International Labour Studies
Edited by Marcus Taylor

Youth in the Former Soviet South
Everyday Lives between Experimentation and Regulation
Edited by Stefan B. Kirmse

Political Civility in the Middle East
Edited by Frédéric Volpi

The Transformation of Tajikistan
Sources of Statehood
Edited by John Heathershaw

Movement, Power and Place in Central Asia and Beyond
Contested Trajectories
Edited by Madeleine Reeves

People Power in an Era of Global Crisis
Rebellion, Resistance and Liberation
Edited by Barry K. Gills and Kevin Gray

EU Strategies on Governance Reform
Between Development and State-building
Edited by Wil Hout

Identity, Inequity and Inequality in India and China
Governing Difference
Edited by Ravinder Kaur and Ayo Wahlberg

The Personal and the Professional in Aid Work
Edited by Anne-Meike Fechter

Rising Powers and the Future of Global Governance
Edited by Kevin Gray and Craig N. Murphy

The Millennium Development Goals: Challenges, Prospects and Opportunities
Edited by Nana Poku

Development Perspectives from the Antipodes
Edited by Susanne Schech

Health, Drugs and Healing in Central Asia
Edited by Alisher Latypov

The Global Politics of Impairment and Disability
Processes and Embodiments
Edited by Karen Soldatic and Helen Meekosha

Negotiating Well-being in Central Asia
Edited by David W. Montgomery

New Actors and Alliances in Development
Edited by Lisa Ann Richey and Stefano Ponte

The Political Invention of Fragile States
The Power of Ideas
Edited by Sonja Grimm, Nicolas Lemay-Hebert and Olivier Nay

Global Land Grabs
History, Theory and Method
Edited by Marc Edelman, Carlos Oya and Saturnino M. Borras Jr.

The Afghan Conundrum: intervention, statebuilding and resistance
Edited by Jonathan Goodhand and Mark Desra

New Actors and Alliances in Development

Edited by
Lisa Ann Richey and Stefano Ponte

Routledge
Taylor & Francis Group
LONDON AND NEW YORK

First published 2015 by Routledge

2 Park Square, Milton Park, Abingdon, Oxon, OX14 4RN
605 Third Avenue, New York, NY 10017

Routledge is an imprint of the Taylor & Francis Group, an informa business

First issued in paperback 2020

British Library Cataloguing in Publication Data
A catalogue record for this book is available from the British Library

ISBN 13: 978-1-138-79975-2 (hbk)
ISBN 13: 978-0-367-73932-4 (pbk)

Typeset in Times New Roman
by RefineCatch Limited, Bungay, Suffolk

Publisher's Note
The publisher accepts responsibility for any inconsistencies that may have arisen during the conversion of this book from journal articles to book chapters, namely the possible inclusion of journal terminology.

Contents

Citation Information

The chapters in this book were originally published in *Third World Quarterly*, volume 35, issue 1 (February 2014). When citing this material, please use the original page numbering for each article, as follows:

Chapter 1
New actors and alliances in development
Lisa Ann Richey and Stefano Ponte
Third World Quarterly, volume 35, issue 1 (February 2014) pp. 1–21

Chapter 2
Business as a development agent: evidence of possibility and improbability
Michael Blowfield and Catherine S. Dolan
Third World Quarterly, volume 35, issue 1 (February 2014) pp. 22–42

Chapter 3
Trade, consumption and development alliances: the historical legacy of the Empire Marketing Board poster campaign
Uma Kothari
Third World Quarterly, volume 35, issue 1 (February 2014) pp. 43–64

Chapter 4
Buying into development? Brand Aid forms of cause-related marketing
Stefano Ponte and Lisa Ann Richey
Third World Quarterly, volume 35, issue 1 (February 2014) pp. 65–87

Chapter 5
The production and construction of celebrity advocacy in international development
Dan Brockington
Third World Quarterly, volume 35, issue 1 (February 2014) pp. 88–108

Chapter 6
The philanthropic state: market–state hybrids in the philanthrocapitalist turn
Linsey McGoey
Third World Quarterly, volume 35, issue 1 (February 2014) pp. 109–125

Chapter 7
The politics of industrial policy: ruling elites and their alliances
Lindsay Whitfield and Lars Buur
Third World Quarterly, volume 35, issue 1 (February 2014) pp. 126–144

Chapter 8
'Donors go home': non-traditional state actors and the creation of development space in Zambia
Peter Kragelund
Third World Quarterly, volume 35, issue 1 (February 2014) pp. 145–162

Chapter 9
Diasporas as development partners for peace? The alliance between the Darfuri diaspora and the Save Darfur Coalition
Alexandra Cosima Budabin
Third World Quarterly, volume 35, issue 1 (February 2014) pp. 163–180

Chapter 10
New development alternatives or business as usual with a new face? The transformative potential of new actors and alliances in development
Nicola Banks and David Hulme
Third World Quarterly, volume 35, issue 1 (February 2014) pp. 181–195

Please direct any queries you may have about the citations to clsuk.permissions@cengage.com

New actors and alliances in development

Lisa Ann Richey[a] and Stefano Ponte[b]

[a]*Department of Society and Globalisation, Roskilde University, Denmark;* [b]*Department of Business and Politics, Copenhagen Business School, Denmark*

'New actors and alliances in development' brings together an interdisciplinary group of scholars exploring how development financing and interventions are being shaped by a wider and more complex platform of actors than usually considered in the existing literature. The contributors also trace a changing set of key relations and alliances in development – those between business and consumers; NGOs and celebrities; philanthropic organisations and the state; diaspora groups and transnational advocacy networks; ruling elites and productive capitalists; and 'new donors' and developing country governments. Despite the diversity of these actors and alliances, several commonalities arise: they are often based on hybrid transnationalism and diffuse notions of development responsibility; rather than being new per se, they are newly being studied as practices that are now coming to be understood as 'development'; and they are limited in their ability to act as agents of development by their lack of accountability or pro-poor commitment. The articles in this collection point to images and representations as increasingly important in development 'branding' and suggest fruitful new ground for critical development studies.

Introduction

This special issue examines the rise of new actors and the configuration of new alliances in development financing and intervention. The nexus of international development has seen a marked shift from public aid to private flows, from primarily North–South relations to multiple polarities of emerging economies and non-Development Assistance Committee (DAC) donors to the ubiquitous debate on China in Africa. The contributions in this collection move beyond the analysis of 'traditional' actors – such as governments, international organisations and NGOs – to highlight how business, consumers, celebrities, philanthropic organisations, diaspora groups, elites and 'non-traditional' state actors work as 'legitimate' development actors to configure the ideas and financing for international development. In the process new spaces are shaped, both opened and constricted, by a changing set of relations and alliances – those between business and consumers; NGOs and celebrities; philanthropic organisations and the state; diaspora groups and transnational advocacy networks; ruling elites and productive capitalists; and 'new donors' and developing country governments.

Not all the actors and alliances examined in this special issue are strictly 'new', as they may have taken new configurations or be operating in new ways, but many have only recently been considered as the targets of study by international development scholars. As concluded by Corbridge in his seminal piece on the field: 'Development studies…cannot escape the dirty worlds of practical policy-making which lend it a reason for being, and which render it impotent, apolitical or supportive of a series of interventions that disempower and even infantilize "the poor"'.[1] Central concerns of the authors in this collection involve the agency of actors whose practices are constituting new forms of engagement in development processes, as well as the structures of constraint and opportunity that shape their engagement. Reflecting on the importance of history for contemporary development policy,[2] the articles included here strive to understand difference historically and to highlight critical changes, but also continuities. They document how these actors and alliances are arising, their potential and limitations, the subjectivities they (re)create and the reconfiguration of worthy recipients of 'help' they stimulate. In doing so, they stake a claim for understandings of development that are critically engaged, while remaining informed by theoretical, historical and empirical research.

Development scholars wedding critical theory insights with international development practices have argued that the perpetuation of universal notions of development are misguided, as these concepts are inextricably linked to the logics of global capitalism.[3] This 'development' apparatus was described in Ferguson's classic book as 'an anti-politics machine, depoliticizing everything it touches, everywhere whisking political realities out of sight, all the while performing, almost unnoticed, its own pre-eminently, political operation of expanding bureaucratic state power'.[4] At its most poignant critical development studies was able to meticulously document how development worked in specific instances to expand the tentacles of the great liberal villain: the state. Then, as neoliberalism and its accompanying structural adjustments emasculated state after state in both North and South, and replaced them with markets, development's critical impulse subsided. Since its peak in the 1990s critical development studies has become increasingly sidelined on ideological grounds, under what Schuurman terms 'neoliberal triumphalism',[5] and on practical grounds of policy irrelevance when critics began to conflate the cultural turn in development studies as constituting the entire scope of 'critical development'.

In its place little has emerged in the way of novel critical scholarship from within international development studies to move us beyond what Ferguson terms 'the politics of the "anti"'.[6] As Ferguson suggests, these politics of denunciation contribute little to understanding the contemporary practices of new actors and alliances involved in the geographical and technical areas that were once the purvey of states, NGOs and consultants acting on their behalf. International development is goal- and target-oriented; it tends to be preoccupied with the future and is thus largely unreflexive,[7] but critical development studies need not suffer the same weaknesses. Meanwhile, most understanding of contemporary development practices remains dominated by economists, who study the policies of states and international organisations with the aim of promoting economic growth, occasionally featuring poverty reduction in post-Millennium Development Goal (MDG) times.

We recognise that considerable knowledge can be gained from parsimonious explanations of when development happens through aid, by whom, and how,[8] yet there is a need to further expand the scope of aid actors to be studied and the disciplinary methods used to understand them. This, we argue, can contribute to critical development studies. This special issue responds to a call for scholarship that engages global issues comparatively but with a proper respect for the differences that place makes (for the legacies of geography and history).[9] Using qualitative methodologies, typically based on fieldwork and empirical data collection, the contributions provide cross-disciplinary and nuanced analyses of the practices of development relations in particular contexts. While this issue focuses on documenting 'new' contemporary actors, the inclusion of grounded historical work is essential in order to 'provide critical responses to the historical effects of colonialism and the persistence of colonial forms of power and knowledge into the present'.[10] The contributors were deliberately chosen for their potential contributions to development studies that are based on empirical, not ontological, critique. Critical development studies cannot decouple theory from policy-oriented development practice – to do so would be to neglect the moral responsibilities held by scholars from various geographical and disciplinary places, who document and argue for changes in policies and politics elsewhere.[11]

Important questions for critical development scholarship and engaged policy are raised by these grounded studies:

(1) Are there important common traits in these new actors and alliances?
(2) To what extent are they 'new' and what are the historical trajectories of current trends?
(3) How do these actors and alliances act as agents of development?
(4) How are new actors and alliances shaping images, communication and representations of development?
(5) What are the implications of these new actors and alliances for critical development studies?

The rest of this introduction will examine a set of key debates addressed by the contributions, as well as indicating some of the answers to the questions posed above. An epilogue to the issue by Banks and Hulme provides a complementary perspective on the articles through the lenses of poverty alleviation and inequality.[12] Through an analysis of the relative roles of state, market and civil society in 'new' development alliances, Banks and Hulme conclude that their transformative potential is limited by their disregard of civil society.

The development aid debate

In the contemporary context in which 'economic scarcity' refers not only to the 'lacking' economies in the developing world, but also to their 'donors', the place of new actors and alliances in development is becoming increasingly relevant. Even development issues of unprecedented popularity for international donor funding have been hit by the global economic crisis. For example, funding for HIV/AIDS fell by 10% in 2010 from the previous year, which is the first time that such funding has dropped in more than a decade (between 2002–08 spending on HIV/AIDS rose more than six fold).[13] Private funding is becoming more important in development as traditional sources are under stress from the effect of a shrinking tax base as a result of the contemporary economic crisis. This is reflected by a historical trend of shifting patterns of resource transfers from North to South. Sources of development financing that are outside official development assistance are growing and diversifying, and this is shaping the funding and agenda of development.

Official development assistance (ODA) is defined by the OECD and the IMF as:

> flows of official financing administered with the promotion of the economic development and welfare of developing countries as the main objective, and which are concessional in character with a grant element of at least 25 percent (using a fixed 10 percent rate of discount). By convention, ODA flows comprise contributions of donor government agencies, at all levels, to developing countries (bilateral ODA) and to multilateral institutions.[14]

ODA is becoming less important in relative terms for both the material and the symbolic meaning of development assistance. Between the 1960s and the late 2000s the public/private patterns of transferring resources from donor countries to development recipients reversed to the point that, in 2007, philanthropy from all OECD donor countries amounted to $49.1 billion, remittances to $14.6 billion and private investment to $325.4 billion: in sum, private flows represented 83% of all flows, while public ODA was only 17%.[15] This reversal in the ways of engaging between North and South, from public aid to private flows, has been acclaimed for providing better 'development'.[16] Yet we know very little about the actual development impact of private flows, even less than we know about the impact of ODA, which remains inadequate.[17] We do know that this material shift in how resources flow has been accompanied by a symbolic shift in the meaning of development, who should be involved and how.

The fundamental debates in development – whether they are conducted by scholars, practitioners, politicians, donor or recipient constituencies – have formed around one main question: 'does development assistance work?' Does a transfer of funding, material resources or services from donor to recipient bring about economic growth and employment, improved governing institutions, better health, education or political participation? Tierney and colleagues review the academic debates since 1990 over aid effectiveness, and summarise them into three schools of thought: 'more aid', 'problem aid' and 'conditional aid'.[18] Given the comprehensiveness of the recent review, we will not repeat the academic grounding for these positions here.[19] However, it is important to keep in mind that academically significant empirical evidence has been published to support contradictory positions. And, as summarised by Tierney et al, 'the roughly one million official development projects and activities over 66 years have brought little certainty about the scope, purposes or effects of development finance. Not for the public whose tax dollars fund aid; not for the foreign aid scholars; not for development practitioners; and certainly not for the recipients of foreign aid.'[20]

The polarisation in the more 'popular' debate on international aid has played along two main parallel axes:[21] (1) aid is bad because there is not enough of it – from this perspective, proposing more aid, a grand plan, or a big push, is needed to get the poorest countries out of their predicament (especially in Africa); and (2) aid is bad because there is too much of it going to the wrong places – this perspective argues that aid is wasted because of bad governance in recipient countries (especially in Africa) and proposes solutions ranging from less or even no aid to promoting more targeted and efficient aid. In practice, supporters of the big push theory (notably, Jeffrey Sachs) tend to underestimate the effect of corruption on aid delivery and growth. Conversely, supporters of smaller, more targeted aid (notably, William Easterly, Robert Calderisi and Dambisa Moyo), tend to place more importance on corruption and argue that less aid, not more, is needed, because more money will inevitably lead to more corruption.

While from a scholarly perspective these debates appear fatally simplistic, engaging in a 'chicken and egg'-type debate over whether increasing aid, or decreasing corruption in fact comes first, they are important for understanding the power of engaging new actors in development. The form of these debates, in which famous authors target audiences of 'non-experts', is significant, but perhaps more significant is the skilful management of affect, of individual desire to 'do good', in these texts. Thus, statements that are both simplified and generalised to the point of being indisputable (one cannot dispute arguments that are not based on evidential claims) form the engagement between a caring public and their international development possibilities. Yet what really counts in these debates in relation to the focus of this special issue is that both camps generate ideological support for the engagement of business as development agent (in ways that go beyond the generation of economic growth and employment), of consumers as donors, of celebrities as key communicators and mediators, and of private philanthropic foundations as rising agenda setters in sectors like health and agriculture in developing countries. The Director of the Hudson Institute argues that there is a dialectical relationship between new actors and alliances and traditional aid: 'Official aid is a minority shareholder in the growth and development of poor countries. As a result, government aid agencies are beginning to change their business models to leverage official aid with activities launched and run by businesses, foundations, charities, religious groups, universities, and even remittances being sent back to hometowns for community projects.'[22]

A new role for business in development

Both the 'aid is bad because it is too little' and the 'aid is bad because it is too much' camps seem to agree that government interventions and 'traditional' aid are not likely to hold the solution to either problem. However, business is held in favourable view by all sides in this debate. We briefly examine three linkages between business and development in this section: (1) development-oriented activities that fall under the broad agenda of Corporate Social Responsibility (CSR); (2) Cause-Related Marketing (CRM); and (3) Bottom of the Pyramid (BOP) business approaches to development.

Corporate Social Responsibility has operated under a number of names and definitions through its rapid practical proliferation and conceptual development.[23] Although the issue of the social responsibility of business can be found in writings that go back centuries, examination of business as a social actor has expanded considerably in the past half century or so.[24] The European Commission defines CSR as 'a concept whereby companies integrate social and environmental concerns in their business operations and in their interaction with their stakeholders on a voluntary basis'.[25] But other definitions of CSR expand responsibility to cover society as a whole, not just the company's immediate stakeholders. Alongside a large literature in business studies, a thriving reflective literature on the role of CSR in international development has also emerged. Much of it concurs that not enough is known on the actual impact of CSR activities in developing countries,[26] or about the complicated relationships linking CSR and desirable developmental outcomes, particularly in Africa.[27] It also argues that CSR often actually distracts attention from the root causes of poverty and environmental destruction.[28] Related to CSR, an equally large literature has examined whether sustainability certifications promote positive outcomes for beneficiaries in developing countries, finding mixed results.[29] But, for all their limitations, at least CSR and sustainability certifications seek – to different degrees – to improve production and trade conditions for Southern producers and other actors who bring a product to the (Northern) market.

In contrast, the link between the social and environmental conditions of production and beneficiaries is dissolved in Cause-Related Marketing initiatives. In CRM the marketing of a brand, company, product or service is tied directly to a cause (including international development causes), with a proportion of the sales going to support the cause. These 'transactional programmes' are classic exchange-based donations, where a corporation agrees to give a specified share of the proceeds for every unit sold.[30] CRM can be used for meeting overarching business goals (including the drive for profits), and strengthening brand reputation and employee loyalty, aiding recruitment and retention.[31] CRM also shifts consumer attitudes, as companies become represented as 'yearning to connect to people and things that will give meaning to their lives'.[32] In the process, business improves brand reputation and sales, without needing to reconsider any of its actual operations and practices.[33]

The most orthodox interpretation of the 'business can solve development problems' argument comes from Bottom of the Pyramid approaches, articulated by Prahalad.[34] In these approaches the key to helping the poor to help themselves is to convince business that BOP markets are important. Business is seen as the key solution in addressing poverty because it can 'create opportunities for the poor by offering them choices and encouraging self-esteem'.[35] Prahalad criticises the traditional approach used to create the capacity for poor people to become consumers – providing products or services for free. He seeks to encourage consumption in BOP markets by making unit packages small and more affordable (because of poor people's unpredictable income flows), and by using new purchase schemes – such as providing credit to consumers in new ways. Not only is there money at the BOP, and profit-making potential, but these markets are also brand conscious. Similarly to CRM, BOP approaches do not address the conditions of inequality and/or poverty that are responsible for their inability to consume in the first place. The difference is that in BOP approaches the focus is on consumers in the South; in CRM approaches the focus is on consumers in the North. In both, the production and trade relations embedded in consumer products disappear.

Contribution to this theme of the articles in this issue

Two articles in this collection specifically focus on the changing role of business in development. Blowfield and Dolan's article provides a comprehensive discussion of how the conceptualisation of business in development has changed over time and where it stands now that poverty has been redefined as a condition amenable to market intervention. They show that business has long been recognised as a key actor in economic development through its traditional roles in investment, production, trade and retail. These activities contribute to job creation, the supply of goods and services, and the funding of social services though taxation. In this classic role as 'development tool', business is active but not responsible for development outcomes. Blowfield and Dolan argue, however, that business is increasingly showing interest not only in developing countries as sites of investment, production, trade or distribution, but in the development of these countries as well. This is often the result of self-interest, but one that can involve 'mutual interest between companies and the poor or otherwise marginalized'.[36] They examine these processes by drawing from a number of studies of what they call 'bottom billion capitalism' initiatives, including that of Fairtrade in tea and flowers in Kenya, and of BOP initiatives such as the CARE Bangladesh Rural Sales Programme (RSP) and Avon South Africa.

'Bottom billion capitalism' according to Blowfield and Dolan is a 'model of inclusive business that recasts poverty as a site of opportunity for both business and the poor', underpinned by the principle that markets can work for the poor. The term is the merging of two other terms coined by Collier[37] – focusing on the population of poor 'bottom billion' countries stuck in poverty traps – and by Prahalad[38] – denoting the aforementioned BOP four billion people earning less than two dollars a day. Blowfield and Dolan highlight that business is involved in a wide range of 'bottom billion capitalism' initiatives not only in terms of engaging with the bottom billions but also in casting them as 'clients', 'partners' and 'entrepreneurs', shifting the discourse of the poor from beneficiaries of aid to active market actors.[39] They conclude critically that, to be a true 'development agent', rather than simply a development actor or tool, business also needs to give primacy to the benefits for the poor and marginalised and to strive to address poverty and marginalisation. Thus, business would be required to become accountable to developing country citizens in ways it currently is not.

McGoey's article shows that business is affecting development-related processes and institutions not only directly, but also by exporting its management models to the non-profit and philanthropic sectors. She draws parallels between the contemporary philanthrocapitalists such as Bill Gates and early 20th-century philanthropists such as Rockefeller and Ford to suggest that the contemporary phase 'is simultaneously far less novel and more novel than proponents suggest'. She points out that shaping philanthropic organisations to operate like business was actually John D. Rockefeller's original idea – what is new about it is 'the unprecedented scale of philanthropic spending'.

McGoey's analysis draws on three case studies based on a wealth of primary interview material on: (1) governmental grants to profitable companies such as Vodafone (for the establishment of M-Pesa, a system first developed in Kenya to allow people to pay bills through text messaging); (2) increased governmental support for 'impact investing' (investment in projects providing environmental and social benefits with the expectation of 'market-rate' financial returns); and (3) the relative roles of the Gates Foundation and of governments in promoting and financing the first Advanced-Market Commitment (AMC) to encourage the development of drugs and vaccines for underfunded diseases.

Using theory from the economists Lazonick and Mazzucato on the 'risk–reward nexus', McGoey shows that, just as government interventions were key to the development of global markets in the 19th and 20th centuries, state support remains essential to the rise of contemporary philanthrocapitalists. 'Governments are, somewhat ironically, instrumental to the success of philanthropic movements strengthened by proclaiming the ineptitude and waning influence of government policies…[they] are extending themselves in new directions in a semblance of surrendering control to private entities that are, in many ways, *less* entrepreneurial than governments themselves'. She concludes that philanthrocapitalists have helped to perpetuate the belief that the private sector is filling public sector gaps in development financing, while in reality it is often governments that subsidise the philanthrocapitalists.

Consumers and celebrities as development actors

Recasting the role of business in development is accompanied by the increasing engagement of consumers and celebrities as development actors. 'Ethical consumers are those whose decisions about what to consume (the "consumption" part) are shaped by their assessment of the moral nature of that context (the "ethical" part)'.[40] There has been increasing interest in, and debate on, various forms of ethical and political consumption over the past two decades. A rich literature has fine-tuned the links between the ethics and the politics of consumption,[41] examined the ethics of 'everyday consumption',[42] or argued that ethical consumption is a dangerous myth.[43] One of the important aspects emerging from this literature is the fact that the possibility of 'consuming ethically' is often based on the consumption of branded products, despite the 'No Logo' battle cry of the anti-globalisation movement. In other words, it is brands' vulnerability to ethical concerns that opens up space for consumer action. But because branded companies seek to minimise such vulnerability, they are also developing initiatives (such as CRM) that detach ethical concerns from the products themselves, and relocate them instead to the ethics of supporting a development cause.

A culture of consumption promotes freedom of choice and consumer sovereignty, and strives to meet needs that are in principle unlimited and insatiable.[44] The consumption of signs and experiences can be the vehicle for the mobilisation of 'meaning', belonging to a 'community', political action and development intervention. Citizen-consumers are increasingly seen as exercising their rights to demand developmental outcomes via individual acts of 'consumption for a cause'. But while consumer agency may take the form of collective action through campaigns and consumer organisations' pressure, the focus of these campaigns is often on the individual act of consumption of branded products. As the value of goods depends increasingly on their 'sign' rather than on their functional or economic value, advertising, marketing and branding become central functions on their own, not subordinate to production.[45] In many cases this kind of consumption is mobilised by celebrities through the management of affect. Consumption can then delineate values and form a partial basis for creating a community that 'cares' for development.

The state-of-the-art understanding of ethical and political consumption rests on the core belief that reconnecting the sites of consumption with those of production will enable a fairer distribution of value along the chains, potentially driven by 'fair trade' and 'ethical consumption' purchases. But while this focus on *products* must not be neglected, it should be accompanied by an understanding of the *causes* (including development) that are increasingly 'sold' together with the products, and of the *celebrities* who translate and embody an ethical leadership role in the management of consumers' desire to do good while shopping well.

From the 'movie star on the famine stage'[46] to the 'AIDS heroes' of China,[47] the past decade has seen a proliferation of celebrities appearing in productions of transnational caring.[48] As celebrities become more relevant, other forms of expertise have followed the celebrity modality, and public figures, academics and business leaders have become 'celebritised' as well. Celebrities have become the faces of doing good, of credibility and of believability. For example, Bono is popular as a rock star and his commitment to development advocacy over time has earned him legitimacy as an expert.[49] This distinguishes some celebrities as particularly effective in cause work from other stars who simply engage in 'do gooding'.[50] Aid celebrities have thus become trusted advisors on issues of health, poverty, the environment or climate change in ways that extend beyond the actual scope of their research or practitioner experience, and their presence is invoked to stand in for important beliefs and social values.[51] In other words, celebrities have become a way of mediating between proximity and distance in the global as well as the specific context.

Contribution to this theme of the articles in this issue

Three articles examine the role of consumers and/or of celebrities in development. Kothari's article shows that linking Third World producers and Western consumers through public campaigns, charity advertising and media promotion is deeply rooted in the history of Empire. Through her analysis of the (British) Empire Marketing Board poster campaign of 1926–33 she argues that popular representations of the 'exotic other' sought to reorder relations between producers and consumers in ways that are not too dissimilar from contemporary campaigns.[52] Kothari shows that it is important to reflect on the historical legacy of the current wave of 'ethical consumption' but without falling into a historically deterministic trap. What is more important is that we should pay specific attention to how the instrumental use of images and representations in these campaigns actually influences development policies, discourses and practices. Kothari shows, literally, through the images of the Empire Marketing

Board, how caring was never considered a relation between equals. Development is sold as yet another product quality trait and contemporary initiatives that use products to link domestic and overseas histories draw on deep imperial roots.

Ponte and Richey's article covers the role of both consumers and celebrities in development, and their new alliance. They formalise a conceptual model for what they have termed 'Brand Aid', the intersection of international development causes, branded products and celebrities – placing it in the context of an institutional framework. Ponte and Richey use this model as a guide to conduct a systematic empirical analysis of contemporary Brand Aid initiatives, including three in-depth case studies of General Mills' 'Win One Give One' campaign, TOMS shoes and Product (RED). They highlight how, in Brand Aid initiatives, celebritised multi-media imaginaries of development are used to sell products to Northern consumers. Development outcomes themselves become so imbued with symbolic and 'ethical' value that they now are used to market consumer goods to Northern buyers, often with celebrities being part of creating 'caring brands' that sell development. Commodities are then sold as the means to achieving development for recipients and good feelings for consumers simultaneously. In the process 'development' becomes ontologically ingrained as 'having the right things'. In Brand Aid initiatives consumers can save distant others who have no connection with the product on sale. Instead of striving to improve production and trade conditions (as in fair trade or other sustainability initiatives), Brand Aid engages the work of a 'story factory', often generated with or through celebrities, producing emotional 'truths' about development and consumer engagement that make development appear simplified and manageable.

Brockington's article argues that our understanding of celebrity and development still lacks an account of how the celebrity industry and the development sector have become intertwined, and a better understanding of the political economy of these relationships. Brockington argues that celebrity in development is important not only because it mediates between Northern consumers and the receivers of 'help', but also because it facilitates access to elites. On the basis of material drawn from over 100 interviews with employees of different NGOs, journalists and agents, managers and public relations staff (mostly in the USA and UK), and from an analysis of articles in the major UK newspapers, Brockington chronicles in detail the emergence of a celebrity–charity–corporate complex as a site of negotiation, clash and overlap of interests, and the emergence of new professional figures managing the celebrity–charity interface. He shows that relations between the development sector and celebrity industries have become more organised and systematic in the past decade, and that, as a consequence, some development NGOs now have dedicated staff who are deeply engaged with agents, publicists, managers and celebrities to build effective relationships. Finally, he shows that the celebrity–charity–corporate complex is also attractive to corporate sponsors because of the valuable publicity it can facilitate, and because of 'the personal pleasure the company of the famous affords'. Brockington concludes that celebrities have become an important set of development actors, and that their presence and influence needs to be better understood by development studies scholars in future work.

State actors, elites and transnational networks

The role of the state, while pushed out of fashion in development theory by 'neoliberal triumphalism',[53] is never absent from understandings of what development might mean in practice and what actors and alliances are necessary to drive it. Thus, development does not emerge spontaneously from the interplay of market forces, but rather requires concerted state interventions. Even in contexts of increasing transnationalism, states are necessary to ensure macroeconomic stability and provide infrastructure, utilities and selective industrial policies. In this collection Whitfield and Buur argue that 'few non-traditional export success stories from anywhere around the world occurred without the help of industrial policies of some sort, such as assisting the absorption and learning of new technologies, export subsidies, and preferential tariff arrangements'.[54] There is increasing agreement on the necessity of industrial policy and the importance of the state, although the details of how this should take place in varying contexts continue to be debated.[55] At the centre of many debates on state actors and elites in development we find the resurgence of African 'exceptionalism'. There is a highly sceptical literature on the capacity of African states to effectively engage as development actors.[56] Specifically it is argued that African states lack capacity because of the prevalence of neo-patrimonial politics and bad political leadership. Within African states ruling elites have often been seen as sources of underdevelopment because they exploit public resources for personal gain and narrow elite or ethnic interests.[57] Structural adjustment programmes sought to undo these alliances, by taking away many of the tools of the state in order to support the emergence, consolidation or expansion of a group of domestic capitalists. Yet, in the era of privatised international development efforts, these very elites, and their relations to industry and the state, are being reconsidered.

The power politics that play into elite alliances and state capacity for development are not limited to those which are geographically bound within developing countries. Transnational networks are increasingly studied for the ways in which they operate a 'boomerang' set of linkages initiated by domestic organisations that 'bypass their state and directly search out international allies to try to bring pressure on their states from outside'.[58] Keck and Sikkink argue that the linkages between international allies and the victim or target group are mutually beneficial, providing access, leverage and money in exchange for credibility for the benefactors as struggling with, not only for, their Southern partners.[59] However, such 'boomerang politics' for development involve extensive complications around resource control and the management of the representation of the development 'problem', termed 'information politics'. As these transnational actors gain in legitimacy on the basis of their perceived access to accurate but often-overlooked information, they enjoy more public trust than states, businesses and the media.[60]

Contribution to this theme of the articles in this issue

In addition to McGoey's intervention already summarised above, three articles in this collection examine state actors, elites and transnational networks and their new, returning and/or reconfigured role in development. Whitfield and Buur's article examines the resurgence of an alliance that has always been central to the process of economic development – that between ruling elites and domestic productive capitalists. These alliances are now experiencing heightened attention from scholars and policy makers with the current revival of debates around industrial policy in developing countries. Whitfield and Buur draw from in-depth and fieldwork-based case studies of the evolution of two successful productive sectors in Africa (sugar in Mozambique and cocoa in Ghana), carried out by the authors as part of the larger research programme 'Elites, Production and Poverty'. They highlight the conditions under which alliances between ruling elites and domestic productive capitalists occur, their specific characteristics and their outcomes. With careful attention to historical and contextual specificity, Whitfield and Buur show that close relations between ruling elites and capitalists are not necessarily 'crony' or unproductive. Under certain conditions, they can lead to positive development outcomes. This happens when the following conditions are met: there are mutual interests between ruling elites and productive capitalists; factional demands within the ruling coalition can be managed in order to create 'pockets of efficiency' in the bureaucracy; and state bureaucrats engage in institutionalised relations with industry actors under a framework providing clear incentives for increasing productivity or expanding an industry. However, Whitfield and Buur also provide a cautionary note – alliances can change with transformations in the configuration of political power or the power of capitalists, and thus their developmental outcomes are far from assured in the long term.

Kragelund's article highlights how non-traditional state actors (emerging donor countries such as China, India and Brazil) contribute to creating 'developmental space' in policy making in Africa. He points out that, while some of these actors have been active in Africa for decades (China in particular), their renewed involvement and the specific modality of this involvement signals the weakening of an old alliance (between African states and DAC donors) and the strengthening of a new one. Kragelund applies Harrison's concept of the 'sovereign frontier'[61] to move us 'beyond the traditional discussion of whether or not African states are indeed sovereign…to a discussion of how a variety of domestic and international actors interact to shape the (changing) development space'. Using his fieldwork-based case study in Zambia, Kragelund examines the role of China, India and Brazil in financing development activities and in promoting alternative development models. He argues that it is not the size of financial flows from these emerging donors that counts – these are still small compared to those from DAC countries. What is most important is that new donors are providing alternative models of development that combine purposive state intervention with market-based economic growth and integration into world markets, while maintaining a high degree of national control. He shows that the Zambian state is taking its first steps in strengthening its 'sovereign frontier' of development, but also that the extent of this movement is still small and development outcomes remain far from assured.

Budabin's article examines the alliance between diaspora groups and transnational advocacy networks. Through her analysis of primary data documenting the relations between the Darfuri diaspora in the USA and the Save Darfur Coalition (an advocacy NGO embedded in a transnational network), Budabin shows that the uneven constitution of alliances between unequally resourced actors limits the abilities of groups like the Darfuri diaspora to act as development agents. The article emphasises that looking simultaneously at the home and host country contexts is key in understanding the strength and viability of transnational alliances. While diaspora groups can provide the emotional 'pull' in the host country for improved visibility, lack of strong ties in the home country, political cleavages and the short-termism of advocacy networks can limit the longer-term development potential of these alliances and lead to an exclusive focus on humanitarian aid. Nevertheless, transnational linkages remain important for diasporas because of their need to align with better-resourced groups that provide necessary financing, communications skills and political access in the host country. For the NGOs engaging in transnational advocacy networks with diaspora groups provides them with an advantage in the 'information politics' of negotiating between legitimate representation of 'others' and policy 'asks' on their behalf.

Conclusion

The contributions to this special issue analyse the rise of new actors, the transformation of old actors and the configuration of new alliances in development. In previous sections we have highlighted the contribution these articles offer in relation to understanding: the new role of business in development; the involvement of consumers and celebrities as development actors; and the complex interactions between state actors, elites and transnational networks. In this last section we provide some answers to the questions raised in the introductory section and suggest future directions for critical development studies.

Are there important common traits in these new actors and alliances?

The articles in this collection demonstrate two main commonalities: hybrid transnationalism and diffuse notions of development responsibility. First, hybrid transnationalism is seen across the studies as resulting from the geopolitical situatedness of the resources generated to support the new actors and alliances in development: funds from global philanthropists, advocacy networks, and development-minded consumers are raised to support causes that are sold as being 'above politics'. This hybrid transnationalism means that development has not become firmly cosmopolitan in ways that would oblige equivalences between distant strangers and close kin and would thus also necessitate struggles against global inequality, in the midst of all the 'helping'. Neither is development geopolitically configured along the traditional lines of DAC donors, bilaterals and multilaterals, or NGOs and states. Many of the new actors and alliances here fall clearly in between; they are neither local nor global – but instead hybrid transnationals.

Second, the new actors and alliances explored in these contributions suggest that most are active as development tools – active, but not responsible for development – and that a diffuse notion of responsibility characterises the relationships between them. As illustrated by Blowfield and Dolan in this issue,[62] the new actors and alliances are 'no more responsible for development outcomes than a hammer is responsible for the carpenter's thumb'. Yet the articles here suggest that a clearer understanding of development responsibility could be better achieved through an empirical analysis of the mechanisms that are producing these new alliances between actors and between processes of development and their supposed beneficiaries.

To what extent are these actors and alliances 'new' and what are the historical trajectories of current trends?

As might be anticipated, nothing we see in contemporary development practices is without specific or combined historical precedent. Most explicitly Kothari shows how the visualisations of self and state created possibilities of empire in ways analogous to how development relations are depicted as a shared struggle for good commodity provision and consumption.[63] Whitfield and Buur demonstrate how ruling elites and domestic productive capitalist relations seen in Mozambique and Ghana have historical precedents in the sugar plantations and smallholder cocoa farms, and that these continue to present challenges for contemporary development.[64] Alliances between new aid actors (China, India and Brazil) and the Zambian state are formed upon the fraught history of that country's domination by its traditional donors and lenders, as shown by Kragelund.[65] And while the scale of contemporary philanthrocapitalism may appear extreme, McGoey traces this to the 19th century development of international markets, with the state remaining central, even though concealed by the relations of 'new' philanthropy.[66] In sum, these actors and alliances are not new *per se*, but they are newly being studied by development studies scholars as practices that are now coming to be understood as an important part of the rubric of what constitutes 'development.'

How do these actors and alliances act as agents of development?

In the positioning of agency in development, we see a new twist in which intentionality or motivation is less important than engagement of one's own (individual or corporate) resources in the risky activity of development. For example, in Blowfield and Dolan's definition of what makes a development agent – willingness to deploy one's assets for development activity, not whether or not there is a profit motive – should be central. In Ponte and Richey's examination of Brand Aid, development's value as a product feature is not lessened by consumer commitment to conspicuous consumption or by businesses capitalisation on the affective need to 'help'. In Brockington's analysis the investment of celebrities' time and publicity capital suggests that they too may be legitimate development agents, and that development causes are also risky endeavours for the profile of an A-list celebrity. Bill Gates (in McGoey's contribution), 'non-traditional state actors' (in Kragelund's), and the Darfuri Diaspora (in Budabin's) are all investing their own assets for developmental activity, and thus meet one of the criteria for constituting them as development agents. However, Blowfield and Dolan's other criteria for defining agency in development – pro-poor primacy and accountability – are much more difficult to meet for many of the development actors examined here.

How are new actors and alliances shaping images, communications and representations of development?

The power of storytelling, including visual representation, has been largely neglected by development scholars.[67] Yet the power of international development representations is not simply a material power that stems from the way that alliances engage business, consumers and other development actors. The impact is also based in images – pictures of the world. Northern shoppers are animated by a confident aid celebrity Bono, who speaks from American television screens claiming: 'We can be the generation that ends extreme poverty. This is our moment to show what we're about.' International development's expansion to include new actors among the so-called 'generation-net' calls for critical consideration of communication, including from the perspective of those affected by it.[68] Drawing on the emotional in political life and on the affective politics of development, some new actors, like celebrities, shape the form of representation of international development and constructions of identity that are always co-constituted through imaginaries of 'us' and 'them'[69] – often with imperial, racist and religious legacies.[70]

Several contributions in this collection speak to these issues. Budabin lends weight to the argument that transnational networks, with their presumptions of legitimacy,[71] rely to a large extent on their ability to furnish compelling stories.[72] As also argued by Keck and Sikkink, the information flows from and around these alliances 'provide not only facts, but testimony – stories told by people whose lives have been affected'.[73] Brockington, however, suggests that celebrity testimonies may be even more important than those of the affected: 'When public figures handle interviews they can speak with more conviction and ease, they are able to tell stories of people they have met, adding much more colour'.[74]

Kothari's and Ponte and Richey's contributions support the argument that 'suffering strangers' and '"iconic figures" of misfortune' are produced, reproduced, formed and transformed according to the stories that need to be told to garner public support.[75] Thus, controversially, it appears that, as international development has become more democratic, including more non-expert voices, it is also becoming increasingly reliant on the silencing of complexity, conflict and on-the-ground realities of development interventions. Through the creation of representational consensus, with the same stories and pictures circulated in various forms of expert and popular media, notions of under-development become popularised via 'reductive repetition',[76] and diverse subjectivities are placed together into the 'suffering slot' that has replaced the 'savage' as the privileged object of cross-cultural attention.[77] Ponte and Richey push this argument even further, arguing that Brand Aid initiatives not only use imaginaries of development to sell products to Northern consumers, but also engage in the work of a 'story factory' – producing truths about international development and consumer engagement that make development appear simplified, manageable and marketable.[78] As Budabin (this issue) explains, in the policy space possible for some diaspora groups and not others, 'not everyone is a good speaker', and as Ponte and Richey illustrate, those whose stories do not compel, do not sell. This has relevant implications for both the performances and the politics of development.

What are the implications of these new actors and alliances for critical development studies?

The articles in this special issue indicate important directions for research in critical development studies by staking a middle ground between post-development/anti-development culturalism and materialist political economy critiques of development as exploitation. First, they suggest that critical research does not have to remain disengaged from development practices – as much of the earlier post-development or anti-development theory had suggested. Critiquing practices and their justificatory premises through Corbridge's provision of Weber's 'inconvenient facts' can provide a better understanding of the implications of the mechanisms through which development works.[79] These practices may well oppress people, but they may also provide the master's tools necessary for taking down his house (to reverse paraphrase Audre Lorde).[80] Second, these contributions point to fruitful new areas for studying international development in its hybrid transnational nature – in addition to the ongoing relationships between international organisations, states and NGOs. Research should look outside the usual scope of development confined by ODA to find out what practices are taking place, what they might mean, and how they might intersect with the practices we conventionally study as international development.

Third, the articles here suggest that development studies could be better understood as part of the intellectual scope of global studies: because the geographical scope of development actors and its recipients is increasingly less confined to 'developing countries'; and because hybrid transnational actors and alliances cross boundaries between state, international organisations and NGOs.[81] This is not a call for less attention to empirical data collection, including fieldwork in developing country sites, but instead a reading of these new actors and alliances through the lens of the global. Fourth, critical development studies must be willing to engage both the material and the representational sides of development interventions. Questions raised around representations of development relate quite directly to the political economy of the 'asks' that form policy and practices in these new alliances and roles of new actors. Who can legitimately ask for what, for whom and from whom? Critical development scholars should bring empirical evidence to bear on political, not merely technical, debates around development, new actors and alliances and changing configurations of North–South relations. A political economy of interests, not an ideological blindness built on the assumptions of altruism, would better guide understandings of development actors and alliances. At the same time the symbolic value of the performance of altruism must be taken into the development calculus.

Acknowledgements

The authors would like to thank the participants in the EADI/DSA conference panel on 'New actors and alliances in development', University of York, 20 September 2011 and Jan Nederveen Pieterse for feedback on this introduction.

Notes on Contributors

Lisa Ann Richey is Professor of International Development Studies in the Department of Society and Globalisation, Roskilde University. She is the author of *Brand Aid: Shopping Well to Save the World* with Stefano Ponte (2011) and *Population Politics and Development: From the Policies to the Clinics* (2008), and the co-editor of "Women and Development: Rethinking Policy and Reconceptualizing Practice" with Frances Vavrus (special issue of *Women's Studies Quarterly*, 2003). She works on new actors in international aid, citizenship and body politics, and gender and the global South.

Stefano Ponte is Professor of International Political Economy at Copenhagen Business School. He is interested in how the global economy is governed and in how developing countries and emerging economies fare in it. In recent research, he has been examining the increasing importance of celebrities and branding in mobilising 'compassionate consumption' and new forms of corporate social responsibility that are 'distant and disengaged'. His most recent books are *Brand Aid: Shopping Well to Save the World* (with Lisa Ann Richey, 2011) and *Governing through Standards: Origins, Drivers and Limitations* (with Peter Gibbon and Jakob Vestergaard, 2011).

Notes

1. Corbridge, "The (Im)possibility of Development Studies," 202.
2. Woolcock et al., "How and Why does History Matter?"
3. See Crush, *Power of Development*; Escobar, *Encountering Development*; Nederveen Pieterse, *Development Theory*; Sachs, *The Development Dictionary*; and Sylvester, "Development and Postcolonial Studies".
4. Ferguson, *The Anti-Politics Machine*, xv.
5. Schuurman, "Critical Development Theory."
6. Ferguson, The Uses of Neoliberalism.
7. Kothari, "Critiquing 'Race' and Racism," 67.
8. See, inter alia, Tierney et al., "More Dollars than Sense."
9. See Corbridge, "The (Im)possibility of Development Studies."
10. Kothari, "Commentary", 69.
11. See Corbridge, "The (Im)possibility of Development Studies."
12. Banks and Hulme "New Development Alternatives."
13. "Investing Wisely in HIV/AIDS." *Lancet Infectious Diseases* 12, no. 1 (2012): 1. http://www.thelancet.com/journals/laninf/article/PIIS1473-3099(11)70357-7/fulltext?rss=yes.
14. http://stats.oecd.org/glossary/detail.asp?ID=6043; and IMF, *External Debt Statistics*.
15. Adelman, "Global Philanthropy and Remittances," 27
16. Ibid.
17. Tierney et al., "More Dollars than Sense."
18. Ibid., 1893–1894.
19. For detailed literature reviews, see also Hansen and Tarp, "Aid Effectiveness Disputed"; and Tarp, *Foreign Aid and Development*; Riddell, *Does Foreign Aid Really Work?*
20. Tierney et al., "More Dollars than Sense," 1891.
21. See, inter alia, Sachs, *The End of Poverty*; Calderisi, *The Trouble with Africa*; Easterly, *The White Man's Burden*; and Moyo, *Dead Aid*.
22. Adelman, "Global Philanthropy and Remittances," 24.
23. Wartick and Cochran, "The Evolution of the Corporate Social Performance Model."
24. Carroll, "Corporate Social Responsibility."
25. See http://ec.europa.eu/.
26. Blowfield, "Reasons to be Cheerful?" Newell and Frynas, "Beyond CSR?"
27. Idemudia, "Corporate Social Responsibility and Developing Countries."
28. Newell, "CSR and the Limits of Capital."
29. Among many others, see Gibbon et al., *Global Agro-food Trade and Standards*.
30. Berglind and Nakata, "Cause-related Marketing."
31. King, *Pink Ribbons, Inc.*, 9.
32. Ibid., 11.
33. Richey and Ponte, *Brand Aid*.
34. Prahalad, *The Fortune at the Bottom of the Pyramid*.

35. Ibid., 5.
36. Ibid.
37. Collier, *The Bottom Billion.*
38. Prahalad, *The Fortune at the Bottom of the Pyramid.*
39. Ponte and Richey, "Buying into Development," show that, while in BOP initiatives the poor are being cast as active market actors, in Brand Aid 'deserving others' are used as marketing tools to sell products to Western consumers. The 'poor', 'African' 'women and children' in these initiatives are passive receivers, who have no agency.
40. Carrier, "Introduction," 1.
41. Clarke et al., "Globalising the Consumer"; Clarke, "From Ethical Consumerism to Political Consumption"; Barnett et al., *Globalizing Responsibility*; and Carrier and Luetchford, *Ethical Consumption.*
42. Miller, *The Dialectics of Shopping*; Barnett et al., "Consuming Ethics."
43. Devinney et al., *The Myth of the Ethical Consumer.*
44. Slater, *Consumer Culture and Modernity.*
45. Bandelj and Wherry, *The Cultural Wealth of Nations.*
46. de Waal, "The Humanitarian Carnival."
47. Hood, "Celebrity Philanthropy."
48. See also Brockington, *Celebrity and the Environment.*
49. Cooper, "Beyond One Image Fits All."
50. See Boykoff and Goodman, "Conspicuous Redemption"; Goodman and Barnes, "Star/Poverty Space"; and Littler, "'I Feel Your Pain'".
51. See Richey and Ponte, *Brand Aid.*
52. See also Trentmann, "An Introduction."
53. Schuurman, "Critical Development Theory."
54. See also Rodrik, *One Economics, Many Recipes.*
55. See Cimoli et al., *Industrial Policy and Development*; and Lin, *New Structural Economics.*
56. Noman and Stiglitz, *Good Growth and Governance in Africa.*
57. See, for example, Mills, *Why Africa is Poor*; Sandbrook and Barker, *The Politics of Africa's Economic Stagnation*; and van de Walle, *African Economies and the Politics of Permanent Crisis.*
58. Keck and Sikkink, *Activists beyond Borders*, 12.
59. Ibid.
60. Wade, "Accountability Gone Wrong", 26.
61. Harrison, "Debt, Development and Intervention in Africa."
62. Blowfield and Dolan, "Business as a Development Agent."
63. Khotari, "Trade, Consumption and Development Alliances."
64. Whitfield and Buur, "The Politics of Industrial Policy."
65. Kragelund, "'Donors Go Back Home'."
66. McGoey, "The Philanthropic State."
67. For notable exceptions, see Smith and Yanacopulos, "Special Issue: The Public Faces of Development"; and Nair, "Governance, Representation and International Aid."
68. See Alhassan and Chakravartty, "Postcolonial Media Policy", for a critical review.
69. See Hall, "The West and the Rest"; and Crush, *Power of Development.*
70. See Kapoor, *Celebrity Humanitarianism*; Harrison, "Campaign Africa"; Nederveen Pieterse, *White on Black*; Kothari, "Commentary"; and Richey and Ponte, *Brand Aid.*
71. Wade, "Accountability Gone Wrong".
72. Budabin, "Diasporas".
73. Keck and Sikkink, *Activists beyond Borders*, 19.
74. Brockington, "The Production and Construction of Celebrity Advocacy."
75. Butt, "The Suffering Stranger"; and Fassin, *When Bodies Remember*, 22.
76. Andreasson, "Orientalism and African Development Studies."
77. Robbins, "Beyond the Suffering Subject."
78. Ponte and Richey, "Buying into Development?"
79. Corbridge, "The (Im)possibility of Development Studies," 201.
80. Lorde's famous essay, "The Master's Tools Will Never Dismantle the Master's House", 10, actually suggests that fundamental critique cannot be based upon existing categories, such as 'woman'; however, our argument is based on the conduct of a practice-based critique. See, for example, Adler and Pouliot, *International Practices.*
81. This collection offers a more practice-based interrogation of development than Nederveen Pieterse's notions of hybridisation as the 'rhizome of culture', drawing a middle ground in descriptions of the effects of cultural globalisation on developing countries. Nederveen Pieterse, *Globalization and Culture.*

Bibliography

Adelman, C. "Global Philanthropy and Remittances: Reinventing Foreign Aid." *Brown Journal of World Affairs* 15, no. 2 (2009): 23–33.

Adler, E., and V. Pouliot, eds. *International Practices*. Cambridge: Cambridge University Press, 2011.
Alhassan, A., and P. Chakravartty. "Postcolonial Media Policy under the Long Shadow of Empire." In *The Handbook of Global Media and Communication Policy*, edited by . R. Mansell, and M. Raboy, 366–382. Chichester: Wiley-Blackwell, 2011.
Andreasson, S. "Orientalism and African Development Studies: The 'Reductive Repetition' Motif in Theories of African Underdevelopment." *Third World Quarterly* 26, no. 6 (2005): 971–986.
Bandelj, N., and F. Wherry, eds. *The Cultural Wealth of Nations*. Stanford, CA: Stanford University Press, 2011.
Banks, N., and Hulme, D. "New Development Alternatives or Business as Usual with a New Face? The Transformative Potential of New Actors and Alliances in Development," this issue.
Barnett, C., P. Cloke, N. Clarke, and A. Malpass. "Consuming Ethics: Articulating the Subjects and Spaces of Ethical Consumption." *Antipode* 37 (2005): 23–45.
Barnett, C., P. Cloke, N. Clarke, and A. Malpass. *Globalizing Responsibility: The Political Rationalities of Ethical Consumption*. Oxford: Blackwell, 2010.
Berglind, M., and C. Nakata. "Cause-related Marketing: More Buck than Bang?" *Business Horizons* 48, no. 3 (2005): 443–453.
Blowfield, M. "Reasons to be Cheerful? What We Know about CRS's impact." *Third World Quarterly* 28, no. 4 (2007): 683–695.
Blowfield, M., and C. S., Dolan. "Business as a Development Agent: Evidence of Possibility and Improbability," this issue.
Boykoff, M., and M. K. Goodman. "Conspicuous Redemption: Promises and Perils of Celebrity Involvement in Climate Change." *Geoforum* 40 (2009): 395–406.
Brockington, D. *Celebrity and the Environment: Fame, Wealth and Power in Conservation*. London: Zed Books, 2009.
Brockington, D. "The Production and Construction of Celebrity Advocacy in International Development," this issue.
Budabin, A. C. "Diasporas as Development Partners for Peace? The Alliance between the Darfuri Diaspora and the Save Darfur Coalition," this issue.
Butt, L. "The Suffering Stranger: Medical Anthropology and International Morality." *Medical Anthropology* 21, no. 1 (2002): 1–24.
Calderisi, R. *The Trouble with Africa: Why Foreign Aid isn't Working*. New York: Palgrave, 2006.
Carrier, J. G. "Introduction." In *Ethical Consumption: Social Value and Economic Practice*, edited by. J. G. Carrier, and P. G. Luetchford. New York: Berghan, 2012.
Carrier, J. G., and P. G. Luetchford, eds. *Ethical Consumption: Social Value and Economic Practice*. New York: Berghan, 2012.
Carroll, A. B. "Corporate Social Responsibility: Evolution of a Definitional Construct." *Business and Society* 38, no. 3 (1999): 268–295.
Cimoli, M., G. Dosi, and J. Stiglitz, eds. *Industrial Policy and Development: The Political Economy of Capabilities Accumulation*. Oxford: Oxford University Press, 2009.
Clarke, N. "From Ethical Consumerism to Political Consumption." *Geography Compass* 2 (2008): 1870–1884.
Clarke, N., C. Barnett, P. Cloke, and A. Malpass. "Globalising the Consumer: Doing Politics in an Ethical Register." *Political Geography* 26 (2007): 231–249.
Collier, P. *The Bottom Billion: Why the Poorest Countries are Failing and What can be Done about It*. Oxford: Oxford University Press, 2007.
Cooper, A. F. "Beyond One Image Fits All: Bono and the Complexity of Celebrity Diplomacy." *Global Governance* 14 (2008): 265–272.
Corbridge, S. "The (Im)possibility of Development Studies." *Economy and Society* 36 (2007): 179–211.
Crush, J. *Power of Development*. London: Routledge, 1995.
Devinney, T., P. Auger, and G. M. Eckhardt, eds. *The Myth of the Ethical Consumer*. Cambridge: Cambridge University Press, 2010.
de Waal, A. "The Humanitarian Carnival." *World Affairs* Fall (2008): 43–55.
Easterly, W. *The White Man's Burden: Why the West's Efforts to Aid the Rest have done so much Ill and so little Good*. New York: Penguin, 2006.
Escobar, A. *Encountering Development: The Making and Unmaking of the Third World*. Princeton, NJ: Princeton University Press, 1995.
Fassin, D. *When Bodies Remember: Experiences and Politics of aids in South Africa*. Berkeley: University of California Press, 2007.
Ferguson, J. *The Anti-Politics Machine: "Development", Depoliticization and Bureaucratic Power in Lesotho*. Minneapolis: University of Minnesota Press, 1994.
Ferguson, J. "The Uses of Neoliberalism." *Antipode* 41, S1 (2009): 166–184.
Gibbon, P., S. Ponte, and E. Lazaro, eds. *Global Agro-food Trade and Standards: Challenges for Africa*. Palgrave: Basingstoke, 2010.
Goodman, M. K., and C. Barnes. "Star/Poverty Space: The Making of the 'Development Celebrity'." *Celebrity Studies* 2, no. 1 (2011): 68–85.
Hall, S. "The West and the Rest." In *Formations of Modernity*, ed. S. Hall. London: Open University, 2011.

Hansen, H., and F. Tarp. "Aid Effectiveness Disputed." *Journal of International Development* 12, no. 3 (2000): 375–398.
Harrison, G. "Campaign Africa: Exploring the Representation of Africa and its Role in British Identity." *British Journal of Politics and International Relations*, doi: 10.1111/j.1467-856X.2012.00520.x.
Harrison, G. "Debt, Development and Intervention in Africa: The Contours of a Sovereign Frontier." *Journal of Intervention and Statebuilding* 1, no. 2 (2007): 189–209.
Hood, J. "Celebrity Philanthropy: The Cultivation of China's HIV/AIDS Heroes." In *Celebrity in China*, edited by. L. Edwards, and E. Jeffreys. Hong Kong: Hong Kong University Press, 2009.
Idemudia, U. "Corporate Social Responsibility and Developing Countries: Moving the Critical CSR Research Agenda in Africa Forward." *Progress in Development Studies* 11, no. 1 (2011): 1–18.
IMF, *External Debt Statistics: Guide for Compilers and Users – Appendix III*. Washington, DC: IMF, 2003, Glossary.
Kapoor, I. *Celebrity Humanitarianism: The Ideology of Global Charity*. London: Routledge, 2012.
Keck, M. E., and K. Sikkink. *Activists beyond Borders: Advocacy Networks in International Politics*. Ithaca, NY: Cornell University Press, 1998.
King, S. *Pink Ribbons Inc: Breast Cancer and the Politics of Philanthropy*. Minneapolis: University of Minnesota Press, 2006.
Kothari, U. "Critiquing 'Race' and Racism in Development Discourse and Practice." *Progress in Development Studies* 6, no. 1 (2006): 1–7.
Kothari, U. "Commentary: History, Time and Temporality in Development Discourse." In *History, Historians and Development Policy: A Necessary Dialogue*, edited by. C. A. Bayly, et al., 65–70. Manchester: Manchester University Press, 2006.
Kothari, U. "Trade, Consumption and Development Alliances: The Historical Legacy of the Empire Marketing Board Poster Campaign," this issue.
Kragelund, P. "'Donors Go Back Home': Non-traditional State Actors and the Creation of Development Space in Zambia," this issue.
Lin, J. Y. *New Structural Economics: A Framework for Rethinking Development and Policy*. Washington, DC: World Bank, 2012.
Littler, J. "'I Feel Your Pain': Cosmopolitan Charity and the Public Fashioning of the Celebrity Soul." *Social Semiotics* 18 (2008): 237–251.
Lorde, A. "The Master's Tools Will Never Dismantle the Master's House." *Sister Outsider*. Berkeley, CA: Crossing Press, 1984.
McGoey, L."The Philanthropic State: Market–State Hybrids in the Philanthrocapitalist Turn," this issue.
Miller, D. *The Dialectics of Shopping*. Chicago, IL: University of Chicago Press, 2001.
Mills, G. *Why Africa is Poor: And What Africans Can Do about It*. London: Penguin Books, 2010.
Moyo, D. *Dead Aid: Why Aid is not Working and How there is Another Way for Africa*. London: Allen Lane, 2009.
Nair, S. "Governance, Representation and International Aid." *Third World Quarterly* 34, no. 4 (2013): 630–652.
Nederveen Pieterse, J. *Development Theory. Deconstructions/Reconstructions*. London: Sage Publications, 2001.
Nederveen Pieterse, J. *Globalization and Culture: Global Mélange*. New York: Rowman & Littlefield, 2003.
Nederveen Pieterse, J. *White on Black: Images of Africa and Blacks in Western Popular Culture*. New Haven, CT: Yale University Press, 1992.
Newell, P., and J. G. Frynas. "Beyond CSR? Business, Poverty and Social Justice: An Introduction." *Third World Quarterly* 28, no. 4 (2007): 669–681.
Newell, P. "CSR and the Limits of Capital." *Development and Change* 39, no. 6 (2008): 1063–1078.
Noman, A., and J. Stiglitz eds. *Good Growth and Governance in Africa: Rethinking Development Strategies*. Oxford: Oxford University Press, 2012.
Ponte, S., and L. A., Richey. "Buying into Development? Brand Aid Forms of Cause-related Marketing," this issue.
Prahalad, C. K. *The Fortune at the Bottom of the Pyramid: Eradicating Poverty through Profits*. Upper Saddle River, NJ: Wharton School Publishing, 2005.
Richey, L. A., and S. Ponte. *Brand Aid: Shopping Well to Save the World*. Minneapolis: University of Minnesota Press, 2011.
Riddell, R. *Does Foreign Aid Really Work?* Oxford: Oxford University Press, 2007.
Robbins, J. R. "Beyond the Suffering Subject: Toward an Anthropology of the Good." *Journal of the Royal Anthropological Institute no.* 19 (2013): 447–462.
Rodrik, D. *One Economics, Many Recipes: Globalization, Institutions and Economic Growth*. Princeton, NJ: Princeton University Press, 2007.
Sachs, W. *The Development Dictionary*. London: Zed Books, 1992.
Sachs, J. D. *The End of Poverty: Economic Possibilities of Our Time*. London: Allen Lane, 2005.
Sandbrook, R., and J. Barker. *The Politics of Africa's Economic Stagnation*. Cambridge: Cambridge University Press, 1985.

Schuurman, F. J. “Critical Development Theory: Moving out of the Twilight Zone.” *Third World Quarterly* 30, no. 5 (2009): 831–848.
Slater, D. *Consumer Culture and Modernity*. London: Polity, 1997.
Smith, M. B., and H., Yanacopulos, eds. “Special Issue: The Public Faces of Development.” *Journal of International Development* 16, no. 5 (2004): 657–749.
Sylvester, C. “Development and Postcolonial Studies: Disparate Tales of the ‘Third World’.” *Third World Quarterly* 20 (1999): 703–721.
Tarp, F. ed. *Foreign Aid and Development: Lessons Learnt and Guidelines for the Future*. London: Routledge, 2000.
Tierney, M. J., D. L. Nielson, D. G. Hawkins, J. T. Roberts, M. G. Findley, R. M. Powers, and B. Parks. “More Dollars than Sense: Refining our Knowledge of Development Finance using AidData.” *World Development* 39, no. 11 (2011): 1891–1906.
Trentmann, F. “An Introduction: Knowing Consumers – Histories, Identities, Practices.” In *The Making of the Consumer: Knowledge, Power and Identity in the Modern World*, edited by. F. Trentmann. Oxford: Berg, 2006.
van de Walle, N. *African Economies and the Politics of Permanent Crisis, 1979–1999*. Cambridge: Cambridge University Press, 2001.
Wade, R. “Accountability Gone Wrong: The World Bank, NGOs, and the US Government in a Fight over China.” *New Political Economy* 14, no. 1 (2009): 25–48.
Wartick, S. L., and P. L. Cochran. “The Evolution of the Corporate Social Performance Model.” *Academy of Management Review* 10, no. 4 (1995): 758–769.
Whitfield, L., and L., Buur. “The Politics of Industrial Policy: Ruling Elites and their Alliances,” this issue.
Woolcock, M., S. Szreter, and V. Rao. “How and Why Does History Matter for Development Policy?” *Journal of Development Studies* 47, no. 1 (2011): 70–96.

Business as a development agent: evidence of possibility and improbability

Michael Blowfiel[a] and Catherine S. Dolan[b]

[a]University of Wolverhampton Business School, Wolverhampton, UK; [b]Department of Anthropology, SOAS, London, UK

An emphasis on making markets work for the poor has thrust companies into the role of 'development agents' – organisations that consciously seek to deliver outcomes that contribute to international development goals. This paper examines what business as a development agent means in terms of the promise, the conceptualisation and the developmental outcomes of several initiatives engaged in 'bottom billion capitalism'. It argues that, while these initiatives are hailed as a solution for poverty, the benefits of such engagement must be weighed against other factors, including exclusion, the emphasis on capital assets and the reinterpretation of positive outcomes. The paper presents an alternative model of business as a development agent that better meets the criteria for a genuine development actor.

Introduction

For much of the postcolonial development period the role of business in development has been confined to its contribution to wealth creation, employment and the provision of goods and services. Business has served the role of a development tool – widely engaged in economic activity in developing countries but assuming little responsibility for the impact of that activity. By the late 1980s this posture had become difficult to sustain. Business came under the glare of public scrutiny for untoward labour, environmental and human rights practices and responded defensively by adhering to voluntary codes of practice that governed the social and environmental impact of its operations. More recently, however, business has move beyond this reactive stance to championing a far more proactive role in development, fostering new business models, partnerships and financial instruments to combat issues ranging from malaria and HIV to trade justice and poverty reduction. Aligning itself with contemporary development approaches of pro-poor business growth and making markets work for the poor (M4P), business is assuming the role of 'development agent' – an organisation that consciously seeks to deliver outcomes that contribute to international development goals.

This paper examines what business as a development agent means in terms of the promise, the conceptualisation, and the developmental outcomes of several existing initiatives engaged in what has come to be known as 'bottom billion capitalism' (BBC). Although BBC comprises a diversity of initiatives (eg Fairtrade labelling, microfinance, bottom of the pyramid (BOP) schemes, commercial social entrepreneurship), each of these harnesses the mechanisms of private enterprise for developmental ends by repositioning business as a development agent. We explain the meaning of 'development agent' and the possibilities it holds for various stakeholder groups, including its intended beneficiaries. Through analysis of empirical studies of BBC initiatives by the authors and others,[1] we identify the structural dimensions of business as a development agent, how the embodiment of 'development agent' differs from other development-related roles associated with the private sector, and the different types of instrumental interaction business has with development issues such as poverty and marginalisation.

The paper advances a new framework for assessing the effectiveness of business as a development agent (capital employed; conscious, accountable development-oriented effort; primacy afforded to development issues), and examines the empirical evidence to determine how this has been applied in a cross-section of initiatives. We demonstrate that, while a powerful discourse hails private sector initiatives as a solution to poverty and marginalisation, the benefits of such engagement must be weighed against other factors, including exclusion, an emphasis on capital assets, and the reinterpretation of positive outcomes, benefits and beneficiaries. We also show not only that developmental accountability is rare in these initiatives, but equally that this is unlikely to change in future because of paradoxes at the heart of the business–development relationship. The paper concludes by positing an alternative model of business as a development agent that better meets the criteria for a genuine new development actor. We set out the characteristics of such an enterprise and describe the type of institutional environment that is required to support the transformation of business into an effective agent of development.

Conceptualising business in development

'Development' can refer to two processes. It can refer to an immanent and unintentional process through which national economies, human well-being and household or individual incomes improve, particularly in poorer countries and former colonies (cf capitalist development). Or it can refer to intentional activities consciously undertaken to improve lives in those same countries.[2] Since the birth of the Bretton Wood institutions commercial enterprise has had a major role to play in development, but mostly as an unintentional actor. Whether it be direct investment by foreign companies, the flurry of activity by local entrepreneurs – not least in the informal sector – the attention given to international trade and capital flows, or the emphasis placed on export-led growth, the private sector has been an important agent in achieving development goals. However, since the 1990s, there can be little doubt that the private sector's role has become more overt as the development discourse has been subsumed within a wider neoliberal discourse about economic growth, prosperity and well-being.[3] A vibrant private sector with well functioning markets is seen as the *sine qua non* of a properly developing economy.

Throughout the private sector's evolution in development theory and policy, the role of business can be characterised as that of a 'development tool'. By business, we mean a conceptual category that embraces any organisation engaging in commerce and trade. This is admittedly very broad, including everything from the start-up enterprise to the multinational conglomerate. However, conceptually at least, the empirical organisations captured by our meaning of the word 'business' share much in common and, as we will show, their primary, unifying function of trade and commerce has particular implications for their development role. In its narrowest form a commercial enterprise creates value for its owners, and in doing so contributes to the public good: creating jobs, obeying the law, supplying goods and services, and helping to fund necessary social institutions.[4] Value creation, therefore, can be said to create growth-driven development; hence business as the primary creator of wealth has a central role to play in development. However, this is the kind of role business could play anywhere in the world, at least wherever there is a functioning private sector. It is not by itself a development-oriented activity; it is no more responsible for development outcomes than a hammer is responsible for the carpenter's thumb.

The notion of business as a development tool – active in developing countries but not responsible for outcomes in these countries – came under closer scrutiny in the late 1980s. This was partly because the Washington Consensus and the role of markets within it were subject to increasing criticism.[5] On top of generic criticisms of the private sector, however, there was an emerging body of evidence associating individual companies with developmentally detrimental outcomes, such as human rights abuses and environmental pollution.[6] This marked the start of a shift from business as an unintentional actor in development (see above) to becoming an actor in intentional development. By the turn of the century multinational companies as diverse as Nike, Freeport Mining, Hershey, Unilever and Home Depot had signed up to voluntary codes of practice relating to one or other aspect of their impact on development. The emergence of voluntary governance initiatives with a developing country focus in the 1990s and early 2000s is well documented,[7] and these represented a notable new element in value chain governance that continues today.[8] However, to what extent does association with these initiatives allow companies to claim they are acting as anything more than a development tool?

It is not our intention to evaluate specific initiatives; there are others who have done this using an array of empirical evidence and analytical frameworks.[9] However, most importantly for this paper, these initiatives to modify the behaviour of companies in developing countries begin to reveal some of the development issues that arise when companies extend the boundaries of the conventional development tool: issues such as inclusivity and exclusivity (eg the position of women, contract labour and indigenous people); and the governing of the poor and marginalised. Although the majority of the literature examines either the enhancement of voluntary governance initiatives,[10] or their efficacy for companies and intended beneficiaries,[11] it has also provoked some debate about the role of business in development overall.[12]

The experience of voluntary governance and the development issues it threw up played a part in a second wave of corporate responsibility initiatives in the 2000s. Perhaps aware that tackling working conditions, pollution, child labour, and so on – while a commendable response to stakeholder pressure – trapped companies in a debate about unethical business and what Kramer and Kania call 'defensive' corporate responsibility,[13] business started to look for 'offensive' opportunities whereby companies could burnish their reputation by tackling development challenges. The mainstreaming of Fairtrade labelling and microfinance, the rapid rise of the BOP concept of the poor as a profitable market, and the accommodation of development into ideas of social enterprise all happened during this decade,[14] and they drove calls for business to take a proactive role in development that went far beyond the original development tool idea.[15] Indeed, in the space of less than two decades, there had been a shift from companies viewing developing countries as a location in which to do business (the role of the development tool), to understanding that to a degree it was not only possible but necessary (for moral or material reasons) for companies to see themselves less as the inanimate hammer and more as the instrumental carpenter, ie to be a development agent.

Criteria for business as a development agent

What does it mean for business to be a development agent? The brief history presented above – to which should be added the extensive experience of extractive industries and others in assisting local community development[16] – shows that, for different reasons, the private sector has an interest not only in developing countries but also in the development of those countries. This interest is often self-interest (eg protecting a corporate reputation; promoting self-regulation to stave off government interference), although self-interest can involve mutual interest between companies and the poor or otherwise marginalised, a premise clearly projected in the BOP concept.[17]

Self-interest (or lack of it) is not a useful criteria on its own for assessing whether business is acting as a development agent. Some people may feel that for a company to act out of self-interest negates the value of its development contribution, but this is a spurious argument. A company makes a profit out of self-interest, but failure to be profitable would remove the company entirely from any development role because it would cease to exist. Some companies make a profit from implementing development programmes, typically on behalf of government clients. Thus there are companies such as Chemonics, PWC and Coffey International that deliver programmes for aid agencies. However, these companies are not investing in development, because they do not deploy their own capital. By contrast, Tropical Wholefoods (Uganda) is a food processor and exporter, which uses its own capital to invest in commercial development projects, while Vodafone/Safaricom (Kenya) matched aid funding with its own capital in setting up the M-Pesa money transfer service.[18] It is the willingness to deploy one's assets for activities with an expected, calculated development benefit that is one criterion for being a development agent, rather than whether or not there is a profit motive.

The second criterion – and one that marks the development agent out from the development tool – is that, in making an investment, the company gives primacy to the benefits for the poor and otherwise marginalised (henceforward 'the poor'). For example, mining companies have often been criticised over the number and quality of jobs they create for local people. Consequently in projects such as BP's Tangguh gas field (Indonesia) companies may invest in building the capacity of local people to carry out skilled functions.[19] Equally the Body Shop consciously invested in Soapworks Ltd (Scotland) because it was located in a deprived community with high unemployment. As we shall discuss later, claims to be acting as a development agent are put to the test when company management has to choose between the seemingly competing interests of different stakeholder groups. For example, if the local labour force is inadequate, should a company such as BP import personnel and, if it does, what responsibility does it have for the pressure migrant worker families might place on local amenities, land rights and the job prospects of local families? Similarly, what is the correct response when the Body Shop is under pressure to close down the Soapworks factory because of falling profits?[20]

The third criterion we suggest is that development agents not only give primacy to benefits for the poor but they consciously and accountably strive to address poverty and marginalisation. This criterion comprises two elements. First, the company goes beyond providing opportunities that would seem to benefit the poor (eg siting factories in deprived areas; funding vocational schools in a mining area), to ensure as far as possible that the poor benefit from these opportunities. This means understanding the nature of poverty and marginalisation so that, for instance, contract workers are just as able to benefit from improved working conditions as permanent ones, or women are not excluded from new political opportunities.[21] Second, a development agent is a company that is accountable for its developmental outcomes just as it is for other core aspects of its business, such as financial performance. This does not mean demonstrating the instrumental benefits for the company of addressing development issues (something that could be accommodated in conventional auditing and accounting processes); it means providing an honest, fair and reliable account to itself and others of what it has achieved in development terms.

These three criteria relating to capital, pro-poor primacy and accountability will inform all the coming sections. Although not without controversy, the notion that business can and should be more than a development tool and something akin to a development agent is gaining ground. What we will demonstrate is that in reality the private sector development agent is an elusive being, for a variety reasons, all of which reveal something about the potential for the criteria to be met in the future. Furthermore, we examine the consequences for the poor of a failure to foster genuine development agents, especially given the current advocacy of the private sector in development.

Business' multiple interactions with poverty

There are three main categories of interaction between business and poverty.[22] The governance initiatives mentioned earlier are a response to companies being regarded as beneficiaries of poverty, infringing on the poor's rights and exploiting the conditions of the poor. In these instances business is blamed for causing or exacerbating poverty. Aside from any moral imperative managers might feel for addressing these issues, there are well documented instrumental reasons for a company not to want to be associated with poverty in this way.[23] Less recognised in the business–development literature is that companies can be victims of poverty. For example, although companies are often accused of benefiting from (and indeed aiding) poor governance,[24] absence of the rule of law may benefit some individual companies but does not benefit business as a whole.[25] In quite different ways companies can be the victim of government policy, of a poorly educated consumer base and workforce, of poor and dangerous infrastructure, and of other conditions characteristic of developing countries. For example, companies such as SAB Miller and L'Oreal have initiated HIV/AIDS prevention programmes in South Africa because of the disease's impact on their workforces, including the management cadre,[26] and companies have funded the Global Road Safety Partnership because of the human and financial cost of unsafe roads.[27] It is possible that some actions business takes because it is either the cause or the victim of poverty could meet the aforementioned criteria of being a development agent. However, in this paper we will focus on the third category of interaction, wherein business sees itself as a solution to poverty, not just through the act of conducting business, but because of decisions informed by an awareness of and a desire to ameliorate poverty. As an exemplar of this we will discuss what Roy terms 'bottom billion capitalism',[28] a term that refers to a significant part of the theory and practice of addressing development through commercial enterprise.

Bottom billion capitalism

As noted, over the past decade business has moved beyond conventional CSR activities to become part of a broader architecture of global development – what Roy terms 'millennial development'.[29] This architecture comprises a different cast of actors and organisational forms – celebrities, business, consumers, philanthropic organisations, new donors and poverty specialists – who aim to revitalise development through new business models, partnerships, modes of finance and development assistance.[30]

It is within this context that a 'new frontier' of business engagement in development has emerged – BBC initiatives that draw the world's poor into global markets through new models of financial inclusion, consumption and entrepreneurship. Although Roy is concerned with how BBC, through the vehicle of microfinance, recasts poverty as a site of opportunity for both business and the poor, the concept builds on the work of Collier and Prahalad,[31] who popularised the phrase 'bottom billion' to refer to those living in extreme poverty. Where Collier advocates a mixed aid and trade approach to improving economic opportunity in bottom billion countries, Prahalad expounds a liberal view, holding up the market-building activities of multinational corporations as a catalyst to reduce poverty among the four billion poor at the so-called base of the pyramid.

Prahalad's vision has been remarkably influential, unleashing a plethora of market-led approaches that seek to reduce poverty in developing countries under the rubric of 'inclusive business' and 'creative capitalism'.[32] For proponents of these initiatives, the role for business in poverty reduction is clear: when business engages in development, the poor benefit. It is an assumption that informs support for several models of BBC, including not only BOP, but also microfinance, inclusive business and Fairtrade approaches, each of which is underpinned conceptually by a neoliberal valorisation of private enterprise, market efficiency, entrepreneurship and the conviction that markets can work for the poor.[33] These models have been embraced by multinational corporations and multilateral development institutions alike, which look to the perceived 'efficiency' of the private sector to do what countless aid dollars and 'absent' states have been unable to do – reduce poverty among the billions of people living on less than two dollars per day.[34]

Although BBC initiatives share an ideological vision to ameliorate poverty through market engagement, in practice they embody different objectives and histories, constellations of actors and institutions, and sectors. Fairtrade, for example, focuses on rectifying 'unfair' markets by reconfiguring supply chains; microcredit aims to redress 'imperfect' markets by providing loans to poor borrowers who typically lack collateral; and BOP systems seek to create markets, bringing new products and services to underserved consumers. Each also includes firms of varying sizes, interests and levels of capitalisation, from multinational corporations and venture capitalists to small and medium enterprises, and spans sectors from food and toiletries to telecommunications and energy. However, while their structure and form differ, each enacts a set of practices, techniques, and ideologies that 'construct, and make productive, a global economy where poverty is a frontier of profit and accumulation'.[35]

A signature feature of BBC is new institutional configurations that pursue 'development through enterprise': market-based models that reflect a shift in poverty discourse from conceptions of the poor as beneficiaries of aid and development expertise to market actors – 'clients', 'partners' and 'entrepreneurs' – who will assume responsibility for their own development.[36] This emphasis on enterprise and entrepreneurship gained traction under a neoliberal policy agenda of privatisation and deregulation, which restructured relationships between states and their citizens, particularly the poor. Efforts to source social provision through private entities, to 'modernise' informal segments of the economy through rationalities of efficiency and responsibility,[37] and to galvanise the participation of the poor in the 'productive' economy, have redefined poverty as a condition amenable to market intervention. Yet, while BBC models are informed by the values of neoliberalism – competition, efficiency and self-governance – they are also premised on an ideology of inclusion, what Roy terms 'neoliberal populism'.[38] They seek to democratise access to markets, extending opportunities to access finance capital, earned income and affordable products to those who have been excluded (or included on unfavourable terms) from the productive opportunities afforded through integration into the global economy.

Clues to the development agent

Although models of BBC are endorsed as 'pro-poor', the degree to which business consciously strives to address poverty and marginalisation through them (ie the extent to which it operates with a logic of pro-poor primacy) is little understood. Empirical evidence on the strategies and impacts of BBC models is variable, ranging from predominantly 'qualitative' case-based studies of BOP and Fairtrade schemes to randomised control trials (RCTs) of microfinance, making generalisation difficult. Indeed, despite increased emphasis on 'evidence-based policy', there is little indication that any of these models has yielded positive impacts that are scalable.[39] In addition, there is a lack of knowledge of how business conceptualises poverty, except in terms of its role as an engine for its alleviation, that is, as a development tool. While conceptions of poverty within development have expanded beyond economic and material indicators to include the realms of health, education and empowerment,[40] management studies have been largely silent on the issue of poverty.[41]

What we do know is confined to the economic impacts of initiatives, either the income gains of beneficiaries or the instrumental benefits to companies (growth, market share and net present value).[42] This focus on a singular metric of output reflects a convergence of trends within business and development, mirroring, on the one hand, the 'epistemic privilege' of the market in an increasingly managerialist development industry, in which alternative ways of measuring benefit are often discounted,[43] and, on the other hand, a business climate in which success is measured on return on investment. Certainly, income growth and economic returns matter; but BBC initiatives that base success on indicators of conventional business performance, or even on the economic benefits (eg access to capital, income) accrued by beneficiaries, not only devalue non-monetised contributions but shed little light on the extent to which business inhabits the position of development agent in the sense of affording primacy to the needs and benefits of the poor.[44]

One way of assessing this is by examining how business defines the field of poverty intervention and to what effect: what normative assumptions underpin the private sector's conception of development problems (ie poverty), development's purported beneficiaries (the poor), and business's role in advancing solutions to improve both?[45] Here, we take our cue from anthropologists Ferguson, Escobar, Li, and Mosse, who have examined how the discourses and practices of development institutions determine the form and possibilities of interventions.[46] Drawing on Foucault, Li describes two key practices that underscore the making of a development intervention.[47] The first, problematisation, refers to the process of 'identifying deficiencies that need to be rectified', making certain types of market intervention knowable and thinkable.[48] It reflects a concern with ontology: how poverty is constructed as a particular type of problem, that of market failure, amenable to solutions at a particular scale (that of the bottom billion) in the context of a particular policy instrument (enterprise).[49] The second is the practice(s) of 'rendering technical' the domain to be governed 'as an intelligible field with specifiable limits and particular characteristics'. This entails 'defining boundaries, rendering that within them visible…and devising techniques to mobilize the forces and entities thus revealed'.[50] This analytic lens has been widely applied to understanding how aid institutions produce and enact development knowledge.[51] Here, we build on this work to examine how business frames its subject matter in the field of poverty reduction, defining what falls within and beyond the scope of attention,[52] and making the object of its intervention knowable, calculable and predictable to global business.[53]

Problematisation: recasting poverty problems as market solutions

In BBC models the process of problematisation is grounded in a normative framework that positions poverty as a product of market failure and its alleviation as the managed integration of the poor into global finance, capital and product markets. In diagnosing the scope of intervention, business tends to recognise only those problems for which a solution within the competence of the enterprise or marketplace can be produced (see also McGoey in this issue). Indeed, in many cases the notion that a particular product will be *the* solution to a development dilemma is a foregone conclusion, as the problem itself is recast in market terms. As the World Economic Forum's report on unleashing the potential of the BOP acknowledges, 'companies can reframe the problems' they encounter in BOP markets by 'finding ways to leverage them into business opportunities', redefining, for example, concerns around water, environmental degradation and disease as market opportunities for soap, cooking stoves and bed nets.[54] For companies operating in bottom billion markets, there is often a tendency to focus on issues that will enhance brand differentiation and competitiveness in poverty markets. As Steven Philips of Exxon Mobil responded, when asked why his company was getting into the business of bed nets in Africa: "'This was not beneficence or corporate social responsibility...We put our resources in places where they earn the best value per dollar, and this had demonstrable shareholder value...Chevron wasn't in malaria. BP wasn't in malaria...Malaria became our differentiator'."[55] Indeed, evidence suggests that the problems business deems significant and the solutions it proffers often accord more with the needs of capital than the needs of the poor. For example, Basheer calls into question the ultimate purpose of the World Bank's Handwashing Initiative, observing that 'The choice of a state that has the lowest incidence of childhood diarrhoea and water-related epidemics could indicate that the project is more about paving the way for the MNCs into the informal personal care market than bringing down the diarrhoeal death rates in the country'.[56]

Similarly, studies of Fairtrade illustrate how the identification of a development problem is shaped by its proposed solution.[57] Research on Ghanaian cocoa producers, for instance, describes how market interests influenced the allocation of Fairtrade's social premium: although producers declared a preference for spending the premium on better roads, cars, televisions, places of worship or simply a cash transfer, these desires did not accord with the poverty solutions envisioned by corporates and Western consumers, for whom a development benefit was equated with 'needs' such as health and education.[58] Similarly, in Kenya, tea producers claimed that, while the projects funded through Fairtrade's social premium were useful, they did not necessarily reflect their priorities – piped water and/or electricity – problems the Fairtrade Labelling Organizations International deemed beyond the proper scope of premium funds. Thus, the market episteme that underpins BBC initiatives tends to discount solutions that are incommensurate with commercial imperatives,[59] that is, which fail to build consumer satisfaction or brand differentiation. What falls outside Western perceptions of poverty reduction, such as converting Fairtrade premium funds to cash or selling 'frivolous' goods (eg lipstick and skin whitening cream) through BOP distribution networks, or what lies beyond the purview of market remediation, is taken off the table as being insufficiently pro-poor. This process, however, shifts the development beneficiary from a rights-bearing subject – a citizen whose rights are bestowed and enshrined by the state – to a 'value-driven consumer' whose needs, desires and preferences are defined and fulfilled by the market.[60] As the director of UK-based Business Fights Poverty described it: 'for too long development has been about treating poor people as recipients, as dependents [sic], and actually for the first time we're seeing them treated as agents of their development…as customers for the first time'.[61]

Rendering technical: expertise and legibility

Discourses and practices of expertise are critical to the problematisation process, as those problems that are identified and corroborated by 'expert' knowledge or that can be made legible through management tools are often prioritised. For example, business's diagnosis of development problems often draws legitimacy from the authority of science, which is harnessed to define problems in ways that require business intervention. The tools of scientific knowledge – surveys, measurements and observations – confer epistemic weight to the diagnoses propounded by business, particularly where a legitimate correlation must be drawn between a development problem and a market/commercial solution. For example, like many market solutions, the 'Health in Your Hands' initiative in Ghana, a partnership between Unilever and NGOs which promotes hand washing and hygiene, invokes scientific 'evidence' to demonstrate the connection between hand washing and child mortality (and thus the need for soap). Indeed, 'robust' assessments of market-based initiatives have become pro forma for companies, who employ business schools, research institutions and consultancy firms to conduct RCTs and impact evaluations to validate proposed product solutions, assessments that are especially prominent 'in public health contexts where the social credentials of a product depend upon evidence of its medical effects'.[62] P&G, for example, now has an army of contracted nurses who travel from school to school in Ghana providing puberty education, a training that addresses hygienic sanitary practices and in which the capacity of different sanitary care products to absorb blood is tested in situ. Such studies enhance the visibility of certain products, according them recognition as the (commercial) remedy for development dilemmas: soap is not simply a cleaning agent but an antidote to infant morbidity and mortality in Ghana; sanitary pads are not only a technology that facilitates the absorption of menstrual blood, they are also a pathway to reduced fertility and teenage pregnancies. In doing this, science legitimates and facilitates certain courses of action: 'the problems chosen, categories used, relationships investigated, and confirming evidence required' all support the material and ideological purpose of business to convert the realm of public provision into private goods,[63] or, as Roy put it, to transform 'economies of need' into 'economies of profit'.[64]

Business also draws legitimacy from partnerships with development 'experts' (humanitarian, multilateral, quasi-governmental and NGOs), whose public credibility shields business from allegations of greenwashing and grants authenticity to their engagement with the poor. NGOs are key nodes in BBC assemblages, their perceived local knowledge and experiences providing a doorway to local markets by making the unfamiliar social practices of the poor knowable and legible to corporations. Uncovering these 'hidden community resources' the World Economic Forum writes, requires 'companies to collaborate with other organizations', as most possess little on-the-ground experience of markets that exist beyond the scope of conventional retail and lack the resources, knowledge or credibility to localise their product solutions for 'poor', rural consumers.[65] NGOs, often in partnership with market research firms, help business to better understand the cultures, habits and behaviours of their target beneficiaries,[66] rendering the problem of poverty comprehensible for purposes of business engagement. Central to this process has been a shift away from surveys and focus groups to the use of ethnography and Participatory Rural Appraisal techniques to hone business's 'native capability', ie its capacity to engage 'in deep listening and mutual dialogue with income-poor communities' and to co-create new business models that resonate with 'the local cultural infrastructure' (http://www.bop-protocol.org).[67] Communities in bottom billion markets are now host to 'Rural Immersion Programs' where MNCs like Danone, Nestlé, Dupont and Pepsi acquire knowledge of local practices through participatory methods and visits to village elders, homes, churches, health and education facilities, and so on.[68] Like the high modernist schemes described by Scott, rural immersion reformats the poor as an object of calculation, enabling business to get a 'handle on its subjects and their environment', while demarcating who falls within and beyond capitalism's domain of concern and/or intervention.[69]

Thus, a considerable amount of 'expertise' goes into making the problem of poverty comprehensible and amenable to business intervention.[70] Yet the process of problematisation goes beyond the identification and framing of a development problem and a product solution. It also specifies and remakes bottom billion beneficiaries as a particular object of governance: the enterprising, self-regulating entrepreneur.

Beneficiaries or instruments of development?

The previous discussion illustrates how what is amenable or not to business intervention as a development agent is commonly premised on a priori conceptions of what the poor need. This in turn is typically needs that are legible to a capitalist worldview, and that can be remedied through solutions that align with commercial imperatives. This normative framing extends to how business defines the target beneficiaries of BBC initiatives. We noted at the beginning that the poor in the past were viewed as 'liabilities', whose ability to transcend deprivation was hitched to aid and philanthropy, or whose conditions posed a risk to corporate reputations. Models of BBC have restructured relationships with the subjects of development, positioning them as sites of opportunity rather than dependence.[71] No longer are the poor portrayed as passive victims of either poverty or of corporations themselves: models of BBC such as Fairtrade, microfinance and BOP are premised on a notion of entrepreneurial development in which the market failure of poverty is overcome by activating the enterprise and entrepreneurship of the poor.[72] The poor are thus recast as agents of development, who can benefit by remaking themselves to conform to the discipline of the market,[73] and by redirecting their capabilities, talents, assets and social networks to market opportunities.[74] For example, BOP entrepreneurs who distribute the products of Unilever, Danone, Coca-Cola, etc door-to-door become 'empowered' entrepreneurial subjects through technologies of management and government that craft 'self-driven' entrepreneurial subjects. In BOP initiatives these technologies assume many forms, from calculative devices such as time management and performance metrics, to pedagogy such as training in sales, recruitment and financial discipline, all of which aim to produce a market subjectivity with clear business acumen.[75] As the Shell Foundation notes, the poor must acquire 'business DNA': those 'skills and entrepreneurial instincts ... that business people everywhere use to identify and assess business opportunities'.[76] However, the talent and initiative that is held to be a 'natural' quality of the entrepreneur is, in fact, produced. While a meritocratic ideal of social mobility – everyone has a shot at being a successful entrepreneur – is widely propounded,[77] it is through integration into the market discipline of BBC markets that the poor develop their capacities for autonomy and self-reliance. To illustrate: BOP entrepreneurs are often assigned a geographic zone, a demarcated target market for which they shoulder responsibility.[78] These zones provide the socio-technical infrastructure of management; it is within them that the poor are observed, inventories are managed, sales and revenues tracked, and accounts assessed. Such data render these sites readable to corporations and provide a blueprint for sales and growth. They do not simply 'relay facts' or make markets more legible; they play an active role in the reconfiguration of bottom billion economies, enabling business and the aforementioned development experts to shape, as well as gauge, the achievement of entrepreneurial attitudes, behaviours and skills. For example, although sales data represent product uptake and market penetration (where, what and how much a product sells), they also recognise the entrepreneurial fitness or otherwise of workers, serving as an instrument of 'value coding' that draws a line between the responsible, enterprising and ambitious, and those who are not.[79]

Although primacy for the poor is often mentioned when business seeks to be a development agent, the meaning of 'poor' is highly circumscribed in ways that have little to do with poverty itself. BOP initiatives are concerned with a particular categorisation of beneficiary – the 'viable poor' – enterprising entrepreneurs who are capable of being integrated into the market and consumer society.[80] Likewise, Fairtrade targets producers who are marginalised, but not so much so that they are unable to invest in the resources necessary to meet the quality standards of Western consumers, thus privileging certain categories of beneficiary (the landed, men, entrepreneurs) while marginalising others (the very poor, landless and certain categories of women). As Mutersbaugh's study of organic coffee producers in Oaxaca, Mexico, demonstrated, Fairtrade can carve out new forms of distinction and uneven development in rural economies, differentiating between those communities and households that possess the resources to engage in certified agriculture and those who do not.[81] In fact, despite the 'democratization of opportunity' that BBC initiatives promote, development institutions and companies target those who will generate maximum return on investment. Similarly, strategies of microfinance promote financial inclusion by winnowing out 'those too poor or too economically inactive to participate', employing a range of technologies to construct and maintain boundaries between the economically active and the underproductive poor.[82] As Moreno concluded in reference to microcredit as a strategy of poverty alleviation in the Philippines, 'microcredit is applicable only to the enterprising poor. The application of microcredit to other poverty groups who actually need subsidies and social safety nets would be a mistake.'[83] While ostensibly a neutral financial calculus of creditworthiness, such judgments make a moral determination of who is worthy of help and who is not.

Conscious, accountable effort

Alongside the investment of capital to address the needs of the poor, another feature of the development agent explained earlier is that business is willing to be accountable for development outcomes, just as the development tool is accountable for its financial performance and its legal responsibilities. Our discussion of problematisation and beneficiaries has highlighted some of the potential problems with any genuine accountability, not least because current theory and practice does not guarantee that companies understand or are willing to act on what is material to the poor. Moreover, as mentioned in the section on stakeholders, the views of the poor are not prioritised, and where they are sought it is through a process of technical rendering by experts with their own epistemologies.[84] Consequently, in marked contrast to conventional notions of accountability, development agents lack the conditions for being accountable to those who are the intended beneficiaries of their actions.

However, even within the limitations imposed by the structural conditions highlighted in relation to problematisation and beneficiaries, accountability is a weak area of the development agent construct, and certainly the forms of accountability practised are much weaker than in other aspects of business where business has to be accountable to others. In part this is because of the difficulties of assigning causation between the investments companies make and outcomes among the poor,[85] but there is also a reluctance on the part of companies to make claims that could be challenged in court. However, the bigger barrier to accountability is that, as with corporate responsibility in general, companies are primarily interested in the instrumental benefits for the firm and its shareholders.[86] Although some companies make available findings from their internal social and economic impact assessments, at present this type of assessment is more concerned with business as a development tool than as a development agent.[87]

One can detect at the centre of the lack of accountability for development outcomes a paradox that cuts across discussions of business as a development agent. There is not space to do this justice here, but it is what we call the 'Porter Paradox', after the work of management theorist, Michael Porter. In recent years Porter has written about a 'higher form of capitalism', where not all profit is equal and commercial activities with a social purpose can expand the total pool of economic and societal value in society. This is called creating shared value.[88] As Porter to an extent acknowledges, creating shared value is at odds with the theory which made his name, ie competitive advantage. Competitive advantage is earned through cost leadership, differentiation and concentration on particular market segments,[89] and is closely linked to cultures of efficiency and productivity that dominate managerial thinking. It excludes many social and environmental impacts, and is blamed by some for leading to unsustainable growth that exploits the poor. It has also helped create some of the key indicators that companies are held to account by, for instance by financial analysts. The Porter Paradox, therefore, is that companies are rigorously held to account for maintaining their competitive advantage, even as this greatly restricts the actions they can take as a development agent. The response to this is that not all companies should engage in creating shared value, and those which do will find that it aids their competitive advantage. As yet, this is an a priori assertion.

There are successful companies that have taken alternative approaches to efficiency and productivity, and created a wider pool of value in the process (eg Lincoln Electric, renowned for its guaranteed employment policy[90]), while companies such as Patagonia have reincorporated themselves as 'benefit corporations' legally required to create general benefit for society as well as for shareholders. It may be that such examples will inspire others to consider the accountability dimension of being a development agent but at present these are very much the exception, and for most companies the Porter Paradox is another trap that hinders them from becoming conscious and accountable agents.

Conclusion: a new generation of development agents?

There appears to be a growing number of commercial enterprises taking development issues into consideration as part of their operations. They are a small minority compared with the number of companies performing the role of the development tool, but they include multinational companies, large international and national companies, and a host of smaller enterprises, many of which were founded on the principle that for-profit entities can deliver positive developmental outcomes. The array of initiatives is broad and falls into a variety of categories, but common to them all is a consciousness that business can deploy its capital for development ends. This is fundamentally different from the use of others' funds to implement development projects, or the use of a company's surplus for philanthropic purposes.

To distinguish such efforts from the development tool role undertaken by other companies, we have used the term 'development agent'. It complements the predominant neoliberal development paradigm, and on current evidence seems likely to be of growing significance for as long as that paradigm flourishes. However, empirical studies show that we need to be cautious about the developmental efficacy of development agent approaches. Not only does their impact tend to be assessed in terms of the instrumental value to business rather than to the poor and marginalised, but the very notions of the poor, poverty, beneficiary, and development worthiness are being constructed around what is material, instrumental and comprehensible to business. In the process the nature of the poor's relationship to development is changing in a powerful shift in kind-making wherein, for instance, people are no longer recipients but customers and agents. It is tempting to look at this shift from a moralistic perspective, as something good or bad, and the role of business is certainly often viewed in this way. However, one does not have to take a stand about whether we are shifting from a better conceptualisation of development to a worse one or vice versa to understand the importance of the fact that a shift is taking place that is influenced by a managerialist, capitalist and populist logic. (For the historical precedents, see Kothari in this issue.) Although this shift is populated with examples of private enterprise demonstrating a pro-poor awareness, the meaning of pro-poor is defined with reference to the normative biases of business and endorsed by private and non-private sector agents that not only fail to reflexively consider the consequences of this, but show no appetite for holding business to account for the outcomes.

Two questions arise from this. First, if the normative conditions that prescribe what business does as a development agent cannot be changed because they are structurally embedded, can anything be done to increase the pro-poor elements of initiatives? This is something that could usefully drive a future research agenda, so that we move from a focus on justifying or criticising business's engagement as a development agent to an understanding of the possibilities and limitations of ideas such as BBC.

Second, and more radically, is it feasible to develop a Mark II (variant or improved) model of the development agent where issues such as pro-poor primacy and accountability are foregrounded? The characteristics of capital, pro-poor primacy and accountability need not change, but there would be two fundamental differences between the Mark II model and its forerunners. First, although it would continue to be a profitable enterprise employing its own capital to optimise development outcomes through commercial activities, its decisions would be based on what the poor would choose. It would, for instance, be likely to include job creation and retention, inclusion and helping people build their capabilities and/or their capital assets (eg social capital). Its products would be selected because they were socially and environmentally positive, as well as providing an acceptable financial return to investors. Overall, its business model would be developed so that it was resilient to the social, economic and environmental cycles that affect business sustainability, and it would be responsive to the needs of the poor as producers and consumers.

There are elements here that are complemented by emerging ideas such as impact investing and benefit corporations. Such ideas are still at the gestation stage but they highlight the need for a congruent and supportive environment of the kind that would lift the development agent out of the trap of the Porter Paradox. Such an environment would require changes to company law to free Mark II agents from the fiduciary and other constraints of mainstream company law. They would also require alternative forms of finance of the kind starting to be seen in impact investing, blended capital, patient capital, venture philanthropy and social venture capital. However, the changes are not simply a matter of replacing the old with the new. Financing the Mark II model implies a renewed role for international finance institutions, especially given the fall in foreign direct investment since 2007. History tells us that the emergence of new business models depends greatly on input from incumbent industries and companies,[91] and this is an area missing from current research. In the second difference from its forerunners, the Mark II model would require the rule of law to protect companies from arbitrary actions by other parties, and to protect citizens from pro-business zealotry.

It is beyond the scope of this paper to assess the feasibility of a Mark II model of the development agent, but it is important to highlight that it is different from what is currently being practised and often held up as an exemplar. The Mark I development agent has had success in engaging business in the issues of poverty and marginalisation, but it has done so by requiring that the primary intended beneficiaries conform to the requirements of business. A Mark II model would continue to encourage commercial enterprise, but it would be built around and judged upon what it achieved for the primary beneficiaries, who to date have been incidental to acting out the role of development agent.

Acknowledgements

The authors wish to thank the National Science Foundation (Grant #0548997), the ESRC/DFID (RES-167-25-0321), the Smith School for Enterprise and the Environment, University of Oxford, and the Oxford University Press John Fell Research Fund for their generous support of this research. We would also like to thank Stefano Ponte and Lisa Ann Richey, and an anonymous referee for their valuable comments on the paper.

Notes on Contributors

Michael Blowfield is Professor of Corporate Responsibility at Wolverhampton University, in addition to being Senior Visiting Fellow at the University of Oxford's Smith School of Enterprise and the Environment and Fellow at the London Business School. His most recent work is focused on business and sustainability and his most recent books are *Turnaround Challenge: Business and the City of the Future* (2013) and *Businessand Sustainability* (2013) both published by Oxford University Press.

Catherine S. Dolan is a Reader in Anthropology at the School of Oriental and African Studies, University of London, and a Visiting Fellow at the Said Business School and Green Templeton College, University of Oxford. She specialises in the cultural economy of development, primarily in Africa, and over the past 15 years has directed and researched interdisciplinary programmes on poverty, globalisation, commodity chains, corporate social responsibility and gender.

Notes

1. The discussion of Fairtrade is based on two multi-sited studies of Fairtrade (tea and flowers) conducted in Kenya from 2004 to 2007. Each study entailed interviews with smallholders, wage employees and industry stakeholders in Kenya, as well as with 'ethical consumers', companies, NGOs, and Fairtrade organisations in Europe. Evidence on BOP initiatives is based on two research projects – the CARE Bangladesh Rural Sales Programme (2008–10) and Avon South Africa (2008–11) – which examined the impact of BOP entrepreneurship on poor women's economic empowerment. Both included interviews with micro-entrepreneurs and their customers, government and civil society stakeholders, as well as participant observation and videography. The paper is also informed by extensive fieldwork conducted on CSR by the authors over the period of 1997–2007.
2. Cowen and Shenton, *Doctrines of Development*, 50.
3. McMichael, "Changing the Subject," 3; and Rankin, "Manufacturing Rural Finance."
4. Friedman, *Capitalism and Freedom*.
5. Rodrik, "Goodbye Washington Consensus"; and Collier, *The Bottom Billion*.
6. Ballinger and Olsson, *Behind the Swoosh*; INGI, "Unjust but Doing It!"; and Morrison and Delaney, "Marine Pollution."
7. Vogel, *The Market for Virtue*; Jenkins et al., *Corporate Responsibility and Labour Rights*; and Kolk et al., "International Codes of Conduct".
8. Ponte et al., *Governing through Standards*.
9. See O'Rourke, "Outsourcing Regulation"; Bendell and Kearins, "The Political Bottom Line"; Hughes, "Learning to Trade Ethically"; and Prieto-Carron, "Women Workers."
10. Locke et al., "The Promise and Perils of Private Voluntary Regulation"; and Mosley, *Labor Rights and Multinational Production*.
11. Knudsen, "Company Delistings"; and Baccaro and Mele, "For Lack of Anything Better?"
12. Newell and Frynas, "Beyond CSR?"; and Reed and Reed, "Partnerships for Development."
13. Kramer and Kania, "Changing the Game."
14. See Blowfield and Dolan, "Outsourcing Governance" on Fairtrade; Prahalad and Hart, "The Fortune at the Bottom" on BOP; and Jackson and Nelson, *Profits with Principles* on social enterprise.
15. See Easterly, *The White Man's Burden*; and Wilson, *Make Poverty Business*.
16. Noyoo, "Corporate Social Responsibility"; and Frynas, *Corporate Social Responsibility*.
17. See Kolk et al., "Reviewing a Decade of Research."
18. See Brett, "Fairtrade, Fair-Trade, Fair Trade" for Whole Foods; and Blowfield and Murray, *Corporate Responsibility* for Vodafone/Safaricom.

19. McKenna and Braithwaite, "Large Corporations and Obstacles to Peace."
20. "The Company File."
21. Blowfield and Dolan, "Fairtrade Facts and Fancies."
22. Blowfield, "Business and Poverty Reduction."
23. Blowfield, *Ethical Trade*; Freidberg, *The Contradictions of Clean*; and Archer and Fritsch, "Global Fair Trade."
24. Fig. *Corporations and Moral Purpose*; and Utting, "The Struggle for Corporate Accountability."
25. Ruggie, "Reconstituting the Global Public Domain"; and Vogel, *The Market for Virtue.*
26. Salomon, "AIDS is Risky Business".
27. Nelson, *Leveraging the Development Impact.*
28. Roy, *Poverty Capital*, 5.
29. Ibid., 6.
30. Richey and Ponte, *Brand Aid.*
31. Roy, *Poverty Capital*; Collier, *The Bottom Billion*; and Prahalad, *The Fortune at the Bottom.*
32. WBCSD, "Inclusive Business is Key"; and Kinsley, *Creative Capitalism.*
33. Ferguson, "The Uses of Neoliberalism"; and Mosse, *Cultivating Development.*
34. UNDP, *Human Development Report.*
35. Roy, "Ethical Subjects," 110.
36. See Elyachar, *Markets of Dispossession*; Ferguson and Gupta, "Spatializing States"; and Rankin, "Governing Development."
37. Ferguson, "Formalities of Poverty."
38. Roy, *Poverty Capital*, 32.
39. See Armendáriz de Aghion and Morduch, *The Economics of Microfinance*; Nelson and Pound, *A Review of the Impact of Fairtrade*; and Ansari et al., "Impact at the 'Bottom'."
40. Sen, "Wellbeing, Agency and Freedom."
41. Bruton's review of leading management journals found that only 11 articles published between 1989 and 2010 contained terms related to poverty. Bruton, "Business and the World's Poorest Billion."
42. See Hall et al., "Entrepreneurship and Innovation" for BOP; Raynolds et al., "Fair Trade" for Fairtrade; and Hermes and Lensink, "Microfinance: Its Impact" for microfinance.
43. Lewis and Mosse, "Encountering Order and Disjuncture," 6; and McMichael, "Changing the Subject," 3.
44. Blowfield and Dolan, "Fairtrade Facts and Fancies."
45. Schwittay, "The Marketization of Poverty," S71.
46. Ferguson, *The Anti-politics Machine*; Escobar, *Encountering Development*; Li, *The Will to Improve*; and Mosse, *Cultivating Development.*
47. Li, *The Will to Improve.*
48. Ibid., 7.
49. Cf. Boyd, "Ways of Seeing."
50. Rose, cited in Li, *The Will to Improve*, 35.
51. See Mosse, "Global Governance"; Escobar, *Encountering Development*; and Ferguson, *The Anti-politics Machine.*
52. Li, *Neo-liberal Strategies of Government*, 4.
53. Rose, *Powers of Freedom*; and Scott, *Seeing Like a State.*
54. World Economic Forum, *The Next Billions*, 6.
55. Quoted in ibid, 51.
56. Basheer, "The Handwashing Initiative," para. 1.
57. Cf. Li, "Practices of Assemblage and Community," 267.
58. Berlan and Dolan, "Of Red Herrings."
59. McMichael, "Changing the Subject," 3.
60. Kuriyan et al., "Consumption, Technology, and Development."
61. University of Oxford, "The 'Bottom of the Pyramid'".
62. Cross and Street, "Anthropology at the Bottom," 6.
63. Taylor and Buttel, "How Do We Know?," 405–406.
64. Roy, "Ethical Subjects," 107.
65. World Economic Forum, *The Next Billions*, 17; Viswanathan, "A Micro-level Approach"; and Hart and London, "Developing Native Capability."
66. Corporate Citizenship, *Inclusive Business*, 14.
67. See also Elyachar, "Next Practices."
68. Kashyap, *Rural Marketing*, 77.
69. Scott, *Seeing Like a State*, 2.
70. Cf. Boyd, "Ways of Seeing."
71. Roy, *Poverty Capital.*
72. Dolan, "The New Face of Development."
73. Roy, "Ethical Subjects," 1.
74. Ivo, "The Redefinition," 81; and Rankin, "Manufacturing Rural Finance."

75. Dolan and Johnstone-Louis, "Re-siting Corporate Responsibility"; and Schwittay, "The Financial Inclusion Assemblage."
76. Shell Foundation, "Enterprise Solutions," 12.
77. Ibid., 207.
78. Dolan, "The New Face of Development."
79. Anagnost, "Strange Circulations," 510; and Dolan and Johnstone-Louis, "Re-siting Corporate Responsibility," 29.
80. Ivo, "The Redefinition," 82.
81. Mutersbaugh, "Ethical Trade and Certified Organic."
82. Schwittay, "The Financial Inclusion Assemblage," 395. See also Roy, *Poverty Capital*, 99; and Rankin, "Governing Development."
83. Moreno, *Good Governance in Microcredit*, i.
84. Blowfield, "Reasons to be Cheerful"; and Lund-Thomsen, "Assessing the Impact."
85. Barrientos and Smith, "Do Workers Benefit?"
86. Margolis and Walsh, "Misery Loves Companies."
87. See Clay, *Exploring the Links*; and Kapstein, *Measuring Unilever's Economic Footprint.*
88. Porter and Kramer, "The Big Idea."
89. Porter, *Competitive Strategy.*
90. Koller, *Spark.*
91. Perez, *Technological Revolutions.*

Bibliography

Anagnost, Ann. "Strange Circulations: The Blood Economy in Rural China." *Economy and Society* 35, no. 4 (2006): 509–529.

Ansari, Shahzad, Kamal Munir, and Tricia Gregg. "Impact at the 'Bottom of the Pyramid': The Role of Social Capital in Capability Development and Community Empowerment." *Journal of Management Studies* 49, no. 4 (2012): 813–842.

Archer, Candace, and Stefan Fritsch. "Global Fair Trade: Humanizing Globalization and Reintroducing the Normative to International Political Economy." *Review of International Political Economy* 17, no. 1 (2010): 103–128.

Armendáriz, Beatriz, and Jonathan Morduch. *The Economics of Microfinance*. 2nd ed. Cambridge: MIT Press, 2010.

Baccaro, Lucio, and Valentina Mele. "For Lack of Anything Better? International Organizations and Global Corporate Codes." *Public Administration* 89, no. 2 (2011): 451–470.

Ballinger, Jeff, and Claes Olsson. *Behind the Swoosh: The Struggle of Indonesians Making Nike Shoes*. Uppsala/Brussels: Global Publications Foundation/ICDA, 1997.

Banerjee, Abhijit, and Esther Duflo. *Poor Economics: A Radical Rethinking of the Way to Fight Poverty*. New York: Public Affairs, 2011.

Barrientos, Stephanie, and Sally Smith. "Do Workers Benefit from Ethical Trade? Assessing Codes of Labour Practice of Global Production Systems." *Third World Quarterly* 28, no. 4 (2007): 713–729.

Basheer, M. P. "The Handwashing Initiative: Selling Soap or Saving Lives?" *Info-Change India*. 2002. http:// infochangeindia.org/other/features/the-handwashing-initiative-selling-soap-or-saving-lives.html.

Bendell, Jem, and Kate Kearins. "The Political Bottom Line: The Emerging Dimension to Corporate Responsibility for Sustainable Development." *Business Strategy and the Environment* 14, no. 6 (2005): 372–383.

Berlan, Amanda, and Catherine Dolan. "Of Red Herrings and Immutabilities: Rethinking Fair Trade's Ethic of Relationality among Cocoa Producers." In *Food Transgressions: Making Sense of Contemporary Food Politics*, edited by M. Goodman, and C. Sage, 39–60. London: Ashgate, 2014.

Blowfield, Michael. "Business and Poverty Reduction." In *Corporate Social Responsibility and Regulatory Governance: Towards Inclusive Development?*, edited by P. Utting and J. C. Marques, 124–150. New York: Palgrave Macmillan, 2010.

Blowfield, Michael. "Ethical Trade: A Review of Developments and Issues." *Third World Quarterly* 20, no. 4 (1999): 753–770.

Blowfield, Michael. "Reasons to be Cheerful? What We Know about CSR's Impact." *Third World Quarterly* 28, no. 4 (2007): 683–695.

Blowfield, Michael, and Catherine Dolan. "Fairtrade Facts and Fancies: What Kenyan Fairtrade Tells Us about Business' Role as Development Agent." *Journal of Business Ethics* 93 (2010): 143–162.

Blowfield, Michael, and Catherine Dolan. "Outsourcing Governance: Fairtrade's Message for C21 Global Governance." *Corporate Governance* 10, no. 4 (2010): 484–499.

Blowfield, Michael, and Alan Murray. *Corporate Responsibility: A Critical Introduction*, 2nd ed. Oxford: Oxford University Press, 2011.

Boyd, William. "Ways of Seeing in Environmental Law: How Deforestation Became an Object of Climate Governance." *Ecology Law Quarterly* 37 (2010): 843–916.

Brett, Adam. "Fairtrade, Fair-Trade, Fair Trade and Ethical Trade: Semantics, Politics and Development." *Food Chain* 1, no. 1 (2011): 117–125.

Bruton, Garry. "Business and the World's Poorest Billion: The Need for an Expanded Examination by Management Scholars." *Academy of Management Perspectives* 24, no. 3 (2010): 6–10.

Collier, Paul. *The Bottom Billion: Why the Poorest Countries are Failing and What Can Be Done about It*. New York: Oxford University Press, 2007.

BBC News. "The Company File: Body Shop Factory Sale." BBC News, June 24, 1999. http://news.bbc.co.uk/1/hi/business/377225.stm.

Corporate Citizenship. *Inclusive Business: The Next Frontier of Corporate Responsibility*. New York: Corporate Citizenship, 2012.

Cowen, Michael, and Robert Shenton. *Doctrines of Development*. London: Routledge, 1998.

Cross, Jamie, and Alice Street. "Anthropology at the Bottom of the Pyramid." *Anthropology Today* 25, no. 4 (2009): 4–9.

Dolan, Catherine. "The New Face of Development: The Bottom of the Pyramid Entrepreneurs." *Anthropology Today* 28, no. 4 (2012): 3–7.

Dolan, Catherine, and Mary, Johnstone-Louis. "Re-siting Corporate Responsibility: The Making of South Africa's Avon Entrepreneurs." *Focaal: Journal of Global and Historical Anthropology* 60, no. Summer (2011): 21–33.

Easterly, William. *The White Man's Burden: Why the West's Efforts to Aid the Rest have Done so much Ill and so little Good*. Oxford: Oxford University Press, 2006.

Elyachar, Julia. "Next Practices: Knowledge, Infrastructure, and Public Goods at the Bottom of the Pyramid." *Public Culture* 24, no. 1 (2012): 109–129.

Elyachar, Julia. *Markets of Dispossession: NGOs, Economic Development, and the State in Cairo*. Durham, NC: Duke University Press, 2005.

Escobar, Arturo. *Encountering Development: The Making and Unmaking of the Third World*. Princeton: Princeton University Press, 1994.

Ferguson, James. "Formalities of Poverty: Thinking about Social Assistance in Neoliberal South Africa." *African Studies Review* 50, no. 2 (2007): 71–86.

Ferguson, James. *The Anti-politics Machine: "Development", Depoliticization, and Bureaucratic Power in Lesotho*. Minneapolis: University of Minnesota Press, 1994.

Ferguson, James. "The Uses of Neoliberalism." *Antipode* 41, no. S1 (2010): 166–184.

Ferguson, James, and Akhil Gupta. "Spatializing States: Toward an Ethnography of Neoliberal Governmentality." *American Ethnologist* 29, no. 4 (2002): 981–1002.

Fig, David. *Corporations and Moral Purpose: South Africa's Truth and Reconciliation Commission and Business Responsibility for Apartheid*. BDS Working Paper 3. Copenhagen: Copenhagen Business School, 2007.

Freidberg, Susanne. *The Contradictions of Clean: Supermarket Ethical Trade and African Horticulture*. London: International Institute for Environment and Development, 2003.

Friedman, Milton. *Capitalism and Freedom*. Chicago, IL: University of Chicago Press, 1962.

Frynas, Jedrzej George. "Corporate Social Responsibility and Societal Governance: Lessons from Transparency in the Oil and Gas Sector." *Journal of Business Ethics* 93, no. 2 (2010): 163–179.

Hall, Jeremy, Stelvia Matos, Lorn Sheehan, and Bruno Silvestre. "Entrepreneurship and Innovation at the Base of the Pyramid: A Recipe for Inclusive Growth or Social Exclusion?" *Journal of Management Studies* 49, no. 4 (2012): 785–812.

Hart, Stuart, and Ted London. "Developing Native Capability: What Multinational Corporations can Learn from the Base of the Pyramid." *Stanford Social Innovation Review* 3, no. 2 (2005): 28–33.

Hermes, Neils, and Robert Lensink. "Microfinance: Its Impact, Outreach, and Sustainability." *World Development* 29, no. 6 (2011): 875–881.

Hughes, Alex. "Learning to Trade Ethically: Knowledgeable Capitalism, Retailers and Contested Commodity Chains." *Geoforum* 37, no. 6 (2006): 1008–1020.

INGI Labour Working Group. "Unjust but Doing It! Nike's Operations in Indonesia." *Inside Indonesia*, 7–9 June, 1991.

Ivo, Anete. "The Redefinition of the Social Issue and the Rhetoric on Poverty during the '90s." In *The Poverty of the State: Reconsidering the Role of the State in the Struggle against Global Poverty*, edited by A. Cimadamore, J. Siqueira, and H. Dean, 73–93. Buenos Aires: Consejo Latinoamericano De Ciencias Sociales, 2005.

Jackson, Ira, and Jane Nelson. *Profits with Principles: Seven Strategies for Delivering Value with Values*. New York: Currency/Doubleday, 2004.

Jenkins, Rhys, Ruth Pearson, and Gill Seyfang. *Corporate Responsibility and Labour Rights: Codes of Conduct in the Global Economy*. London: Earthscan, 2002.

Kashyap, Pradeep. *Rural Marketing*, 2nd ed. Delhi: Pearson Education, 2012.

Kinsley, Michael. *Creative Capitalism: A Conversation with Bill Gates, Warren Buffett, and Other Economic Leaders*. New York: Simon and Schuster, 2008.

Kolk, Ans, Miguel Rivera-Santos, and Carlos Rufin. "Reviewing a Decade of Research on the 'Base/Bottom of the Pyramid' (BOP) Concept." *Business & Society*, doi 10.1177/0007650312474928, forthcoming.

Kolk, Ans, Rob Tulder, and Carlijn Welters. "International Codes of Conduct and Corporate Social Responsibility: Can Transnational Corporations Regulate Themselves?" *Transnational Corporations* 8, no. 1 (1999): 143–180.

Koller, Frank. *Spark: How Old-fashioned Values Drive a Twenty-first Century Corporation: Lessons from Lincoln Electric's Unique Guaranteed Employment Program*. New York: Public Affairs, 2010.

Knudsen, Jette Steen. "Company Delistings from the UN Global Compact: Limited Business Demand or Domestic Governance Failure?" *Journal of Business Ethics* 103, no. 3 (2011): 1–19.

Kramer, Mark, and John Kania. "Changing the Game: Leading Corporations Switch from Defense to Offense in Solving Global Problems." *Stanford Social Innovation Review* Spring (2006): 20–27.

Kuriyan, Renee, Dawn Nafus, and Scott Mainwaring. "Consumption, Technology, and Development: The 'Poor' as 'Consumer'." *Information Technologies and International Development* 8, no. 1 (2012): 1–12.

Lewis, David, and David Mosse. "Encountering Order and Disjuncture: Contemporary Anthropological Perspectives on the Organization of Development." *Oxford Development Studies* 34, no. 1 (2006): 1–13.

Li, Tania. *Neo-liberal Strategies of Government through Community: The Social Development Program of the World Bank in Indonesia*. IILJ Working Paper 2006/2. New York: New York University School of Law, 2006.

Li, Tania. "Practices of Assemblage and Community Forest Management." *Economy and Society* 36, no. 2 (2007): 263–293.

Li, Tania. *The Will to Improve: Governmentality, Development, and the Practice of Politics*. Durham, NC: Duke University Press, 2007.

Locke, Richard, and Monica Romis. "The Promise and Perils of Private Voluntary Regulation: Labor Standards and Work Organization in Two Mexican Garment Factories." *Review of International Political Economy* 17, no. 1 (2010): 45–74.

London, Ted, and Stuart Hart. "Reinventing Strategies for Emerging Markets: Beyond the Transnational Model." *Journal of International Business Studies* 35, no. 5 (2004): 350–370.

Lund-Thomsen, Peter. "Assessing the Impact of Public–Private Partnerships in the Global South: The Case of the Kasur Tanneries Pollution Control Project." *Journal of Business Ethics* 90, no. 1 (2009): 57–78.

Margolis, Joshua, and James Walsh. "Misery Loves Companies: Rethinking Social Initiatives by Business." *Administrative Science Quarterly* 48, no. 2 (2003): 268–305.

Mckenna, Kylie, and John Braithwaite. "Large Corporations and Obstacles to Peace in Papua." In *Comprehending West Papua*, edited by P. King, J. Elmslie, and C. Webb-Gannon, 318–338. Sydney: University of Sydney, 2007.

McMichael, Philip. "Changing the Subject of Development." In *Contesting Development: Critical Struggles for Social Change*, edited by P. McMichael, 1–13. New York: Routledge, 2009.

Miller, Clark. "Democratization, International Knowledge Institutions, and Global Governance." *Governance: An International Journal of Policy, Administration, and Institutions* 20, no. 2 (2007): 325–357.

Moreno, Frede. *Good Governance in Microcredit Strategy for Poverty Reduction: Focus on Western Mindanao, Philippines*, 2004. http://eprints.rclis.org/16617/.

Morrison, R. J., and J. R. Delaney. "Marine Pollution in the Arafura and Timor Seas." *Marine Pollution Bulletin* 32, no. 4 (1996): 327–334.

Mosley, Layna. *Labor Rights and Multinational Production*. Cambridge: Cambridge University Press, 2011.

Mosse, David. *Cultivating Development: An Ethnography of Aid Policy and Practice*. London: Pluto Press, 2005.

Mosse, David. "Global Governance and the Ethnography of International Aid." In *The Aid Effect*, edited by D. Mosse, and D. Lewis, 1–28. London: Pluto Press, 2005.

Mutersbaugh, Tad. "Ethical Trade and Certified Organic Coffee: Implications of Rules-based Agri-cultural Product Certification for Mexican Producer Households and Villages." *Transnational Law and Contemporary Problems* 12, no. 1 (2002): 89–108.

Nelson, Jane. *Leveraging the Development Impact of Business in the Fight against Global Poverty*. CSR Initiative Working Paper 22. Boston, MA: John F. Kennedy School of Government, 2006.

Nelson, Valerie, and Bill Pound. *A Review of the Impact of Fairtrade over the Last Ten Years*. London: Fairtrade Foundation, 2010.

Newell, Peter, and George Frynas Jedrzej. "Beyond CSR? Business, Poverty and Social Justice: An Introduction." *Third World Quarterly* 28, no. 4 (2007): 669–681.

Nikolas, Rose. *Powers of Freedom: Reframing Political Thought*. Cambridge: Cambridge University Press, 1999.

Noyoo, Ndangwa. "Corporate Social Responsibility and Social Policy in Zambia." Paper presented at the Conference on Business, Social Policy and Corporate Political Influence in Developing Countries, Geneva, November 12–13, 2007.

O'Rourke, Dara. "Outsourcing Regulation: Analyzing Nongovernmental Systems of Labor Standards and Monitoring." *Policy Studies Journal* 31, no. 1 (2003): 1–30.

Perez, Carlota. *Technological Revolutions and Financial Capital: The Dynamics of Bubbles and Golden Ages*. Cheltenham: Edward Elgar, 2002.

Ponte, Stefano, Peter Gibbon, and Jakob Vestergaard eds. *Governing through Standards: Origins, Drivers and Limitations*. London: Palgrave Macmillan, 2011.

Porter, Michael. *Competitive Strategy: Techniques for Analyzing Industries and Competitors*. New York: Free Press, 1980.

Porter, Michael, and Mark Kramer. "The Big Idea: Creating Shared Value." *Harvard Business Review* 89 (2011): 1–2.

Prahalad, C. K. *The Fortune at the Bottom of the Pyramid: Eradicating Poverty through Profits*. State College, PA: Wharton School Publishing, 2004.

Prahalad, C. K., and Stuart Hart. "The Fortune at the Bottom of the Pyramid." *Strategy+Business* 26 (2002): 54–67.

Prieto-Carrón, Marina. "Women Workers, Global Supply Chains and Corporate Codes of Conduct." *Journal of Business Ethics* 83, no. 1 (2008): 5–17.

Rankin, Katherine. "Manufacturing Rural Finance in Asia: Institutional Assemblages, Market Societies, Entrepreneurial Subjects." *Geoforum* 39, no. 6 (2008): 1965–1977.

Rankin, Katherine. "Governing Development: Neoliberalism, Microcredit, and Rational Economic Woman." *Economy and Society* 30, no. 1 (2001): 18–37.

Raynolds, Laura, Douglas Murray, and Peter Taylor. "Fair Trade: Building Producer Capacity via Global Networks." *Journal of International Development* 16, no. 8 (2004): 1109–1121.

Reed, Ananya, and Darryl Reed. "Partnerships for Development: Four Models of Business Involvement." *Journal of Business Ethics* 90, no. 3 (2009): 3–37.

Richey, Lisa Ann, and Stefano Ponte. *Brand Aid: Shopping Well to Save the World*. Minneapolis: University of Minnesota Press, 2011.

Rodrik, Dani. "Goodbye Washington Consensus, Hello Washington Confusion? A Review of the World Bank's Economic Growth in the 1990s: Learning from a Decade of Reform." *Journal of Economic Literature* 44, no. 4 (2006): 973–987.

Roy, Ananya. *Poverty Capital: Microfinance and the Making of Development*. London: Taylor and Francis, 2010.

Roy, Ananya. "Ethical Subjects: Market Rule in an Age of Poverty." *Public Culture* 24, no. 1 (2012): 105–108.

Ruggie, John. "Reconstituting the Global Public Domain—Issues, Actors, and Practices." *European Journal of International Relations* 10, no. 4 (2004): 499–531.

Salomon, Martha. "AIDS is Risky Business: Examining the Effect of the Aids Crisis on Publicly Traded Companies in South Africa and the Implications for both South African and US Investors." *Vanderbilt Journal of Transnational Law* 37, no. 5 (2004): 1473–1510.

Schwittay, Anke. "The Financial Inclusion Assemblage: Subjects, Technics, Rationalities." *Critique of Anthropology* 31, no. 4 (2011): 381–401.

Schwittay, Anke. "The Marketization of Poverty." *Current Anthropology* 52, no. S3 (2011): S71–S82.

Scott, James. *Seeing Like a State*. New Haven, CT: Yale University, 1988.

Sen, Amartya. "Wellbeing, Agency and Freedom: The Dewey Lectures 1984." *Journal of Philosophy* 82 (1985): 169–221.

Foundation, Shell. *Enterprise Solutions to Poverty: Opportunities and Challenges for the International Development Community and Business*. London: Shell Foundation, 2005.

Taylor, Peter, and Frederick Buttell. "How Do We Know We Have Global Environmental Problems? Science and the Globalization of Environmental Discourse." *Geoforum* 23, no. 3 (1992): 405–416.

United Nations Development Program (UNDP). *Human Development Report*, 2007. http://hdr.undp.org/en/media/hdr_20072008_en_complete.pdf.

University of Oxford. "The 'Bottom of the Pyramid' Approach: Responsible Capitalism or Business as Usual?" Public Debate, Said Business School, University of Oxford, May 3, 2012.

Utting, Peter. "The Struggle for Corporate Accountability." *Development and Change* 39, no. 6 (2008): 959–975.

Viswanathan, Madhubalan. "A Micro-level Approach to Understanding BOP Markets." In *Next Generation Business Strategies for the Base of the Pyramid: New Approaches for Building Mutual Value*, edited by T. London, and S. Hart, 129–164. Upper Saddle River, NJ: Pearson, 2011.

Vogel, David. *The Market for Virtue: The Potential and Limits of Corporate Social Responsibility*. Washington, DC: Brookings Institution Press, 2005.

Vogel, David. "Private Global Business Regulation." *Annual Review of Political Science* 11 (2008): 261–282.

WBCSD. "Inclusive Business is Key for Companies to Engage in Developing Countries, WBCSD Executive Dialogue Reveals." November 7, 2008. www.wbcsd.org.

Wilson, Craig. *Make Poverty Business: Increase Profits and Reduce Risks by Engaging with the Poor*. Sheffield: Greenleaf, 2006.

World Economic Forum. *The Next Billions: Unleashing Business Potential in Untapped Markets*. Geneva: World Economic Forum, 2009.

Trade, consumption and development alliances: the historical legacy of the Empire Marketing Board poster campaign

Uma Kothari

Institute for Development Policy and Management, University of Manchester, UK

This article examines the historical legacy of contemporary development alliances through an analysis of the British government's Empire Marketing Board poster campaign from 1926 to 1933. The primary aim of these posters was to instil in the British public a preference for buying empire-grown goods and the significance of their role as consumers in maintaining the Empire. By conveying messages of a common humanity and invoking a visual language of interdependence between Britain and its colonies, the posters attempted to open up new connections and create new moral communities across distance in ways that are not dissimilar to fair trade campaigns today.

Introduction

Since the 1980s new kinds of relationships have been forged between Third World producers and Western consumers through various ethical consumption initiatives. These have, in part, been enabled through the vast proliferation of public campaigns, charity adverts, fair trade marketing posters and media promotions. Much recent scholarly attention has investigated the growing significance of these public and popular campaigns in influencing the role of consumers in supporting development related concerns.[1] These studies have, importantly, identified the extent to which ethical consumption creates new global alliances and consumers have become new development actors.[2] While there is no doubt that there is something unique about contemporary fair trade initiatives and ethical consumerism campaigns, encouraging Western consumers to support development concerns, and the use of popular campaigns to mobilise them, is not wholly new. Indeed, there is a significant historical genealogy to the present-day relationship between trade, consumption and development and the use of popular and visual representations of development issues to strengthen these connections.[3] This paper explores how particular global connections and development alliances were initiated during the colonial period through the forging of new consumer identities and consciousness. More specifically, it demonstrates how an understanding of this colonial legacy can shed light on contemporary ethical consumption initiatives through an analysis of the British government's Empire Marketing Board (EMB) poster campaign, which ran between 1926 and 1933.[4]

The primary aim of the EMB posters, displayed on large billboards throughout the UK, was to instil in the British public a preference for buying empire-grown goods. However, the posters also had an important function in encouraging them to recognise the significance of their role as consumers in maintaining the Empire. By conveying messages of a common humanity and invoking a visual language of interdependence between Britain and its colonies, the EMB attempted to establish an ethos of care and responsibility towards people in the Empire overseas as a means to encourage the British public to buy empire-grown produce. By encouraging the British public to become responsible consumers, the EMB posters endeavoured to open up new connections and create new moral communities across distance. While the ambivalent moralities of trade, consumption and development, underpinned by the visual reproduction of often racial and cultural stereotypes, inevitably compromised the form and extent of this, the posters did reveal to the British public the significance of their new role in civilising, modernising and developing the colonies.

Analysis of these posters can offer important insights for the advertising and marketing campaigns of international development charities and NGOs today.[5] These are saturated with images, some of which are provocative and challenging, but many of which continue to reproduce essentialised representations of formerly colonised people and places. As such, an analysis of the relational ethics between consumers and distant producers depicted in the posters can contribute to a critical analysis of new development alliances and the framing of new consumer identities. However, while it is important to explore the legacy of these representations today, this cannot be done outside of an understanding of the historical, economic and cultural context in which they were produced.[6] Additionally critiquing contemporary discourses by identifying their roots in a colonial past has often led to contrived historical comparisons that have not only run the risk of misrepresenting the past but also of distorting the present. Notwithstanding this cautionary note, and while acknowledging that understandings of the past are inevitably an act of the present,[7] historical research has, importantly, located imperial themes in contemporary popular culture and raised awareness of the interconnectedness of domestic and overseas histories.

This article is based on archival research on the Colonial Office Records at the National Archives in Kew, London, which holds extensive documentation, photographs and correspondence spanning Britain's colonial era and includes material on the policies, procedures and debates of the British government's Empire Marketing Board. It draws upon a collection of the posters donated by the EMB in 1933 to the Manchester Art Gallery and it adopted a critical approach to visual imagery to examine the practices, technologies and knowledges through which these images had been constructed.[8] While some posters refer to the settler colonies of Australia, Canada and New Zealand, for the purposes of linking the EMB campaign to contemporary campaigns for ethical consumption, this study focused on those depicting scenes from Africa, Asia and the Indian Ocean.

The EMB was established in 1926 by the Colonial Secretary, Leopald Amery, and directed by Stephen Tallents. It was anticipated that the EMB would stimulate trade and satisfy the demands of the colonies and dominions for greater access to the British market for their agricultural and industrial goods. The EMB represented the British government's first peacetime propaganda campaign, advocating non-tariff preference as a way of addressing conflicts between those promoting free trade, protectionism and preferences. In its attempt to promote 'imperial preference without tariffs' the EMB spent £1.1 million between 1926 and 1932.[9] However, the EMB was short-lived, abolished in 1933 when a system of imperial preference replaced free trade following the signing of trade agreements on the Commonwealth Tariff Preference by Britain and its 'empire nations' in Ottawa in 1932.[10]

In order to publicise and promote Empire trade, the EMB organised exhibitions, poster campaigns, films, 'Empire Shopping Weeks', Empire shops, lectures, radio talks, a library, advertisements in the national and local press and shop window displays. The most important and visible work of the EMB was its poster publicity campaign, which commissioned and displayed some 800 posters between 1926 and 1933. These posters signify one of the most systematic and paradigmatic examples of a public consumer campaign, the primary purpose of which was to increase sales of Empire-produced goods throughout the British Empire.[11] Images and texts of the people and places of the Empire overseas were depicted on large hoardings, changed every week, displayed in public spaces and thoroughfares; sent to over 25,000 schools and posted in football stadiums throughout Britain. By 1933 frames were placed at 1800 different sites in 450 British towns. So extensive was the geography of the campaign that Constantine remarked: 'no British consumer could have been unaware' of it.[12] The posters are historically significant not only as early examples of modern public relations and consumer marketing campaigns,[13] but also because of their aesthetic and artistic qualities.[14] In order to ensure the popularity and marketing success of the poster campaign, the EMB committee solicited the help of London's major design houses.[15] The EMB 'became a major patron of commercial art',[16] relying on a range of personnel, including those from the media, public relations and the advertising industry. The posters themselves are large and visually stunning, created by some of the most famous artists of the time (such as Frank Newbould, Keith Henderson and Hugh Williamson). As such, they represent unique examples of industrial art of the late 1920s and early 1930s.

It is important to recognise the difficulties of measuring popular opinion with reference to the EMB, and that in the end speculation is unavoidable, since 'hard data on popular attitudes towards Empire and the wider world is lacking'.[17] With no market research at the time, it was difficult to evaluate the extent to which the advertising efforts of the EMB were successful in changing the consumption patterns of the British masses to make purchasing decisions based on where goods came from rather than on price, although it is likely that the EMB, as a popular and public campaign, enjoyed some success in implanting its ideological message about Empire.[18] Despite difficulties in gauging the impact and influence of the EMB campaign, it is possible, through an analysis of the posters, to identify the attempts that were being made to create new imperial relations and how these were expressed and communicated.

The following section explores the relationship between public campaigns and consumer culture before highlighting how trade was promoted through changing consumer practices, identities and behaviours. The paper goes on to examine the EMB campaign's efforts to forge new forms of global interconnectedness that shaped the British public's ideas about a common humanity and their role in supporting the development of the empire overseas. It concludes by suggesting that some of these representations and discourses parallel that of Fair Trade campaigns today in terms of reconfiguring relations between consumers and producers, demonstrating how an analysis of the EMB campaign provides useful insights into contemporary ethical consumption initiatives.

Public campaigns and consumer culture

The EMB posters were forms of advertising that produced particular kinds of commodity culture built on visual images. Based on his study of advertising campaigns in Mumbai, Mazzarella suggests that commodity images attempt to redefine culture and, in so doing, market not merely the product but culture itself.[19] In this way a cultural value is given to material goods and the commodity image is the signifier produced by an advertisement when it becomes part of the public domain.[20] Advertising campaigns then incorporate culture into consumerism and hence capitalism is not simply an economic, but also a cultural, process. The links between consumer culture and capitalism, identified by Benjamin for example, are characterised by visual inscriptions of modernity in which commodity culture is a projection, not a reflection, of the economy.[21] Particularly useful for understanding how global connections are established through consumption, furthermore, is the idea that the commodity image can be used not only to project culture but to create cultural difference. Since 'every commodity reproduces the ideology of the system that produced it',[22] this commodification of culture may fix and naturalise inequalities between and within cultures and societies. In the contemporary context of ethical consumption, as Abrahamsen suggests, 'the idea of Africa appears as a commodity, its poverty and illness symbolic goods in a global economy of signification that allows (predominantly) Western consumers not only to express their identity, but also to reproduce social hierarchies'.[23] Thus, advertising does not just sell things but also creates structures of meaning and difference. Importantly 'commodities function at several levels – as signs and symbols, as regulating agents, as meaning conferring things, as markers of the categories of a culture. As such they connect with many corresponding levels of behaviour and identity.'[24] Advertising then reflects complex relationships between images, practices and uses that change over time, are context-specific and always ideological.

In the context of Empire advertising, as an influential mode of social reading,[25] became a medium capable of enforcing and enlarging Britain's power in the colonial world.[26] Visual colonialism extended into the everyday lives of people through posters, as advertising took 'scenes of empire into every corner of the home stamping images of colonial conquest on soap boxes, matchboxes, biscuit tins, whiskey bottle, tea tins and chocolate bars'.[27] In *Imperial Leather* McClintock provides a detailed study of how mass advertising in the 19th century sold not only the product but the political culture of imperialism.[28] With reference to Pears soap she writes that the advertising posters invested 'the aesthetic space around the domestic commodity with the commercial cult of empire'. Thus, 'commodity kitsch made possible, as never before, the mass marketing of empire as an organised system of images and attitudes'.[29]

Colonial consumption was largely characterised by the conspicuous consumption of 'exotic', luxury goods such as tea, gold, spices and sugar by the upper classes. The EMB campaign, however, extended into the realm of the everyday, highlighting the role of the wider British public in consuming empire-grown produce. It took visual representations of the Empire into the mass realm, suffusing British cultural life and public space.[30] For this to be possible the cultural resource had to 'offer points of pertinence through which the experience of everyday life can be made to resonate with it';[31] and, for public communication to be popular, it had to speak to the quotidian. However, in the context of the mass media, which Herman and Chomsky argue serves 'as a system for communicating messages and symbols to the general populace…to amuse, entertain and inform', there is also the function of inculcating 'individuals with the values, beliefs and codes of behaviour that will integrate them into the institutional structure of the larger society'[32]. Thus, popular and public representations have the power to reshape national life and public relations.[33] It is these aims that underpinned the objectives and ideology of the EMB poster campaign.

While popular ideas about the Empire are diffused through literature,[34] the visual offers an unrivalled form of 'sensual immediacy'.[35] As such, through these visually arresting images, the EMB campaign bridged the furthest spatial, economic and emotional distances of the global food system at the time. Indeed, the desired economic effects of the campaign would not have been achieved unless the posters had been able to demonstrate to the British public their links to the empire overseas thereby shifting their consumer behaviour. So, for example, the 'picking empire grown tea' and 'drinking empire grown tea' posters (Figure 1) create a transnational (gendered), interconnected sphere of production and consumption as well as resonating with, the everyday sensibilities and proclivities of, especially middle class, British consumers. The EMB posters were, thus, 'a set of cultural technologies',[36] which commodified and marketed Empire to an increasingly consumer-conscious, and globally aware, British public. And the campaign simultaneously forged new global linkages and consumer identities.

Promoting trade and creating new consumer identities

Richey and Ponte have identified the new ways in which commerce, consumption and 'doing good' are being linked in a present in which helping distant others has become 'a way of constructing a postcolonial Western identity,

Figure 1. Two posters showing the picking and drinking of empire-grown tea.
Sources: Williamson, H. S. "Picking Empire Grown Tea." Manchester Art Gallery. Accessed August 25, 2013. http://www.manchestergalleries.org/the-collections/search-the-collection/display.php?EMUSESSID=6f0b417e8713a5ff36b570af8bf1a7f8&irn=4356; and Williamson, H. S. "Drinking Empire grown tea." Manchester Art Gallery. Accessed August 25, 2013. http://www.manchestergalleries.org/the-collections/search-the-collection/display.php?EMUSESSID=6f0b417e8713a5ff36b570af8bf1a7f8&irn=4190.

producing a responsible form of corporate engagement in the market, and selling products at the same time'.[37] This has an important legacy in the EMB campaign, whose principal aim was to stimulate trade by promoting and marketing Empire products (Figure 2). This section explores how the EMB promoted trade by creating new consumer identities, forging new imperial connections and marketing a reworked idea of Empire. The following section examines in more detail how the campaign furthered its aims by demonstrating to British consumers their roles and responsibilities in helping develop distant others in their empire overseas.

The main objective of the EMB campaign was to increase British consumption of Empire foodstuffs and raw materials and it did this by depicting and explaining the interconnectedness of Empire and the importance to Britain of sustaining the Empire. All forms of EMB publicity were designed to showcase either specific imperial goods or the virtues of an individual nation – with the related goals of boosting sales and developing a product-based imperial consciousness.[38] It did this through the text on posters, which provided messages encouraging imperial trade and details of the product and country being promoted. At the same time the campaign promoted the idea that empire purchasing

Figure 2. Highways of Empire: "Buy Empire Goods from Home and Overseas", Empire Marketing Board.
Source: Library and Archives Canada.

would create increased demand for the manufactured products of the UK and thereby stimulate employment at home. This dual message, connecting the idea that being an 'empire buyer' enabled empire building, is evident in Figure 3.

In order to build new consumer identities and, importantly, to legitimise the Empire 'for another generation',[39] new connections between producers and consumers were built. However, given the high level of ignorance among the British public about the places and extent of empire, stimulating empire trade required the EMB to take on the role of educating consumers about the geographical spread, benefits, successes and interconnectedness of Empire. As Chair of the Empire Marketing Board, Amery mounted a campaign projecting an image of the British Empire to the general public,[40] while Tallents, similarly dismayed by the lack of public knowledge about the Empire, 'devised a publicity campaign that would provide didactic instruction on what the British Empire was and why it was important to people in Britain'.[41] This significant educational function meant that many advertisements promoting a particular product from the Empire included information about the good or the colony from which it comes (see Figure 3). And, to ensure that the message could be easily understood, statistics and figures were kept to a minimum.[42] Thus, the EMB 'campaign became like a series of geography lessons, a patriotic pageant and an economic spectacle all rolled into one'.[43] This attempt to bring 'the Empire alive' was based on creating new commercial links between Britain and its colonies; borne out of a desire to promote trade, it simultaneously created and reflected the changing consciousness among the British public about the role and purpose of Empire.

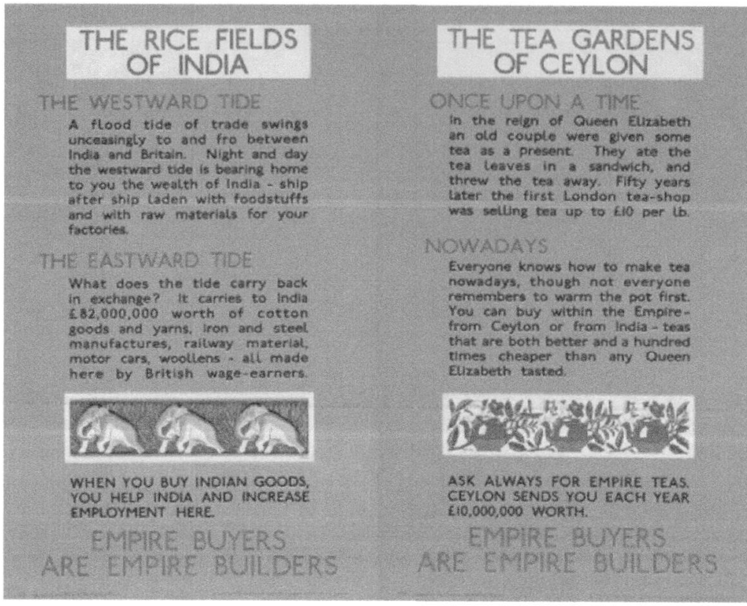

Figure 3. The Rice Fields of India; The Tea Gardens of Ceylon, Empire Marketing Board.
Source: Library and Archives Canada.

Thus, while the campaign did not market a 'brand' as such, it sold a reworked *idea* of empire as the source of the nation's strength, status, unity and pride.[44]

It was this recasting of Empire that was central to instilling in the British public a preference for empire-grown produce and their role in sustaining the Empire. The sentiment implied by some of the posters was that this was a new dawn in imperial relations; as such, it demonstrates well the multiple, varied and changing nature of colonialism over time.[45] The specific moment of the establishment of the EMB in Britain's imperial history was thus significant. The posters were produced when the metropole, and its colonies, were witnessing a transition that eventually culminated in independence for many colonies and the setting up of the Commonwealth. From the 1920s it was this process that the EMB sought to explain, reflect and, to some extent, promote. Indeed, the posters' content, design and display provide examples of how changing constellations of networks and reconfigurations of people, ideas and things shaped 'Britain's changing place in, and involvement with, the rest of the world'.[46] The posters show how the British Colonial government wanted British citizens to identify with the Empire in the later days of colonialism. Along with colonial films they promoted an enterprise of mutual prosperity, creating an image, albeit largely idealised, of imperial interconnectedness and cooperation between 'more than 40 separate territories, more than 60 million people'.[47] The EMB campaign thus represented attempts by the British government to foster new connections between the metropole and its colonies and to recast the Empire as a modern interdependent whole. The posters articulate an ambivalence between diverse colonial projects shaped simultaneously around ideas of the 'white man's burden', the economic needs of a dwindling empire, and civilising missions, in which the colonised are 'out there' yet also part of a collective project for the establishment of a common wealth of people across the Empire. In order to reimagine Empire as a force for justice and progress, Amery further expounded this idea of an integrated common wealth.[48] This was developed by Tallents who, following the demise of the EMB, drew a parallel between the Board and UNESCO, noting that the EMB had come to think of the British Empire primarily as a cooperative concern.[49] Grierson, head of the EMB film unit, similarly suggested that the EMB was like the League of Nations.[50] Utilising public relations techniques and propaganda, the posters' underlying message was to 'move Britain's view of empire away from notions of domination',[51] and in so doing to remodel the British Empire as a benevolent, progressive mission towards a 'commonwealth' of people.

The campaign thus articulated a shift from Empire as domination 'to convey the message that the British Empire constituted a single family of diverse yet united peoples'.[52] In order to achieve this modernising of Britain's image, Tallents and the EMB promoted the idea of an imperial family in which 'Britain was like the parents, the Dominions were the brothers and sisters and the Colonies were like the children'.[53] The family analogy and implied interconnections were evident in posters that urged 'Keep Trade in the Family' and 'Remember your Cousins'.[54] In depicting the interconnectedness of the economic interests of the metropole and colonies, and invoking the metaphor of a single family, the posters attempted to establish links between different parts of the Empire through the economies of production and consumption as well as through the development of other mutual interests.

Through the posters a vision for the Empire was integrated into the everyday spaces of people's lives and imaginations. As forms of advertising that promoted a product, the posters revealed to the British public the places, people and produce of Empire, and crucially underlined their contribution to its ongoing success. They served to instil national pride in Britain as an imperial power, while also educating Britons as to the importance of Empire and to their role in sustaining it. In this way they attempted to create new alliances between the British public and the Empire overseas through consumption. In summary, the poster campaign had multiple purposes: to promote greater trade between Britain and its colonies, to identify the interconnectedness of Britain and the Empire overseas and to increase understanding of the relationship between producers and consumers. This meant not just selling the Empire to the British but also selling the British to the peoples of the Empire. In endeavouring to turn the British public into empire-conscious consumers, the EMB encouraged them to conceive of the Empire as an ethical and interconnected concern.[55] But these posters reflected a further important tangent: Amery and Tallents, as shown above, were keen to depict a more modern version of Empire and this necessitated explicitly invoking a language of care and responsibility towards imperial subjects and the promotion of ideas of progress and development for all.[56] Consequently many posters intertwined the promotion of economic trade with a 'civilising mission'. As public, visual representations during later British imperial rule, they were, therefore, also a medium through which ideas and forms of humanitarianism towards, and development of, the colonies could be articulated, as detailed below.

Constructions of a common humanity and promoting ideas of development

Notions of a common humanity and global interconnectedness, which underpin modern ideas of development, began to emerge through the EMB posters. They provide a paradigmatic example of a public consumer campaign in which views of development were conveyed,[57] thus signifying a seminal moment in the advancement of a connection between consumption and development. As such, the EMB poster campaign was the precursor of Britain's new commodity culture,[58] and marked the emergence of a modern development discourse, one that was imbricated with, but simultaneously began to move away from, earlier imperial representations of otherness. Thus, the promotion of markets, trade and consumption, through public advertising, spread ideas about developing the colonies and attempted to create and sustain moral communities of care across distance. These new relations, defined and visually manifest in the EMB posters, are evident in ethical consumption campaigns today in which the belief that, through commerce, Western consumers can help develop distant others is promoted. This message resonates with what Richey and Ponte refer to as 'Brand Aid', which today helps sell and improve the ethical profile and value of a (brand) product, while at the same time, 'like other cause-related marketing initiatives, a proportion of the profit or sales is devoted to helping others'.[59] This section explores in more detail how messages conveying this responsibility towards the development of others were historically depicted and established.

Ideologies such as those underpinning the EMB, which connect people across vast spaces, have often shaped notions of caring for distant others.[60] For Amery, it was this development of the colonies that represented 'a most wonderful piece of work upon which we are engaged. I think it is the most direct and practical contribution that we, the White peoples of the Empire, can make to the general welfare of mankind.'[61] The posters were infused with notions of a common humanity, care for distant others and forms of economic and social development that reflected progressive strands based on socially liberal and welfarist ideas that were gaining ground in metropolitan thought in the late colonial period. Keen to shift the image of Empire away from associations with subjugation, violence and conflict, the EMB used its posters to depict the sorts of opportunities the Empire could offer its subjects. At the same time, as public exhibits and symbols of Empire, these notions were conveyed through the transmission of images that further embedded the superiority of Britain and the British. By communicating ideas about the 'backwardness' of colonial people and places, and depicting the rightness and beneficial nature of Empire, the posters alluded to the need for Britain to advance social, economic and technological progress in the overseas Empire.

This is evident, for example, in posters that presented production processes in the colonies as non-industrial, backward and inefficient, processes which consequently necessitated and legitimised the purportedly modern, progressive and humanitarian interventions by the metropole. What is evident in these

Figure 4. Colombo, Ceylon from the 'Our Trade with the East' series, Empire Marketing Board.
Source: Library and Archives Canada.

posters is an acknowledgment that colonised people are hardworking (Figure 4). Their problem, then, is not an unwillingness to work, but ignorance and a lack of the necessary skills, expertise and technology to develop. The posters thus appealed to the need to share Britain's modern, industrial expertise and, importantly, served to justify further imperial intervention.

The role of the metropole in helping the colonies to develop is evident through a range of visual strategies but most obviously through depictions of a white man educating, supporting, guiding and bringing modernity and technology to the colonies. This is particularly striking in the disturbing racialised imagery of the larger-than-life white man imparting wisdom to the black child while overseeing agricultural processes in the 'Colonial Progress Brings Home Prosperity' series poster (Figure 5) below.

These popular representations of development were based on a belief that Britain was a pioneering nation that had built for itself an advanced human culture and a model of civilisation.[62] Progress and modernity were important aspects of British colonial identity at home and overseas, and the posters reflected the moral responsibility of helping colonies develop their societies to achieve the kinds of progress exemplified by Britain. Based on a belief in this superiority of British culture and economy, the EMB placed great emphasis on what it believed was Britain's role as the Empire's enabler. Referring to the achievements of the EMB's development work abroad, Tallents commented that, 'Every colonial civil servant knows how much could and should be done in helping backward peoples to learn new and more scientific ways of rearing their children, tilling their soil and improving their health'.[63] Significantly key themes of development, religion, art and economics suffused their campaign and provided causes onto which British consumers could project their liberal values and take pride in their benevolent intentions.

Figure 5. Empire Tobacco from Northern Rhodesia and Nyasaland from the 'Colonial Progress brings Home Prosperity' series, Empire Marketing Board.
Source: The National Archives. Accessed August 26, 2013. http://www.nationalarchives.gov.uk/default.htm.

The metaphor described above, in which the Empire is depicted as a family so as to encourage the British public to buy goods in support of their colonial 'kith and kin'. was also an important component of the humanitarian message of the EMB campaign, which effectively linked consumption and development. In the EMB posters, films and writings, 'British people were represented as both father-like and mother-like, teaching their colonial family about progress and industry as well as supporting and nurturing its welfare and growth'.[64] In this large extended Empire family married British women in the metropole were the imperial housewives whose shopping practices bound the familial empire together (Figure 6).[65]

The EMB 'turned metropolitan homes into sites of imperial consumption'.[66] Women were designated 'empire builders', suggesting that, when 'housewives cared for their nuclear families by purchasing and preparing empire foods they

Figure 6. The Good Shopper, Empire Marketing Board.
Source: Library and Archives Canada.

also helped to build and sustain the extended family of the British Empire'.[67] Within this domesticated Empire, although the 'parents' are in charge, they also have responsibilities towards their 'children', and the posters encouraged the British consumer to play the part of the good parent by buying goods from the colonies to help their colonial children grow. Furthermore, as their welfare needed to be protected, notions of care and trusteeship became central to ideas of development. These visual depictions of the progressive benefits of the colonial project, as well as familial dependency, connected people in ways that emphasised the 'progressive rather than aggressive mission of colonialism'.[68]

The EMB's creation of a more humanitarian imperial project in the minds of the metropolitan public, however, relied on 'circulating false images of imperialism and of the British Empire, and...inaccurately comparing the empire to a family'.[69] Indeed, mapping the aesthetics of the Victorian family onto this large Empire family produced paternalistic relations between coloniser and colonised that were deeply hierarchical, since caring was never considered a relationship between equals.[70] At best this inequality was represented as benevolence and paternalism, at worst the posters articulated deeply racist stereotypes that reflected the colonial government's racialised approach to colonial development. Mackenzie questions the extent to which the posters actually created and manipulated popular racialised opinions, since by the time they were produced 'many of the popular attitudes towards Empire were [already] deeply embedded'.[71] Thus, rather than *creating* the racial character of popular imperialism, perhaps the posters were merely *reflecting* it.[72] The 'Buy Empire Goods' campaign, or indeed the fair trade movement more recently, was not therefore neutral but a means by which political traditions could be reworked and mobilised and through which value systems that favour particular identities and relationships could be reasserted.[73]

That the EMB campaign was ultimately about changing consumer preferences and identities in order to sustain the Empire is evident in one of the last series of posters, which presents a radical shift in popular representations of imperial relations, alliances and development. The promotion of trade within the Empire was given a boost in 1932 when, at an Imperial Economic Conference held in Ottawa, 'Imperial Preference' was introduced. In the light of this the Empire Marketing Board was closed down in 1933 as there was no longer a need to actively promote and advertise Empire trade. Yet the 'Advance Empire Trade' series reproduced below (Figure 7) provides provocative and striking imagery of the future Commonwealth, displaying a common and shared vision of progress, enlightenment and development that disrupts many of the previous images dis-

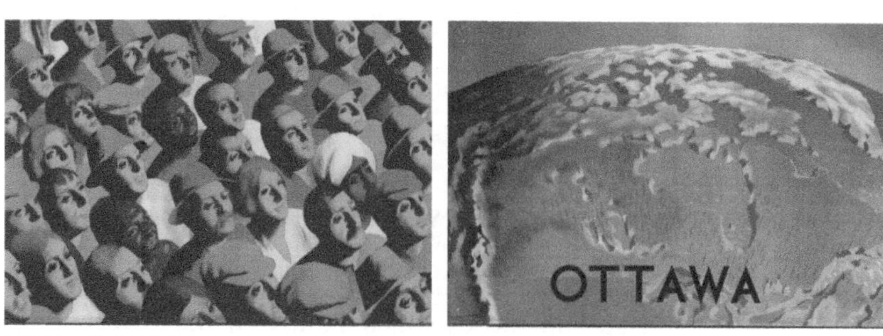

Figure 7. The Advance Empire Trade Series, Empire Marketing Board.
Source: Library and Archives Canada.

cussed above. Here, symbolically, a multiracial group, together, look up towards what appears to be a light symbolising a collective and unified future project of progress – the Commonwealth.

Historical legacy of contemporary alliances and ethical consumption identities

Postcolonial critiques of development have revealed the colonial legacy of contemporary institutions, discourses and practices.[74] These studies, illuminating the relevance of Empire and colonialism to, for example, contemporary perceptions of development, have interrogated hegemonic understandings of geography, history and representations, demonstrating how these emerged out of colonial projects and the multiple ways in which they continue to be played out in the present.[75] It remains important to engage with historical material to explore the legacy of present-day ideas, to counter the persistence of negative representations and to reveal how they reproduce hierarchies over time. However, this has to be done within an understanding of the historical, economic and cultural context in which they were produced.

The EMB campaign, with its focus on promoting the consumption of produce from the Empire overseas, demonstrated the interconnectedness of consumers and producers and highlighted the responsibilities of consumers to help the colonies develop. This has important resonances with contemporary ethical consumption, branding and cause marketing. Specifically how trade, consumption, global alliances and development were linked through the EMB campaign provides important insights into how these connections are being forged in present-day campaigns, particularly in terms of raising consumers' awareness of their role in supporting the development of others. This is evident in the way the EMB campaign in the past fostered a geographical development imaginary that connected Western consumers with distant producers in much the same way as fair trade campaigns today promote alternative modalities of trade and development through new commodity networks.[76] Importantly, however, forging these connections was enabled and sustained by reifying differences and relying on racialised representational tropes of colonised peoples, strategies which, though less pernicious, continue to be invoked today.

In the EMB campaign, together with the metaphor of the Empire family, linking consumers to a geography of production created various geographical attachments and entanglements.[77] In an attempt to combine the economic imperative inherent in the promotion of empire-grown goods with a moral responsibility towards development the EMB campaign evoked a visual language of care, interdependence and a common humanity. As ubiquitous public displays, the posters' imagery and ideology suffused British everyday space, shaped the British public's ethical disposition towards an integrated Empire and fostered the emergence of moral communities across distance. In this way it aimed to build a 'community' by promoting connections between the metropole and its colonies. It is at this level that the past can be considered in some senses to have something to offer to the contemporary version of ethical trade and consumption, and in particular to an understanding of how new global alliances are being created. The construction of this geographical imaginary through the creation of spatial connections, networks and alliances was a significant component of the EMB campaign and is evident in contemporary fair trade campaigns. Furthermore, some of the colonial ideas and images described above represent historical antecedents of those mobilised in contemporary marketing campaigns, as they work to promote ethical consumerism by raising awareness about development issues.

The dual meaning of consumption, as in purchasing goods, and absorbing and imbibing ideas, is similarly invoked in historical and contemporary campaigns. The complex relations of embodied, material encounter and engagement between, for example, the British public and the posters did not only shape their consumer practices and behaviours.[78] It also affected how they envisaged the Empire overseas and their roles and responsibilities towards colonised people. Through visual illustrations of Empire created through the posters of the EMB attempts were made by the British government to recast the Empire as a modern, interdependent and interconnected whole. This was, in part, articulated through the projection of a humanitarian project to encourage an ethos of care among the British public, albeit one that was wrapped around particular notions of superiority, modernity and progress. The posters illuminated how the British public could assume a role in developing the colonies as consumers and demonstrated the importance of creating connections and alliances with the Empire overseas. As a means of advertising that promoted a product together with ideas of development, the EMB 'took its place at the vanguard of Britain's new commodity culture and its civilising mission'.[79]

These popular representations, which simultaneously sought to reorder relations between producers and consumers through the promotion of a project of caring for distant others, are not too dissimilar to contemporary fair trade campaigns. Trentmann provides a poignant comparison in his study of the relationship between the EMB and the present-day fair trade campaign in terms of the ways in which they both address the interconnectedness of trade, consumerism and development.[80] He argues that the EMB campaign represented a precursor of care and reciprocity evident in the contemporary fair trade movement, showing the genealogy of current norms and practices of ethical consumerism. An analysis of the EMB campaign demonstrates how it shaped the British public's ideas about progress, humanity and development and their relationship to the Empire overseas in much the same way as the fair trade campaign today influences ideas about global connections and humanity and reconfigures relations between consumers and producers. Indeed, fair trade adverts are replete with symbols of an interconnected world, in which images and representations attempt to 'connect cultures globally'.[81]

Fair trade campaigns are often based on what Goodman refers to as 'conditions of consumption' in which 'where one's purchase is going and how consumption affects the social and ecological conditions of production, are made visible on fair trade commodities'.[82] While these conditions of consumption were evident in some of the EMB posters, they were focused more on the economic benefits to the metropole and the British public collectively rather than to the individual specifically. Yet self-perceptions and self-interest underlie these historical and contemporary campaigns. By informing the British public about colonised places and spreading the idea of an empire family, the EMB created 'for the British a world view which was central to their perceptions of themselves' as globally powerful.[83] This self-interest is evident in campaigns today, when 'private giving and charity...has become part of the relentless self-invention of a particular kind of modern consumer' as do-gooder.[84] Additionally, reconnecting producers and consumers through the creation of a transnational moral economy,[85] requires heavy investment in consumer education, which played as significant a role during the EMB campaign as it does today.

Promoting global interconnectedness through texts and images is a significant component of these campaigns, often revealing particular meanings and values of difference, otherness and inequality that continue to underpin discourses of development. Despite a language of a common wealth and interdependence, the posters continued to reify a hierarchical imperial system and reproduce paternalist and unequal relationships between coloniser and colonised. Mackenzie suggests that the EMB campaign occurred within the broader context of imperialist attitudes in Britain and demonstrated that 'jingoism was an omnipresent' cultural facet of everyday British life.[86] Thus the ambivalent moralities of trade, consumption and development were often underpinned by a racialised discourse that inevitably compromised the extent to which moral communities of care could be created and sustained across distance. Overall, therefore, the posters did promote ideas of development and interconnectedness but only in the context of ensuring and sustaining economic benefits to the metropole, very much like the contemporary Brand Aid initiatives analysed by Ponte and Richey.[87] Indeed, as Cecil Rhodes once put it, 'imperialism was philanthropy plus a 5 per cent dividend on investment'.[88] While modelling overseas development on Britain's technological and scientific advancement did instigate some humanitarian support, it also confirmed the cultural and economic superiority of Britain. The EMB posters reified racial hierarchies through visual images of modern, benevolent colonial whites depicted alongside inferior, yet industrious, colonised others. In debating the purpose and value of exhibiting these posters today, the Manchester Art Gallery acknowledged that 'the EMB's sentiments in some ways illustrate the formation of the Commonwealth, but in other ways they reflect many older imperial ideas and prejudices'.[89] Linking the past to the present, Harrison reminds us that 'when we think about Brand Aid, and its connections between the virtuous consumer and the fate of distant others, we would do well to remember how deeply embedded in (post-) imperial public norms this subjectivity is' as an 'African imagery served to generate a sumptuary sensibility: of patriotic purchase, mainly promoted through the Empire Marketing Board'.[90] Today, when Africa is seen as symbolic of all that is depraved, and with representations of Africa becoming increasingly stylised, such that 'the tribal/savage trope is still cleaved to by many journalists in their disaster reportage',[91] the legacy of colonial depictions is ever more apparent. These forms of representation of interconnectedness paradoxically reaffirm distinctions between consumers and distant producers.

In terms of relations between consumers, these campaigns have varied and multiple consequences. As marketing displays, despite their appeal primarily to middle class women who had the economic power to effect changes in their domestic consumption patterns, the posters acted as a focus for the convergence between classes, genders and elite and popular culture. Nevertherless, the only appeal from the EMB to the working classes would have been to instil imperialistic beliefs, as the latter had limited purchasing power. One of the less stated reasons for launching the EMB was the belief that imperialism provided an ideological counter to socialism for the working class, since the project touted imperialism as a solution to the economic problems in Britain.[92] In this way, as Constantine has written, art was 'harnessed to a political purpose' to ensure the ongoing legitimacy of the Empire.[93] Today, as Abrahamsen argues,[94] 'commodities aid in securing, advancing and reproducing class cohesion but they also facilitate movement within and between class positions'. As such we are witnessing the 'emergence of a new modality of aid...allowing sections of contemporary consumer society to produce and maintain their identity and class positions'.[95]

The expanding range of actors and forms of new alliances today are in some senses new and different. Even though contemporary representations merge the old with the new, there have also been significant changes over time. As Richey and Ponte suggest, 'Brand Aid' is 'based on three pillars: a brand, a cause, and one or more celebrities'.[96] It is the increasingly central role of the celebrity that marks out contemporary campaigns from their earlier manifestations.[97] Furthermore, in many fair trade campaigns today the voice and agency of producers is advertised in order to demonstrate recognition and to promote forms of 'solidarity in difference'.[98] This is contrary to the EMB campaign, in which producers are accorded no agency in presenting their ideas about trade, consumption or indeed their development. However, there is clearly an historical dimension to current marketing campaigns and this article has suggested that the legacy of contemporary ideas about a common humanity and global interconnectedness, which underpin modern ideas of development, has circumscribed relations between consumers and producers. The EMB represents a seminal moment in the evolution of responsible consumption. As such, analysis of the posters can offer food for thought to the advertising and marketing campaigns of international development charities and NGOs today that are saturated with images, some of which are provocative and challenging, but many of which continue to reproduce essentialised representations of formerly colonised people and places. The EMB provides an opportunity to critically reflect on the historical legacy of the current, and increasingly important, role of advertising and marketing campaigns of international development charities, NGOs and fair trade initiatives in drawing in new actors, and forming new alliances.

Acknowledgements

I would like to thank Dr Melanie Horton at Manchester Metropolitan University and Ruth Shrigley, Principal Manager of Collections Access at Manchester Art Gallery, for their support and for sharing with me their invaluable knowledge of the EMB posters.

Notes on Contributor

Uma Kothari is Professor of Migration and Postcolonial Studies in the School of Environment and Development, University of Manchester. Her research interests include development histories and theories, colonial and postcolonial analyses and transnational migration and diaspora. This research has involved a number of externally funded projects and has resulted in the publication of numerous articles and guest editorships. Her edited books include *Participation:*

The New Tyranny?, *Development Theory and Practice: Critical Perspectives* and *A Radical History of Development Studies*. She is currently carrying out research on perceptions of climate change and migration, the military as new development actors and the impacts of international volunteering.

Notes

1. Silverstone, *Media and Morality*; Sparks, *Globalisation*; and Goodman, "The Mirror of Consumption."
2. Littler, *Radical Consumption*; and Morgan, "Local and Green."
3. Trentmann, "Before Fair Trade."
4. Barnett et al., "Political Ethics of Consumerism," 45–51.
5. Nash, "Global Citizenship"; and Richey and Ponte, "Brand Aid."
6. MacKenzie, *Orientalism*.
7. Driver, "Geography's Empire," 36.
8. Heywood and Sandywell, *Handbook of Visual Culture*; Pink, "Applied Visual Anthropology"; and Rose, *Visual Methodologies*.
9. Meredith, "Imperial Images," 30.
10. Cronin, "Selling Irish Bacon."
11. Grierson, *Edited Version*, G2.8.4.
12. Constantine, *Buy and Build*.
13. Ibid.
14. Cronin, "Selling Irish Bacon."
15. Ibid., 134.
16. Constantine, *Buy and Build*, 7.
17. Ibid., 223.
18. Ibid., 219–224.
19. Mazzarella, *Shovelling Smoke*.
20. Ibid., 16.
21. Benjamin, *Illuminations*.
22. Fiske, *Understanding Popular Culture*, 14.
23. Abrahamsen, "Africa," 141.
24. Clammer, "Consuming Bodies," 217.
25. Wicke, *Advertising Fictions*.
26. Richards, *The Commodity Culture*, 127.
27. McClintock, *Imperial Leather*, 209.
28. McClintock, *Imperial Leather*.
29. Ibid., 213, 209.
30. MacKenzie, *Orientalism*.
31. Fiske, *Understanding Popular Culture*, 129.
32. Herman and Chomsky, *Manufacturing Consent*, 1.
33. Anthony, *Public Relations*.
34. See Jackson and Tompkins, *Illustrating Empire*.
35. Mirzoeff, *The Visual Culture Reader*, 9; and Evans and Hall, *Visual Culture: The Reader*.
36. Bennett, "The Exhibitionary Complex," 78.
37. Richey and Ponte, "Brand Africa," 135. See also Richey and Ponte, this issue.
38. Cronin, "Selling Irish Bacon," 133.
39. Constantine, quoted in Horton, *Propaganda, Pride and Prejudice*, 38.
40. Meredith, "Imperial Images," 30.
41. Horton, *Propaganda, Pride and Prejudice*, 3.
42. Ibid.
43. Ibid., 4.
44. Self, "Treasury Control," 157.
45. See Lester, "Imperial Circuits."
46. Ogborn, *Global Lives*, 7.
47. Constantine, quoted in Horton, *Propaganda, Pride and Prejudice*, 38.
48. Amery, quoted in Self, "Treasury Control," 156.
49. Horton, *Propaganda, Pride and Prejudice*, 137.
50. Grierson, *Edited Version*, G2.8.4.
51. Horton, *Propaganda, Pride and Prejudice*, 114.
52. Mackenzie, "The Popular Culture of Empire," 217.
53. Manchester Art Gallery, *Empire Marketing Board Posters*.
54. MacKenzie, *Imperialism and Popular Culture*, 217.

55. Horton, *Propaganda, Pride and Prejudice.*
56. Merchant, "The Imperial Housewife."
57. Anthony, *Public Relations.*
58. McClintock, *Imperial Leather.*
59. Richey and Ponte, "Brand Africa," 136. See also Richie and Ponte, this issue.
60. Trentmann, "Before Fair Trade."
61. Amery, *My Political Life*, 352.
62. Hobsbawm, *The Age of Empire.*
63. Horton, *Propaganda, Pride and Prejudice*, 137.
64. Manchester Art Gallery, *Empire Marketing Board Posters.*
65. Merchant, "The Imperial Housewife," 1.
66. Merchant, "The Imperial Housewife", 4.
67. Ibid., 3.
68. Horton, *Propaganda, Pride and Prejudice*, 124.
69. Meredith, "Imperial Images," 32.
70. Trentmann, "Before Fair Trade."
71. MacKenzie, *Propaganda and Empire*, 118.
72. MacKenzie, *Propaganda and Empire.*
73. Trentmann, "Before Fair Trade."
74. Power, *Rethinking Development Geographies*; Kothari, "Spatial Imaginaries and Practices"; McEwan, "Material Geographies and Postcolonialism"; and Duffield and Hewitt, *Empire, Development and Colonialism.*
75. Havinden and Meredith, *Colonialism and Development*; Chakrabarty, *Provincializing Europe*; and Slater and Bell, "Aid and the Geopolitics of the Postcolonial."
76. Goodman, "Reading Fair Trade," 908.
77. Pike, "Placing Brands and Branding"; and Miller, "The Unintended Political Economy."
78. Rose and Tolia-Kelly, *Visuality/Materiality.*
79. McClintock, *Imperial Leather*, 208.
80. Trentmann, "Before Fair Trade."
81. Dogra, "Reading NGOs Visually," 161.
82. Goodman, "Reading Fair Trade," 900.
83. MacKenzie, *Propaganda and Empire*, 2.
84. Abrahamsen, *Africa*, 140.
85. Goodman, "Reading Fair Trade," 891.
86. MacKenzie, *Propaganda and Empire.*
87. Ponte and Richey, this issue.
88. Rhodes quoted in Lawlor, *Murder on the Verandah*, 63.
89. Manchester Art Gallery, *Empire Marketing Board Posters*, 12.
90. Harrison, "Images and Representations," 143.
91. Ibid., 144.
92. See MacKenzie, *Propaganda and Empire.*
93. Constantine, quoted in Horton, *Propaganda, Pride and Prejudice*, 38.
94. Abrahamsen, "Africa," 141.
95. Ibid., 142.
96. Richey and Ponte, "Brand Africa," 136. See also Ponte and Richey, this issue.
97. See Brockington, this issue.
98. Goodman, "Reading Fair Trade," 906.

Bibliography

Abrahamsen, R. "Africa in a Global Political Economy of Symbolic Goods." *Review of Africa Political Economy* 39, no. 131 (2012): 140–142.

Amery, L. S. *My Political Life*. London: Hutchinson, 1953.

Anthony, S. *Public Relations and the Making of Modern Britain*. Manchester: Manchester University Press, 2011.

Barnett, C., P. Cloke, N. Clarke, and A. Malpass. "The Political Ethics of Consumerism." *Consumer Policy Review* 15, no. 2 (2005): 45–51.

Benjamin, W. *Illuminations*. London: Pimlico, 1999.

Bennett, T. "The Exhibitionary Complex." *New Formations* 4 (1988): 73–102.

Chakrabarty, D. *Provincializing Europe: Postcolonial Thought and Historical Difference*. Princeton: Princeton University Press, 2000.

Clammer, J. "Consuming Bodies: Constructing and Representing the Female Body in Contemporary Japanese Print Media." In *Women, Media and Consumption in Japan*, eds. L. Skov, and B. Moeran, 197–218. Richmond: Curzon Press, 1995.

Constantine, S. *Buy and Build: The Advertising Posters of the Empire Marketing Board*. London: HMSO, 1986.

Cronin, M. "Selling Irish Bacon: The Empire Marketing Board and Artists of the Free State." *Eire-Ireland* 39, no. 3–4 (2004): 132–143.

Dogra, N. "'Reading NGOs Visually'– Implications of Visual Images for NGO Management." *Journal of International Development* 16, no. 2 (2007): 161–171.

Driver, F. "Geography's Empire: Histories of Geographical Knowledge." *Environment and Planning D* 10, no. 1 (1992): 23–40.

Duffield, M., and V. Hewitt eds. *Empire, Development and Colonialism*. James Currey: Rochester, NY, 2009.

Evans, J., and S. Hall eds. *Visual Culture: The Reader*. London: Sage, 2004.

Fiske, J. *Understanding Popular Culture*. London: Routledge, 1994.

Goodman, M. "Reading Fair Trade: Political Ecological Imaginary and the Moral Economy of Fair Trade Foods." *Political Geography* 23, no. 7 (2004): 891–915.

Goodman, M. "The Mirror of Consumption: Celebritization, Developmental Consumption and the Shifting Cultural Politics of Fair Trade." *Geoforum* 41, no. 1 (2010): 104–116.

Grierson, J. *Edited Version of Typed Copy of Annual Report on the Activities of the Empire Marketing Board Film Unit*, ref G2.8.4, 1931. Accessed August 25, 2013. http://www.is.stir.ac.uk/libraries/collections/spcoll/media/ownwordsemb.php.

Harrison, G. "Images and Representations of Africa: Old, New and Beyond." *Review of African Political Economy* 39, no. 131 (2012): 142–145.

Havinden, M., and D. Meredith. *Colonialism and Development*. London: Routledge, 1993.

Herman, E., and N. Chomsky. *Manufacturing Consent: The Political Economy of the Mass Media*. London: Vintage, 1994.

Heywood, I., and B. Sandywell eds. *The Handbook of Visual Culture*. London: Berg, 2012.

Hobsbawm, E. *The Age of Empire, 1875–1914*. London: Abacus, 1999.

Horton, M. "*Propaganda, Pride and Prejudice*." Manchester Metropolitan University: Unpublished doctoral thesis, 2010.

Jackson, A., and D. Tompkins. *Illustrating Empire: A Visual History of British Imperialism*. Oxford: Bodleian Library, 2011.

Kothari, U. "Spatial Imaginaries and Practices: Experiences of Colonial Officers and Development Professionals." *Singapore Journal of Tropical Geography* 27, no. 3 (2006): 235–253.

Lawlor, E. *Murder on the Verandah: Love and Betrayal in British Malaya*. London: Flamingo, 2000.

Lester, A. "Imperial Circuits and Networks: Geographies of the British Empire." *History Compass* 4, no. 1 (2006): 124–141.

Library and Archives Canada. Government of Canada. Accessed August 26, 2013. http://www.bac-lac.gc.ca/eng/Pages/home.aspx.

Littler, J. *Radical Consumption: Shopping for Change in Contemporary Culture*. London: Open University Press, 2008.

MacKenzie, J. *Propaganda and Empire The Manipulation of British Public Opinion 1880–1960*. Manchester: Manchester University Press, 1984.

MacKenzie, J. ed. *Imperialism and Popular Culture*. Manchester: Manchester University Press, 1986.

MacKenzie, J. *Orientalism: History, Theory and the Arts*. Manchester: Manchester University Press, 1995.

Mackenzie, J. "The Popular Culture of Empire in Britain." In *The Oxford History of the British Empire: The Twentieth Century*, edited by. J. Brown, and W. R. Louis, 212–231. Oxford: Oxford University Press, 1999.

Manchester Art Gallery. *Empire Marketing Board Posters*. London: Scala, 2010.

Mazzarella, W. *Shovelling Smoke: Advertising and Globalization in Contemporary India*. Durham, NC: Duke University Press, 2003.

McClintock, A. *Imperial Leather: Race Gender and Sexuality in the Colonial Contest*. London: Routledge, 1995.

McEwan, C. "Material Geographies and Postcolonialism." *Singapore Journal of Tropical Geography* 24, no. 3 (2009): 340–355.

Merchant, E. "*The Imperial Housewife and the Familial Empire: The Empire Marketing Board's Family Analogy, 1926–1933*". Paper presented at the Gender in the Archive graduate student workshop: University of Michigan, April, 2004.

Meredith, D. "Imperial Images: The Empire Marketing Board, 1926–32." *History Today* 37, no. 1 (1987): 30–36.

Miller, D. "The Unintended Political Economy." In *Cultural Economy: Cultural Analysis and Commercial Life*, edited by. P. Du Gay, and M. Pryke, 166–184. London: Sage, 2002.

Mirzoeff, N. ed. *The Visual Culture Reader*. London: Routledge, 2002.

Morgan, K. "Local and Green, Global and Fair: The Ethical Foodscape and the Politics of Care." *Environment and Planning A* 42, no. 8 (2010): 1852–1867.

Nash, K. "Global Citizenship as Show Business." *Media Culture & Society* 30, no. 2 (2008): 167–181.

Ogborn, M. *Global Lives: Britain and the World 1550–1800*. Cambridge: Cambridge University Press, 2008.

Pike, A. "Placing Brands and Branding: A Socio-spatial Biography of Newcastle Brown Ale." *Transactions* 36, no. 2 (2011): 206–222.

Pink, S. *Doing Visual Ethnography*. London: Sage, 2007.
Power, M. *Rethinking Development Geographies*. London: Routledge, 2003.
Richards, T. *The Commodity Culture of Victorian England: Advertising and Spectacle, 1851–1914*. Stanford, CA: Stanford University Press, 1990.
Richey, L., and S. Ponte. "Brand Africa: Multiple Transitions in Global Capitalism." *Review of African Political Economy* 39, no. 131 (2012): 135–150.
Richey, L., and S. Ponte. *Brand Aid: Shopping Well to Save the World*. Minneapolis: University of Minnesota Press, 2011.
Rose, G. *Visual Methodologies: An Introduction to the Interpretation of Visual Materials*. London: Sage, 2007.
Rose, G., and D. P. Tolia-Kelly. *Visuality/Materiality: Images, Objects and Practices*. Aldershot: Ashgate, 2012.
Self, R. "Treasury Control and the Empire Marketing Board: The Rise and Fall of Non-tariff Preference in Britain, 1924–1933." *Twentieth Century British History* 5, no. 2 (1994): 153–182.
Silverstone, R. *Media and Morality: On the Rise of the Mediapolis*. London: Polity Press, 2006.
Slater, D., and M. Bell. "Aid and the Geopolitics of the Postcolonial: Critical Reflections on New Labour's Overseas Development Strategy." *Development and Change* 33, no. 2 (2002): 335–360.
Sparks, C. *Globalisation, Development and the Mass Media*. London: Sage, 2007.
Trentmann, F. "Before Fair Trade: Empire, Free Trade and the Moral Economies of Food in the Modern World." *Environment and Planning D* 25, no. 6 (2007): 1079–1102.
Wicke, J. A. *Advertising Fictions: Literature, Advertisement, and Social Reading*. New York: Columbia University Press, 1988.

Buying into development? Brand Aid forms of cause-related marketing

Stefano Ponte[a] and Lisa Ann Richey[b]

[a]*Department of Business and Politics, Copenhagen Business School, Denmark;* [b]*Department of Society and Globalisation, Roskilde University, Denmark*

Consumers, partnering with corporations and celebrities, are forming new alliances in international development through what we call 'Brand Aid' initiatives. At a time of shifting relationships between public and private aid, commodities are sold as the means of achieving development for recipients and good feelings for consumers simultaneously. In this article we first formalise our conceptual model of Brand Aid at the triple interface of causes, branded products and celebrities. Then we conduct a systematic empirical analysis of contemporary Brand Aid initiatives, including three in-depth case studies of 'Win One Give One', TOMS shoes and Product (RED). We argue that these not only use imaginaries of development to sell products to Northern consumers but also engage in the work of a 'story factory' – producing truths about international development and consumer engagement that make development appear simplified, manageable and marketable. We conclude that, in Brand Aid, the problems themselves and the people who experience them are branded and marketed to Western consumers (through celebritised multimedia story-telling) just as effectively as the products that will 'save' them.

Introduction

What links a bottle of vodka with a pair of Emporio Armani (RED) sunglasses, or a pair of canvas shoes with a box of Fruit-Flavor Shapes Transformers? Bono assures us that a percentage of the profits of all (RED) co-branded products goes directly to the Global Fund to Fight HIV/AIDS, TB and Malaria. Dr Michele Borba, celebrity educator, advises parents that Betty Crocker fruit flavored snacks can contribute to kids' altruism. Blake Mycoskie identified a development 'need' in Latin America linked to his performance in the US television show, 'The Amazing Race' and launched a youth movement and TOMS shoes. All these products are marketed through celebrities to consumers who want to shop for a better world. These consumers, allied with corporations, are becoming new actors in international development through what we call 'Brand Aid' initiatives. Brand Aid entails specific forms of cause-related marketing (CRM), where the purchase of a product triggers a business donation (typically to a non-profit organisation) for the purpose of solving a social, environmental or animal welfare 'cause'. Unlike other CRM campaigns, Brand Aid initiatives address specific 'international development' causes and involve celebrities in their launch, mediation and/or management.

Brand Aid, the combination of causes, branded products and celebrity, is one of the newest alliances in international development, and it comes at a time of shifting relationships between public and private aid.[1] Private funding is becoming more important as traditional sources are under stress from the contemporary economic crisis. This is reflected in a historical trend of shifting patterns of resource transfers from North to South. Sources of development financing outside traditional official development assistance (ODA) are growing,[2] and this is shaping the funding and agenda of development. As we argued in the introduction to this issue, the activities of new actors and alliances is becoming increasingly relevant. However, the power of Brand Aid in shaping international development is not simply a material one. On the basis of substantial empirical work on CRM initiatives supporting the 30 most recognisable non-profit organisations dealing with 'international needs', a recent article in this journal found that the promotional aspects of partnering with corporations were more important than the actual financial benefits arising from the CRM engagement.[3] These findings raise important questions about the role of consumption in funding international development initiatives: in short, if it is not for the money, then why would development organisations benefit from CRM?

To begin to answer this question, we develop a conceptual model of 'Brand Aid', where 'brand' incorporates material value and fantasy. Companies are of course the core actors in branding for profit. Celebrities are personified through their own brands or personae. And it is slowly becoming recognised that non-profit organisations working in international development are also branded entities.[4] Our purpose in this article is to provide a framework to help understanding how development actors such as consumers and celebrities overlap in new alliances.[5] We also test the model empirically through a systematic study of contemporary Brand Aid initiatives in order to examine its possibilities and limitations.

We distinguish between the selling of ideas together with the 'cargo' of development,[6] and using imaginaries of development to sell products to Northern consumers. We focus on the latter. Development as a commodity for exchange can be linked to trajectories as diverse as selling improved seeds in the Green Revolution or selling condoms through social marketing initiatives for family planning. But the increasing 'privatisation of helping' has made engaging in development such a desirable practice that admission to such a process can be sold to consumers as one might sell entrance tickets to a concert or amusement park. Development outcomes themselves – such as primary education for a child, vaccines provided to a health clinic or a community well for clean water – become so imbued with symbolic and 'ethical' value that they are used to market consumer goods to Western buyers. Trusted celebrities are important for creating the caring brand that sells development.[7] Commodities are sold as the means of achieving development for recipients and good feelings for consumers simultaneously. In the process 'development' becomes ontologically ingrained as synonymous with 'having the right things'.

Our analysis of Brand Aid initiatives focuses on those with a direct purchase–contribution link. This is a choice that reflects the different kinds of social relations surrounding these forms of CRM. First, the focus on buying a particular product directly links a product with a cause in ways that draw on the awareness raised by decades of activism for fair trade and ethical consumption. But this also pushes the meaning of ethical consumption away from the attributes of the product itself (the social, environmental or animal welfare conditions of its production) and places them onto the worthy cause, as the basis for 'ethical' engagement.[8] Second, the focus on purchase-linked donation encourages increasing consumption.[9] As you spend money, purchase products and consume, you are actively 'helping'. Third, in the direct purchase–contribution model, the point of action or engagement is clear and distinct. It is the point of purchase. This clear action for consumers is a way of defining development 'goods' and the entry point for everyday consumers into activism, providing 'development' or just 'helping' needy others. When the purchase has been made, the consumer has completed her/his job in the process of helping, and the product itself becomes a marker of that good act. You buy something so that someone else can have something, and imaginaries of development, 'yours' and 'theirs,' are constructed on the basis of these 'things.'

In the next section, we briefly review the current debates on cause-related marketing, celebrity and development. The third and fourth sections lay out our conceptual model and methodology and in Section 5 we present three case studies of Brand Aid initiatives. This is followed by a conclusion.

Cause-related marketing, celebrity and development

Brand Aid initiatives are CRM campaigns that employ an international development 'cause' and celebrities as mediators. In earlier work we argued that this specific configuration of CRM is new and can be ascribed to the birth of Product (RED) in 2006.[10] However, CRM campaigns have a much longer history and are accompanied by a well developed literature in business studies,[11] only recently expanding to development studies.[12] In its simplest form CRM is essentially marketing – it is devised to sell a product or service to consumers by highlighting the fact that part of the profit or sale price will be donated to a 'good cause'. The size of the donation is typically linked to the volume of sales during the CRM campaign.

The birth of CRM dates back to the American Express campaigns of the early 1980s, when card-holders were encouraged to use their credit cards in specified campaign periods to support a number of US local causes.[13] The success of these initiatives led American Express to legally trademark the term 'cause-related marketing' in 1983, when it began piloting the approach nationally with a three-month campaign to restore the Statue of Liberty. This campaign cost $4 million in advertising, raised $1.7 million for the cause and also triggered a 27% rise in American Express card use and a 45% increase in new card applications.[14] The experience demonstrated to American Express, and many other companies after it, that they could 'do well by doing good'.

The business studies literature concurs that the number and size of CRM campaigns have experienced a consistently upward trend since their beginning.[15] Historically CRM has evolved from being predominantly a one-off tactic to increase sales to an approach aimed at building brand reputation and customer loyalty through a deeper long-term commitment linking a brand with a cause organically, and even to becoming the public face of 'responsibility' for the most advanced companies in this realm.[16] The explosion of CRM has been fuelled by the expansion of social media and the 'word- of-mouth' marketing that it enables.[17] It has also moved from an almost exclusive focus on local causes to also cover 'distant' ones. Part of the attractiveness of CRM from the point of view of consumers is that it triggers a donation with every purchase.[18] Einstein argues that tying a product to a cause not only increases profits but also leads to 'increased sales for the *entire line of products connected to the brand...* These sales increases bring in earnings well above the cost of the company's charitable donations.'[19]

Critics question the consequences that CRM campaigns have on the power dynamics, distribution and redistribution of resources, portrayals of 'communities in need' and the possibility of stimulating social change. Nickel and Eikenberry, for example, argue that CRM is especially insidious as it 'creates the appearance of giving back, disguising the fact that it is already based in taking away'.[20] From an analysis of dozens of mostly US-based CRM campaigns, Einstein concludes that most are self-congratulatory and serve to further corporate interest, while rarely affecting real change, and that they lead to an expectation of return when acting magnanimously because 'when you give you get'.[21] King's work on the Pink Ribbon breast cancer campaigns to support the Komen Foundation shows how CRM is based on the 'assumption that quick, convenient, and relatively inexpensive acts of giving have nonetheless powerful effects and deep spiritual meaning'.[22] Critics also argue that CRM campaigns often describe donations in terms of 'lives saved' or 'litres of water purified' – making it more difficult to monetise the donation size and highlight the contradictions between profit and donation. They also perpetuate gender stereotypes of both consumers and recipients.[23]

CRM with a development cause has also been heavily criticised. Brei and Bohm analysed 10 brands of bottled water that claim to contribute to campaigns aimed at providing drinking water to 'poor African people', concluding that these companies are mainly attempting to create a better image for an industry beset by environmental and social criticism.[24] Hawkins suggests that women in the South are typically portrayed as being closer to nature, but at the same time unable to fulfil their role of responsible mothers as a result of environmental conditions. She highlights how CRM campaigns emphasise individual action and market-based solutions to complex issues and how 'everyday lives in the North are constituted as separate from natural environments *except* through consumption choices, a dangerous idea that constitutes the market as the only route to "participate" in development interventions, caring, and environmentally responsible actions'.[25]

These critiques focus thoughtfully on the relations between profitable companies, products and the causes they claim to support; however, they do not engage the role of public approval – a point of important access for celebrity advocates. Celebrities are often found advertising the products, representing the benefits of the cause while co-branding helping as cool, and are important for the 'fit' between a cause and a company.[26] It is through the celebritisation of development information that the cause in CRM becomes marketable.

Celebrity marketing of development causes can be linked to the rise of global celebrity 'do-gooding',[27] the growing engagement of celebrity politics in the USA[28] and the UK,[29] and to the rise of celebrity diplomacy internationally.[30] Celebrities are themselves commodities: 'produced, traded and marketed by the media and publicity industries'.[31] They are brands whose images are packaged, bought and sold across national borders.[32] Celebrities are also 'politics made flesh' – as both commoditisers and commodities – and an important element of why international development causes are being bought by Western consumers.[33]

Debates on how causes can be wrapped around consumer products with the mediation of celebrity to deliver 'development' have so far been mostly compartmentalised. The business literature has examined CRM, but has mostly focused on its marketing aspects. The emerging literature on celebrities as global actors has focused primarily on famous Hollywood celebrities, not on the aid celebrities whose expertise becomes celebritised and marketed as part of the product of development intervention.[34] The large political and ethical consumption literature has thoroughly examined the role of fair trade and other labels in promoting (or in failing to promote) 'development', but has so far failed to recognise that CRM and Brand Aid initiatives are moving attention away from the social and environmental conditions of production and towards the beneficiaries of causes that have little or no relation to the product itself. In the rest of this article we argue that there are important overlaps between these aspects that need to be examined systematically. In next section we develop a conceptual framework for such analysis, followed by a methodological and empirical example of how it can be applied.

Conceptual model

In our previous work we developed the concept of 'Brand Aid' to describe how branded products are sold as ethical items through their mediation by celebrities who link them to worthy causes in developing countries.[35] Brand Aid, we argued, is 'aid to brands' because it helps sell products and improve a brand's ethical profile and value. It is also 'brands that provide aid' because a proportion of the profit or sales is devoted to helping others.

Here we introduce a conceptual model, as illustrated in Figure 1, where Brand Aid appears at the triple interface of causes, branded products and celebrities. The model also shows other forms of interaction: generic CRM (the combination of branded products and causes); celebrity-driven issue campaigns (the combination of celebrities and causes – for example, George Clooney's Save Darfur campaign); and marketing campaigns using celebrities (the well established combination of celebrities and branded products). These other categories fall outside the scope of this article, but structured comparisons between them are part of our agenda for future research.

Each of the circles in our conceptual model represents a regime of value that contains both material and symbolic forms. Appadurai described the arrangements of meanings created by signifying images and objects as 'regimes

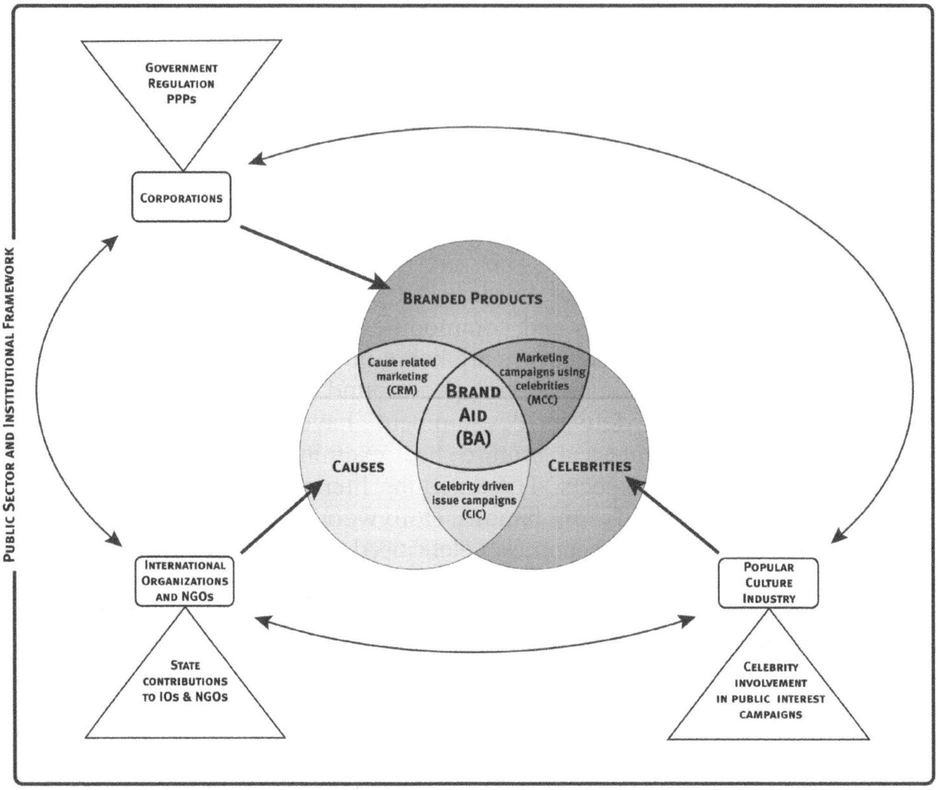

Figure 1. Brand Aid Conceptual Model.

of value' – constructs of the social imaginary which give significance to experience through discourse.[36] Value for Appadurai refers to both economic and material value and also to the non- economic categories and understandings of particular commodity arrangements. New imaginaries of development are created in which consumption becomes the mechanism for action and purchase creates a partnership between individual consumers, corporations, non-profits and ultimately beneficiaries in developing countries. The relationship is created, not simply documented, through the discourses, images, narratives and truths communicated as part of Brand Aid.

Regimes of value exist within an institutional framework that constitutes and supports them (see actors and relations in Figure 1 outside the overlapping circles). Traditionally international development operated through public and private sector interactions between international organisations, NGOs and states. However, as corporations and the popular culture industry become actors in promoting international causes, new alliances are formed and new forms of institutional embedding takes place. In relation to the lower right corner of Figure 1, for example, celebrities engaging in Brand Aid initiatives should be understood through the mediated context of the popular culture industry, which now includes agencies that match the right product/brand/corporation to the right celebrity, or the right international development cause/NGO to the right celebrity, or both.[37] Celebrities also interact directly with the public sector when they are called to endorse public-service campaigns or, more controversially, when they move residence to lower taxation locations. Similar observations can be made on the interactions between corporations and the public sector (eg via public–private partnerships; see top left corner in Figure 1) and between NGOs and their public donors (see lower left corner). Thus, Brand Aid enacts complex regimes of value on the basis of an expanded institutional framework – both forging new alliances and linking new actors in 'development'.

In our model we are engaging with 'development' as an interactive process of material exchange and conceptual engagement that links the technical and specialised activities practiced in the South by particular 'experts' and 'organisations' with a network and communication media of non-expert publics in the North. Our focus is on what Smith and Yanacopulos describe as the 'public faces of development' or the various ways in which development organisations convey meanings and representations of the global South and the concept of development itself to a Northern public.[38] Celebrity remains a key component of our conceptual model for its role signifying the communication of development causes specifically to an audience of non-specialists. As described by Brockington in this issue, the increasing presence of corporate actors in relationships between NGOs and celebrities reflects the rise of CRM initiatives: 'it is good business sense to build relationships with NGOs, particularly if it then results in associations between that business and famous faces'.

Methodology

We use the conceptual model of Brand Aid provided in Figure 1 to analyse empirical material documenting contemporary CRM initiatives that have an international development cause and celebrity involvement. Because consumer initiatives are not documented as sources of development financing, which would appear in the AidData database (http://aiddata.org/research/releases/) and because many are linked to private corporations whose financial reports are not public information, systematic documentation faced serious challenges.[39] We settled on a selection process based on existing databases and lists constituted by definition from at least one selection criterion of the Brand Aid model.[40]

Our first data search focused on the combination of two elements of Brand Aid: 'product' and 'cause'. After examining a dozen sites dedicated to CRM, we selected the most comprehensive list of 'new CRM campaigns' compiled by Cause Marketing Forum (CMF).[41] We conducted a data search covering the period from January 2011 (when CMF started to compile a comprehensive list) to April 2012. The CMF search generated 99 hits that were analysed by reading the campaign press releases and the websites dedicated to them. In order to qualify as Brand Aid, however, these initiatives needed to address not just any cause, but an international development cause. This filter left us with 21 instances – a sizeable minority, given that the CRM literature in business studies typically advises corporations to link their campaigns to local causes. Of these 21 CRM campaigns, seven mentioned a celebrity prominently in their press release and therefore fully qualified as 'Brand Aid' according to our conceptual framework. Of these, we selected the four that were 'transactional' in nature (they required the purchase of a product, not just a 'brand experience' such as visiting a website, leaving a message, or 'liking' a Facebook page) for further analysis.

Our second data search focused on the 'celebrity' involvement criterion and was targeted to identify other initiatives that may have not been captured by the CRM search. We collected data from a prominent set of celebrity newsletters, sent several times a week to subscribers by the UK-based site 'The Red Pages' (www.theredpages.co.uk), over the same time period covered by the CMF database. This led to the compilation of a list of 1822 news items on celebrity endorsement, charity work and involvement in marketing and other events. These items were filtered to assess whether the celebrity was involved in a Brand Aid initiative as defined above. This yielded three new Brand Aid entries and two entries that had already been captured in the CMF database. A final step entailed merging these two filtered databases and eliminating double-entries, which produced a short list of eight case studies (Table 1).

We carried out three case studies (see entries 1 to 3 in Table 1) from the short list in order to provide meaningful detail in our analysis. We selected those that represent all three models of business engagement in CRM: the commercial model, the social enterprise model and the umbrella model. The first case is General Mills' 'Win One Give One' initiative, involving a 'commercial model' in which existing companies select specific products to enhance their ethical value through their link with development causes. The second case is TOMS shoes, which follows a 'social enterprise model' in which social value is the *raison d'être* of the business itself. The third case covers the Penfolds and Belvedere Product (RED) campaigns, which are part of the 'umbrella model' where ethical value is mediated and managed by a co-branding initiative. As we have analysed Product (RED) extensively elsewhere,[42] we only update and summarise its main features in this article.

Case Studies

'Win one give one': Betty Crocker® Fruit Flavored Snacks

The 'Win One Give One' campaign is an instance of Brand Aid because it combines a cause, a branded product and a celebrity (see Figure 1, central overlap), but with an important twist – the beneficiaries of the cause are simultaneously American children (and their moms) and Rwandan school children. The mechanism enacting Brand Aid in this case is as follows: from 15 November 2011 until 31 July 2012, consumers who entered a UPC code from boxes of General Mills' 'Betty Crocker® Fruit Flavored Snacks' ('the branded product') would be registered to win an XO Laptop (the commodity carrying the solution to 'the cause': addressing poor educational infrastructure) provided by an organisation founded in 2005 by Nicolas Negroponte ('the celebrity'). Linked to this 'instant win game', for every 100 UPC codes entered on the website, Betty Crocker® Fruit Flavored Snacks pledged to donate one XO laptop to a child in Africa, up to 1725 laptops, or in the USA, up to 259 laptops. These fruit-flavoured snacks come in 38 varieties, ranging from 'Fruit-Flavored Shapes My Little Pony' to 'Fruit Gushers Mood Morphers Fruit Punch'.[43] Almost all the 38 varieties are made from the same ingredients: a combination of concentrated pears, corn syrup, modified corn starch, preservatives, and red, yellow and blue colouring. Sugar constitutes roughly half the total product weight.

Table 1. Selection of Brand Aid initiatives.

ID nr.	Cause				Product	Celebrity
	Details of international development cause	*Nonprofit Involved*	*Name of Campaign*	*Donation*	*Product/brand/company*	*Main celebrities involved*
1	Provision of laptop computers to school children in Rwanda	One Laptop Per Child	Win One Give One	in Africa, up to 1725 laptops; in the US, up to 259 laptops	General Mills (Betty Crocker Fruit Flavored Snacks)	Dr. Michelle Borba; Nicholas Negroponte OLPC founder and aid celebrity
2	Shoes for chilren in need	TOMS/ onedaywithoutshoes.com	One to One	over 1 million new pars of shoes	TOMS + The Row (shoes)	Ashley and Mary-Kate Olsen designed for TOMS; other celebrity links for the 'one day without shoes' campaign; Blake Mycoskie, the founder of TOMS, is a celebrity himself
3	AIDS medication to selected Global Fund programs in Africa	Global Fund to Fight AIDS, Tuberculosis & Malaria	(Product) RED: Penfolds and Belvedere	15% of sales of two varieties of wine during promotional periods (Penfolds); 50% of profits (Belvedere)	Penfolds Wines, Belvedere Vodka	Bono, Mary J. Blige, Usher and many other photo-op celebs on website launch
4	Fight hunger in the Horn of Africa	Save the Children, International Rescue Committee and Mercy Corps	We Can Be Heroes	Up to $ 1 million	DC Comics and Warner Bros. Entertainment (superhero gadgets)	Superhero characters and US Vice-Pres. spouse Dr. Jill Biden
5	Support the healthy development of mothers and babies while also addressing the basic care needs of families during crisis situations	Save the Children	Johnson's Baby Cares	unknown	Johnson & Johnson (Baby Care packs)	Hilary Duff
6	Helping children through sport in violence prone areas	Fight for Peace	LUTA clothing	unknown	LUTA clothing (boxing clothing)	Former boxing champion Luke Dowdney owns the clothing business; actor Idris Elba supports it

(*Continued*)

Table 1. (*Continued*).

ID nr.	Cause				Product	Celebrity
	Details of international development cause	*Nonprofit Involved*	*Name of Campaign*	*Donation*	*Product/brand/company*	*Main celebrities involved*
7	Specially deisgned shoes donating funds to charity	OneKid OneWorld	Celebrity Shoe Design Program for Charity	unknown	ShoeDazzle (shoes)	Kristin Cavallari
8	Free T-shirts to children in Africa (and art programs for low-income children in the U.S.)	Young Audiences Arts for Learning, Starkey Hearing Foundation	Support the Youth	unknown	Akomplice Clothing (selected lines)	NFL star and playmaker Vernon Davis

Table 2: Other cause-related marketing and -branding initiatives with an international development cause

ID nr.	Cause				Product	Celebrity
	Details of international development cause	*Nonprofit Involved*	*Name of Campaign*	*Donation*	*Product/brand/company*	*Main celebrities involved*
9	Fighting hunger around the world	World Food Programme	From Hunger to Hope	Unknown - self-described "largest private sector hunger relief effort"	KFC, Pizza Hut and Taco Bell, Front Row Motorsports	NASCAR driver David Gilliland; Christina Aguilera
10	Provision of books for children in third world countries, mentorship for teens, and scholarships to women	The Step Up Women's Network, the Venus Goddess Fund for Education and the Maribel Foundation	Venus Goddess	$70,000	P&G/Gillette Venus Brand	Jennifer Lopez
11	Provision of clean water in developing countries	Charity water, Disabled American Veterans, National MS Society, St. Jude Children's Research Hospital	Ultimate Burger Experience	$40,000-$100,000	Omaha Steaks	none
12	One of the 4 charities selected provides clean water and sanitation in developing countries and the US	American Forests; Keep America Beautiful; National Park Foundation; Water.org	Lowe's Community Giving Campaign	$1 million	Lowe's	none
13	Donation of TB test tubes	Foundation for Innovative New Diagnostics and the Earth Institute at Columbia University	World TB Day Donation Campaign	20,000 BD BACTEC™ MGIT™ tubes	Becton, Dickinson and Company	none

14	Support to victims of war, natural disasters and people living in poverty in the U.S. and around the globe	Soles4Souls	Allen Edmonds National Shoe Drive	Unknown	Allen Edmonds	none
15	Installation of solar powered generators to light two Guatemalan schools	Integral Heart Education Program	Heart Cart	Unknown	ToonUps	none
16	Clean water provision in developing countries	charity: water	Get Dirty	Up to $5,000	Rubicon Property	none
17	Encouraging travelers visiting selected developing countries to reserve five pounds of space in their luggage for items needed in schools and clinics near their destination	Pack for a Purpose	Luxury Link/Pack for a Purpose	Unknown	Luxury Link	none
18	Serves as the national sponsor of the 2012 UNICEF Tap Project, to help provide the world's children with access to safe, clean water	U.S. Fund for UNICEF	Acqua for Life	Up to $100,000	Giorgio Armani	none
19	Microloans for women in the U.S. and overseas	Kiva	Financial Independence Through Entrepreneurship	$500k	Dermalogica	none
20	Funding CARE programs in Malawi & India, where they help lift women & girls out of poverty through education, health, & economic empowerment projects.	CARE	Join My Village	$1million	General Mills and Merck	none
21	Logistics company donating six meals for every client shipment delivered in March	Feed My Starving Children	Morgan Delivers for Starving Kids	Goal: 50,000 meals	D. W. Morgan	none
22	Funds for Community Health Workers in Africa in the Millennium Villages Projects	Millennium Promise	Spokes of Change	Title Sponsorship	USA Pro Cycling Challenge	none
23	Improving maternal and newborn health in Uganda	Safe Mothers, Safe Babies	Light the Night	Unknown	Humless	none
24	Donating 'hours of light' in 2011 to rural communities in need around the world	One Million Lights	Energizer Night Race for a Brighter World	Donations of solar powered lights and batteries to power 11 million hours of light	Energizer	none

What could link fruit-flavoured snacks and concerned American mothers with a top-down development techno-fix and 'kids in Africa'? The homepage of the initiative's 'Win & Give' website (www.winonegiveone.com/Default.aspx) centres on a portrait of a young Rwandan boy in a well pressed school uniform in front of the Rwandan flag. The child has tightly shaved hair, looks to be around eight years old, and wears an expression of alertness. He is framed with the caption, 'Take a trip to Rwanda with Jean-Luc. See how XO Laptops™ are making futures brighter'. You can click the bold link under the photo reading 'Explore'. To the left of Jean-Luc is a photo of the computer with a smiling Black boy on the screen, and three boxes of fruit-flavoured snacks. Their caption reads 'Enter a UPC code'. These are linked to the words 'Enter Here!'. To the right is a photograph of a Rwandan boy in the same starched uniform, who may or may not be 'Jean-Luc'. His portrait is superimposed slightly behind a portrait of a smiling, supposedly American, boy in a striped casual collared shirt with pale skin and freckles, under the caption 'See the impact you can make'. These boys have a link that reads, 'Learn More'. In small text in the right bottom corner of the page is an old-fashioned propeller aeroplane, pulling a banner that reads, 'Hey kids, this is Advertising'. While the advertising for the fruit snacks is obvious, the subtler, and arguably more hard-sell, approach is an imaginary of international development delivered through the provision of a commodity.

In terms of the institutional framework within which this Brand Aid initiative operates, it is important to point out that the XO Laptop comes from 'One Laptop per Child' (OLPC), an international development initiative that has backing from the computer industry and works in more than 30 developing countries, with the idea of producing a durable laptop computer costing only $100 that could make technology accessible to developing country children. OLPC has been controversial since its inception by the development celebrity Nicolas Negroponte. In this development scheme the low-cost laptop would result from a 'tripartite perfect storm' where both business and the public sector play an important role: first, sales would only be to governments and in quantities above one million; second, open-source software would bypass Microsoft software and Intel processors; third, commodity parts would keep the price low. Funding was sought from education ministries using Negroponte's mantra: 'It's an education project, not a technology project'.

One line of criticism has been directed at the technology itself. The best thing about the OLPC computer is that it is inexpensive. However, it has yet to meet the price point of $100, and has remained at twice that price. The physical computer was designed to prevent water and soil damage, to be readable in direct sunlight for children who attend school outside, and to operate on less power consumption to allow for possible solar or crank powering. A scathing technology critique in *The Economist* described how the laptop has bugs that cause occasional crashes.[44] Additionally the 'cumbersome operating system' makes it quite difficult, even in a world of abundant electricity and bandwidth, to perform basic activities. This initiative has been characterised in the press as 'a high-profile deal of one man evangelizing top government officials on how he can save their poor children and in the end these politicians abandoned him'.[45]

The politics of global trade and local power relations have also proved problematic for OLPC across its interventions. Consumers in industrialised economies, many of whom still also lack computer access at school, wanted the possibility of buying cheap laptops as well. Countries like Nigeria and Brazil wanted locally produced laptops. Libya and Nigeria cancelled their informal commitments to purchase the computers when they realised that they were untried, cost more than $100 and were not the only cheap laptops available. Other businesses such as Intel wanted to produce their own cheap laptops and, thus, OLPC came to be perceived as creating a monopoly in the market. Another line of criticism has been OLPC reflects some of the traditionally 'worst practices' in international development. It is a top-down model, developed without consultation on the needs or interests of the local recipients, and it is implemented in a blueprint formula in countries that are extremely diverse.

In Rwanda, where the Win One Give One computers are donated, OLPC began with a specific deal reached between the country's government in 2007 and OLPC. By March 2012 80,000 laptops had been donated to schools around the country. The OLPC Coordinator in the Ministry of Education 'pointed out that the use of laptops on a daily basis in all schools was going to drastically increase with the current deployment of servers in schools. They will enable all lessons to be covered through digital courses'.[46] However, *The Economist* concluded that 'giving a child a computer does not seem to turn him or her into a future Bill Gates – indeed it does not accomplish anything in particular'.[47] An evaluation done of OLPC in Peru by the Inter-American Development Bank found that children receiving the 850,000 computers, in which the government had invested $225 million, did not show any improvement in maths or reading.[48] The Bank's report found no evidence that access to a laptop increased motivation or time devoted to homework or reading.[49]

Businessweek declared OLPC a failure in 2007, something it attributed to the project's rejection of the fundamental rule of product development: 'design from the bottom up, not top down…Near-finished prototypes were tested out late in development, brought to village kids as a "gift"'.[50] Nonetheless, OLPC continues to operate. In spite of the criticism of the laptop's aesthetic design, awkward software and inappropriate business model for technology diffusion, and with no mention of the relatively high sugar and colouring content of the supposedly 'healthy' fruit snacks, the links between them as part of a Brand Aid version of CRM were effective.

Whatever the impact on African children, the Win One Give One initiative assures American mothers that 'any kid can help'. When you click to 'Learn More', instead of information on OLPC or Rwanda, there are two links: the first is to the 'Kid's Altruism Indicator'. This is described as 'a joint research initiative with *Parenting Magazine* to uncover children's views on giving back and helping others. As a component of the partnership, The Parenting Group's MomConnection® research provided insights on how moms instill altruistic values in their kids.' The questions and 'findings', reported as 'According to Kids: Who do you think you can help?', are interesting. Eighty-three per cent of children responded that they could help 'Kids in another country, such as Haiti, Africa [sic], or Chile'. This is only slightly fewer than those who reported confidence in helping 'kids at my school' or 'my family' (see www.winonegive

one.com_pdf_wingive-parentingresults.pdf). The second webpage link takes you to a 'What's your giving style' quiz, to determine your family's giving style and 'receive special tips from Dr Michele Borba, parenting expert'.[51] After you take the quiz, you can also download a coupon for Betty Crocker® Fruit Flavored Snacks. In Win One Give One a first celebrity expert promotes a technological solution to a problem, embedded into the laptop, while a second celebrity expert guarantees that this modality of consumption is linked to the development of altruism in American children so, in this development imaginary, giving donors will produce development in villages like Jean-Luc's in Rwanda. Whether the results indicate that you are a 'global do-gooder', 'neighborhood helper' or 'project seeker' the same tips appear, including the final suggestion: 'Find easy ways to help others around the world through opportunities such as the Betty Crocker Fruit Flavored Snacks "Win & Give" campaign'. And with each opportunity, large buttons at the top of the webpage encourage you to 'Print a Coupon', 'Share on Facebook' or 'Post on Twitter', because it is not sufficient to become more empathetic, or 'incorporate giving into your everyday life'; rather you should share your brand of giving with others.

TOMS Shoes

TOMS shoes is a social entrepreneurship model in which the cause itself is inextricably linked to the objective of the business. TOMS was founded in May 2006 by Blake Mycoskie ('the celebrity' in our conceptual framework, see Figure 1), who became famous for his participation in the US TV show, 'The Amazing Race'. The genesis story of the brand is that Mycoskie was in Argentina playing polo when he joined a group of foreigners donating used shoes in a village. This was a life changing experience, and he started a company that sells an alpargata shoe ('the branded product') inspired by those worn by Argentinian farmers, priced at twice the product value, to permit the company to donate a pair of shoes 'to a child in need' for every pair purchased by the consumer (see http://www.toms.com). (According to TOMS, shoes are a fundamental resource for protecting children's health, 'the cause'). This 'Buy One, Give One' marketing strategy links the purchase and donation directly with the product and brand of TOMS. It is now advertised as 'One person buys. One person is helped', and the company has expanded its product line to include TOMS glasses, which works in partnership with the Seva foundation.[52] Along with Win One Give One, TOMS' version of Brand Aid entails the delivery of a commodity to address a development 'cause'.

TOMS operates in an institutional framework where interactions with the public sector are mostly absent, invisible or indirect (see its engagement with schools below); where a complex set of alliances and mechanisms govern shoe production, sale and giving; and where a multitude of supporting 'communities' brings together consumers-cum-activists as 'development actors'. TOMS is allied with a variety of 'giving partners', works in over 60 countries, and 'as of June 2013, TOMS has given more than 10 million pairs of new shoes to children in need'.[53] The 'given pair' of shoes is most frequently 'a black, unisex canvas slip-on with a sturdy sole', except in Argentina, where TOMS gives shoes 'similar to our colorful Classics' and in Ethiopia, where they give 'a variety of locally produced shoes'.[54]

Its donation missions, termed 'giving trips', reward TOMS' staff and contest winners with the opportunity to visit their 'Giving Partners' in developing countries. These trips are well documented on the blog, with colourful photos of young, attractive students travelling to places like El Salvador to distribute shoes together with organisations like Save the Children. Photos of thin, beautiful university students kneeling at the feet of Third World children to place a shoe, literally, on the feet of the poor, invoke images of Christian culture that play on Western consumers' imaginaries of beneficence.[55]

Linked to TOMS is also the 'One for One'™ Movement, where 'compassionate young people' are 'getting involved' through campus clubs, internships and branded interactions on social media. The most famous TOMS brand activity is the 'One Day Without Shoes' campaign, in which supporters go barefoot to 'spread awareness of the impact a pair of shoes can have on a child's life'. On this day supporters are encouraged by the brand to walk barefoot, photograph their feet, stencil-shirts ('Go without shoes so kids don't have to!' and 'Ask me about my feet'), share the TOMS giving videos, and hold concerts with shoeless musicians.

TOMS effectively manages many of the features of 'new marketing', such as word-of-mouth, through social media, real and virtual events, video storytelling, education-cum-marketing, and engaging a movement of consumer-activists. Mycoskie himself is extremely apt at navigating the popular culture industry and its current need for multi-product and multimedia strategies. He has authored a book, *Start Something That Matters*, with a teaching guide that can be downloaded free. TOMS includes a 'Campus Programs Department' to provide resources for students and teachers who have 'embraced the TOMS philosophy and shared it with their communities inside and outside the classroom'.[56] Detailed instructions are given on how to form a TOMS campus club, including registering all events with the company, and hosting at least one event per semester to 'raise awareness of the TOMS story.'

With a catchy slogan and easy to understand truisms, TOMS has become the brand of compassion for many American young people. The author of the popular book and blog, *Where Am I Wearing* (www.whereamiwearing.com/?s=Toms&x=0&y=0) sums up how TOMS fits with American values: 'I've met so many raving TOMS fans that have no idea where TOMS are made [in China]. All they know is that a pair was given away somewhere – probably Africa – because they bought a pair. And that's enough for them to feel swell about their shoes'. The development imaginary linking the USA and Africa is complicated by the inclusion of productive (not merely recipient) 'Others' in China who are actually making TOMS feel-good shoes.

TOMS uses a multi-channel integration strategy to bring awareness to their cause, and to sell their products, framed in terms of inspirational story-telling, not advertising. It relies heavily on its online community for marketing, and has an extensive network on Facebook with over 1.5 million 'likes', including over 4000 people who have added their own photos or videos to the page. Additionally TOMS is active on Twitter and has its own YouTube channel. Its charismatic founder Mycoskie has a popular blog (http://www.toms.com/blog), which he uses to keep consumers informed on the products and their social impacts, and where he often characterises himself as the 'chief giver'. He is also a popular speaker at American church groups, university TOMS clubs and on US television.

TOMS has been critiqued for labour conditions in shoe production in China (where it sources its shoes for sale), Ethiopia and Argentina (where it sources its shoes for donation). The company has responded that it is third-party audited to ensure that no child labour is used and fair wages are paid.[57] In response to the sustainability of shoes for children whose feet grow, TOMS 'strives to set up long-term giving partnerships that allow us to keep giving as children grow'. How often this is practically achieved, given the mobility of families and development partners is not documented. Little is actually known about TOMS giving partners' work, beyond the distribution of shoes, and even less about the actual details of production, volume of sales and nature of partnerships between the company and its beneficiaries. Other serious critiques are also levied against TOMS because giving in kind distorts local economies of production.[58] A counter-campaign to TOMS' 'A Day Without Shoes' was launched on the blog 'Good Intentions are not Enough' and entitled 'A Day Without Dignity' (http://goodintents.org/in-kind-donations/a-day-without-dignity). It asked aid workers, the diaspora and people from areas that receive shoe drops and other forms of charity to speak up on blogs, Twitter and at school. They posted numerous interventions from critics of the initiative, including videos and photos documenting the widespread availability of shoes in local Third World markets.

Nevertheless, Mycoskie has won awards from the Smithsonian Institution in 2007 and the US Secretary of State's award for Corporate Excellence in 2009 (www.toms.com/blakes-bio). TOMS imaginary of development is one in which growing up barefoot is the primary obstacle to receiving education and avoiding disease: 'Shoes are a fundamental resource for protecting children's health and providing them with opportunity' (www.toms.com/our-movement-why). TOMS is an award-winning social enterprise model built around CRM, transmitted in a three-minute video with emotional music, smiling brown children with white saints sitting at their feet. As aptly termed by Vivek Nemana, 'Aid-vertising' clearly works to get a buy-in from consumers, based on stories they tell themselves (http://aidwatchers.com/2011/04/barefoot-on-broadway-warning-gross-feet-pics).

Product (RED) Belvedere vodka and Penfolds wine

The Product (RED)™ initiative was launched by Bono the Irish rock star ('the celebrity') at the World Economic Forum in Davos in 2006. According to www.joinred.com, Product RED is 'a brand created to raise awareness and money for the Global Fund to Fight AIDS, Tuberculosis and Malaria by teaming up with iconic brands to produce RED-branded products'. With the engagement of iconic brands, such as American Express, Apple, Armani, Gap and Starbucks ('the branded products'), consumers can help HIV/AIDS patients in Africa ('the cause'). From a RED Bugaboo baby stroller to a RED iPod™ and from (Starbucks) RED whole bean coffee to a Belvedere special edition RED vodka, a percentage of the profits from the sale of all RED co-branded products is contributed by the 'iconic' partners directly to the Global Fund.

As we have documented in detail elsewhere,[59] understanding the dynamics of RED is tightly linked to the institutional framework surrounding it, and specifically the actual and perceived roles of public and private donors in financing the Global Fund. The Global Fund is an international mechanism to channel aid financing to developing countries, and it controls the second largest pool of donor funds in the world (after the UN itself). Companies that come under the RED umbrella pay a licensing fee and commit themselves to a multi-year partnership. According to RED's website, as of August 2013, it had donated nearly $210 million to the Global Fund. RED grants are made through the Fund's standard disbursement processes and have been dedicated to its best-performing programmes for AIDS in Africa.

Two of the RED products were captured in our sampling framework.[60] The first, Belvedere Vodka, has a RED website that can only be accessed after the input of your country and birthday, because viewers must be of legal drinking age in their country, or 18 years old if the country has no drinking age. The vodka company has partnered with RED to produce a Special Edition Bottle, the sale of which will cause 50% of the profits to be donated to the Global Fund. The artist and celebrity Usher has teamed up with Belvedere RED Vodka 'to encourage consumers to support programs that offer education and medication on the ground in Africa'.

The second, Penfolds Wines from Australia, has a similar contribution and communication model, and has partnered with RED for its Koonunga Hill and Thomas Hyland wines for 'Inspired Wine, Inspi (RED) Purpose'. In June 2012 Penfolds launched a Special Edition bottle: 'for every bottle purchased Penfolds will make a contribution on your behalf to the Global Fund to help eliminate AIDS in Africa. Keep an eye out for this Special Edition pack this summer and help us deliver an AIDS free Generation by 2015' (www.penfoldsusa.com/?p=1206). During the promotions period only, Penfolds contributed 15% of its profits to the Global Fund.

The Brand Aid modality of merging shopping and helping, which we have described as a new frontier in international development,[61] is maturing into a hybrid institution with the likelihood of longer duration. The modalities of engagement within Product RED are expanding: now the model includes CRM, corporate philanthropy (with the new Coca Cola sponsorship which has no direct product link) and activism (now that RED is officially a division of ONE, the international NGO also founded by Bono). The supporting cast of celebrities changes with each event under RED, but the grounding of Bono remains stable.

Product RED now has two levels of cooperation with business: 'partners' and 'Special Editions'. Additionally, since 1 December 2011, a new partnership between RED and Coca-Cola was set up, to 'fund marketing awareness campaigns activated through global Coca-Cola music initiatives and programs'. The company will donate more than $5 million over the next four years, with a minimum of $3 million to be donated directly to the Global Fund to purchase antiretroviral medicine and distribute literature.[62] RED continues to brand celebrity events such as concerts and a virtual AIDS quilt, and the Global Fund has taken up the RED story-telling model in its fundraising campaigns.[63]

Analysis and conclusion

A fundamental problem with Brand Aid initiatives is that they are teaching people how to give from a narrowly individualistic and consumption-oriented perspective. Products are manufactured and then linked to 'needs' identified in the developing world, primarily Africa, which supplies a convenient trope for 'needy'. In this process 'development' itself is sold as commodity transfer: development interventions equal donations of commodities, things that needy people need. Companies that both produce these necessary goods and sacrifice their corporate profit to share them with the global poor invite consumers to 'partner' with them through the purchase of the Brand Aid products. Through real time and virtual events, where people come together to share experiences with others who share their deep frame values,[64] these companies not only provide the commodities themselves, but also construct an entire realm in which these products become meaningful – Appadurai's regimes of value.[65]

Large, media-savvy development organisations (primarily international NGOs) 'partner' by constructing these regimes of value for development, which resonate with years of promotion of public–private partnerships. 'Private' has now fused with 'corporate', celebrities are becoming the public faces of development, and the distinction between non-profit and for-profit is obfuscated. In this article we have provided a conceptual model that can help examine increasingly complex sets of actors, alliances and relations in development interventions, in the context of a broader institutional framework. We focused on the new overlap between international development causes, branded products and 'celebrities' and applied the conceptual model to analyse three case studies of Brand Aid.

Brand Aid provides an easy solution to current crises by linking the global economy to international development – a development that enables corporations to brand themselves as 'caring' without substantially changing their normal business practices, while consumers engage in low-cost heroism without meaningfully increasing their awareness of the struggles of people they are supposed to be helping. In Brand Aid the problems themselves, be they low educational achievement, shoelessness or AIDS, and the people who experience them, are branded and marketed to Western consumers through celebritised multimedia story-telling just as effectively as the products that will 'save' them.

Brand Aid initiatives tend to reduce 'development' to a process of identifying a lack, locating a supplier, providing a commodity and managing the distribution of the needed commodity to its intended recipients. Our case studies were selected to explore different models of Brand Aid – the commercial business, social enterprise and umbrella models. Yet they showed little variation in the imaginary of development as 'providing needed commodities'. In all these initiatives products (laptops, shoes, pills) are given to beneficiaries without regard to the underpinning relations of production, consumption or donation. The ethical value is placed exclusively in the realm of the Northern consumer through the purchase of a particular product or the donation within a branded experience. 'Buying' is 'buying into' an imaginary of development in which consumers can make a difference. Making a donation in a branded environment, or sharing a story that will trigger a matching donation by a branded host, is a way of blending the experience of giving and the feeling of empathy with that brand, reflecting calls for corporate philanthropy to become more strategically related to brand reputation.[66] Thus, engagement in Brand Aid pulls the marketing, corporate philanthropy and brand management sides of business together. Corporate philanthropy becomes shared with the consumer, publicised and celebritised – it is not anonymous, as in past forms. Instead, Brand Aid is embedded in the public relationship between the consumer and the branded product through the mediating role of the celebrity. Given that consumers authorise the development interventions through their purchases, there is no concern in Brand Aid for participation by the recipient communities or accountability to these supposed beneficiaries.

Whether business is good for development is an ongoing debate;[67] like the larger debates on aid effectiveness, it often suffers from the basic flaw of over-aggregation.[68] However, the scope and diversity of contemporary Brand Aid initiatives suggest that 'buying into development', at least in some form, is good for business. In this article we have offered a material and a symbolic interpretation of why this may be the case. A material interpretation is that when consumers 'buy into' development through the purchase of CRM products that support international causes, they could encounter opportunities to link material consumption with global production relations in distant places. In this interpretation Brand Aid could act as a sort of gateway into more substantial changes in consumption patterns, as supported by fair trade forms of engagement. However, on the basis of our empirical analysis of contemporary Brand Aid, there are few indications that this is the case. Thus far, Brand Aid has not opened up significant space for greater public debate over the production of goods in developing countries or the development interventions that are supposed to 'help' the global poor. If individuals are becoming more aware, through their role as consumers of Brand Aid goods, they are keeping this fact to themselves.

A symbolic interpretation of why 'buying into development' may be good for business is linked to the increasing involvement of business and corporate philanthropy in financing development aid and in shaping its agenda. Individuals are unlikely to have a 'Gates effect' on development as consumers;[69] however, in the aggregation of preferences defined by purchase, Brand Aid may add a democratic perception that links to the current trend of market-led development goals and practices. Consumers could, through their purchases, have the potential to shape aid agendas in ways that are more participatory for Northern publics than the traditional forms of engagement through ODA (which has also never been driven by particularly democratic engagement). Thus far, however, it appears that Brand Aid initiatives tend to drive rather than be driven by consumer's visions of international development. While Brand Aid products are tapping into expanded definitions of 'quality' that include the product's ability to support consumer values (justice and help), they do not seem to have any direct link to the modalities of 'helping' for the causes being supported.

Most complicated are the ethical dimensions of the Brand Aid initiatives. As a recent critique of neoliberalism succinctly stated: 'Consumerist activism, development discourse, and pink-ribbon feminism all partake of the liberal fallacy that good will and cooperation and compromise will suffice to fix the intractable problems of poverty and inequality – problems that are imagined to be static and given, as if outside the realm of history and politics'.[70] All of contemporary Brand Aid initiatives we analysed engage in what has been characterised by Flannery as the work of a 'story factory' – producing truths about international development and consumer engagement that make development appear simplified and manageable and outside history or politics.[71] As a critic of TOMS has put it (www.whereamiwearing.com/?s=Toms&x=0&y=0): 'We take the nugget of a story that can be printed on a shoebox and we make up our own story'.

When branded products become the mechanisms for action needed to save suffering strangers in our personal stories, we have sold out our values and our non- commodified ways of living those values. Consumption becomes the legitimate place for manifesting meaning, and companies and celebrities are taking on the roles traditionally assigned to philosophers and religious leaders of defining 'the good life'. Negroponte, Mycoskie and Bono define the values around which we are called to mobilise and the branded mechanisms that provide the answers when individuals want to 'take action' on global problems. The way of building relationships, making meaning and living the good life rests on having the right things. In a symmetry that belies equivalences, their development and our development both become based in the things we have.

Acknowledgements

The authors would like to thank the International Development Research Group at Roskilde University, the participants of the Sustainability Seminar series at Copenhagen Business School and an extremely helpful reviewer for their feedback on earlier versions of this paper.

Notes on Contributors

Stefano Ponte is Professor of International Political Economy at Copenhagen Business School. He is interested in how the global economy is governed and in how developing countries and emerging economies fare in it. In recent research, he has been examining the increasing importance of celebrities and branding in mobilising 'compassionate consumption' and new forms of corporate social responsibility that are 'distant and disengaged'. His most recent books are *Brand Aid: Shopping Well to Save the World* (with Lisa Ann Richey 2011) and *Governing through Standards: Origins, Drivers and Limitations* (with Peter Gibbon and Jakob Vestergaard 2011).

Lisa Ann Richey is Professor of International Development Studies in the Department of Society and Globalisation, Roskilde University, Denmark. She is the author of *Brand Aid: Shopping Well to Save the World* with Stefano Ponte (2011), *Population Politics and Development: From the Policies to the Clinics* (2008), and the co-editor of "Women and Development: Rethinking Policy and Reconceptualizing Practice" (special issue of *Women's Studies Quarterly* with Frances Vavrus 2003). She works on new actors in international aid, citizenship and body politics, and gender and the global South.

Notes

1. Richey and Ponte, *Brand Aid*.
2. Adelman, "Global Philanthropy and Remittances."
3. Hawkins, "A New Frontier in Development?," 1797.
4. See Biccum, "Interrupting the Discourse of Development."

5. Hawkins, "A New Frontier in Development?"; and Brockington, "The Production and Construction of Celebrity Advocacy."
6. See the classic Long and Van Der Ploeg, "Demythologizing Planned Intervention."
7. See Brockington, "The Production and Construction of Celebrity Advocacy"; and Cameron and Haanstra, "Development Made Sexy."
8. See Richey and Ponte, "Better (Red)™ than Dead?"; and Richey and Ponte, *Brand Aid.*
9. See Goodman, "The Mirror of Consumption."
10. Richey and Ponte, *Brand Aid.*
11. See, inter alia, Adkins, *Cause-related Marketing*; Berglind and Nakata, "Cause-related marketing"; and a recent review in Vanhamme et al., "To Do Well by Doing Good".
12. See Hawkins, "One Pack = One Vaccine"; Hawkins, "Shopping to Save Lives"; and Hawkins, "A New Frontier in Development."
13. Daw, *Cause Marketing for Nonprofits*, 3.
14. Ibid.
15. Daw, *Cause Marketing*; CSR, *Cause Related Marketing*; and Einstein, *Compassion, Inc.*
16. Daw, *Cause Marketing.*
17. Einstein, *Compassion, Inc.*
18. Integer Group, "M/A/R/C Research."
19. Einstein, *Compassion, Inc.*, 35. Emphasis in the original.
20. Nickel and Eikenberry, "A Critique of the Discourse of Marketized Philanthropy."
21. Einstein, *Compassion, Inc.*, 137.
22. King, *Pink Ribbons, Inc.*, 73.
23. See Hawkins, "One Pack = One Vaccine"; Hawkins, "Shopping to Save Lives"; Hawkins, "A New Frontier in Development"; King, *Pink Ribbons, Inc*; and Richey and Ponte, *Brand Aid.*
24. Brei and Bohm, "Corporate Social Responsibility as Cultural Meaning."
25. Hawkins, "Shopping to Save Lives," 758. Emphasis in the original.
26. See Hawkins, "A New Frontier in Development"; and Brockington, 'The Production and Construction of Celebrity Advocacy."
27. Littler, "I Feel Your Pain."
28. See, for example, Marks and Fisher, "The King's New Bodies."
29. See, for example, Marks and Fisher, "The King's New Bodies"; Street, "Do Celebrity Politics and Celebrity Politicians Matter?"; and Street, "Celebrity Politicians."
30. Cooper, *Celebrity Diplomacy.*
31. Turner, *Understanding Celebrity.*
32. Littler, "Introduction," 1.
33. Boykoff and Goodman, "Conspicuous Redemption?"
34. For an exception, see Goodman and Barnes, "Star/Poverty Space."
35. Richey and Ponte, *Brand Aid.*
36. Appadurai, "Commodities and the Politics of Value."
37. See Brockington, "The Production and Construction of Celebrity Advocacy."
38. Smith and Yanacopulos, "The Public Faces of Development."
39. For example, after several trials, we decided that we could not use an internet search focused on a set of words or concepts to establish a 'long list' of CRM initiatives, because of the many different definitions used for CRM -like initiatives and the transience of these initiatives on webpages (after CRM initiatives end, they are typically 'disappeared' from companies' websites). Hawkins 'A New Frontier in Development' describes similar data challenges.
40. To be defined as Brand Aid, initiatives must: (1) be CRM initiatives; (2) involve at least one celebrity; and (3) have a cause related to 'international development' broadly defined. See Richey and Ponte, *Brand Aid.*
41. The database used comes from www.causemarketingforum.com, a website established in 2002 with the stated goal of: 'increasing the number of successful company/cause alliances by providing businesses and nonprofit executives with the practical information and connections that they need to succeed'.
42. Richey and Ponte, *Brand Aid.*
43. http://www.generalmills.com/home/brands/baking_products/betty_crocker/brand%20product%20list%20page.aspx#{588DE128-522B-4712-9F21-ED8D2EF2CA90}.
44. "One Clunky Laptop per Child: Great Idea, Shame about the Mediocre Computer." *The Economist* January 4, 2008. www.economist.com/node/10472304.
45. www.businessweek.com/innovate/NussbaumOnDesign/archives/2007/09/its_time_to_cal.html.
46. F. Kanyesigye, "Rwanda: Project to Distribute 100,000 More Laptops." *The New Times*, 6 March 2012. allafrica.com/stories/printable/201203060083.html.
47. "Education in Peru: Error Message – A Disappointing Return from an Investment in Computing." *The Economist* April 7, 2012.
48. http://www.iadb.org/en/research-and-data/publication-details,3169.html?pub_id=IDB-WP-304.
49. Ibid.
50. www.businessweek.com/innovate/NussbaumOnDesign/archives/2007/09/its_time_to_cal.html.

51. Dr Michele Borba is 'an internationally renowned educator, award-winning author, and parenting and child adolescent expert' (according to the product website). Among her most signalled credentials are that she has 'appeared more than 100 times as a parent expert on "Today" as well as countless talk shows including "Dr Phil," "Dateline," "The View," "Dr Drew," "FOX & Friends," "The Doctors," "CNN," and "The Early Show"'.
52. See http://www.toms.com/eyewear/our-movement. The other 'giving partners' are not listed in TOMS public information, but Partners in Health, Paul Farmer's celebritised NGO has been a partner since 2009.
53. TOMS One for One Giving Report, 2013.
54. Ethiopia has a competitive footwear industry run by Ethiopians, but this does not figure in the TOMS marketing imaginary.
55. See Richey and Ponte, *Brand Aid* for an analysis of how this works in Product RED.
56. Letter from TOMS Founder and Chief Shoe Giver, Blake Mycoskie, 3.
57. See http://apersonaldiaspora.blogspot.it/2011/04/toms-discussion-on-bad-aid.html.
58. See www.goodintents.org/in-kind-donations/a-day- without-dignity.
59. Richey and Ponte, *Brand Aid*. On Product RED, see also Banet-Weiser and Lapsansky, "RED is the New Black"; Giardina, "One Day, One Goal"; Himmelman and Mupotsa, "(Product) RED: (Re)Branding Africa?" and other contributions to the same special issue; Littler, *Radical Consumption*; Wirgau et al., "Is Business Discourse Colonizing Philanthropy?"; and Youde, "Ethical Consumerism or Reified Neoliberalism?".
60. All product information from the official website, www.joinred.com/partners/#.
61. Richey & Ponte, *Brand Aid.*
62. www.thecoca-colacompany.com/dynamic/press_center/2011/12/red-partnership.html.
63. See Richey, "Mobilizing for Global AIDS Treatment."
64. Darnton and Kirk, *Finding Frames*.
65. Appadurai, "Commodities."
66. Frumkin, *Strategic Giving*.
67. See Blowfield and Dolan, "Business as a Development Agent."
68. See Tierney et al., "More Dollars than Sense."
69. See McGoey, "The Philanthropic State."
70. Hickel, "Liberalism and the Politics of Occupy Wall Street."
71. Flannery, "Kiva at Four."

Bibliography

Adelman, C. "Global Philanthropy and Remittances: Reinventing Foreign Aid." *Brown Journal of World Affairs* 15, no. 2 (2009): 23–33.

Adkins, S. *Cause-related Marketing: Who Cares Wins*. Boston, MA: Butterworth- Heinemann, 1999.

Appadurai, A. "Commodities and the Politics of Value." In *The Social Life of Things: Commodities in Cultural Perspective*, edited by. A. Appadurai, 3–63. Cambridge: Cambridge University Press, 1986.

Banet-Weiser, S., and C. Lapsansky. "RED is the New Black: Brand Culture, Consumer Citizenship and Political Possibility." *International Journal of Communication* 2 (2008): 1248–1268.

Berglind, M., and C. Nakata. "Cause-related Marketing: More Buck than Bang?" *Business Horizons* 48, no. 3 (2005): 443–453.

Biccum, A. "Interrupting the Discourse of Development: On a Collision Course with Postcolonial Theory." *Culture, Theory and Critique* 43 (2002): 33–50.

Blowfield, M., and C. Dolan. "Business as a Development Agent: Evidence of Possibility and Improbability," this issue.

Boykoff, M., and M. Goodman. "Conspicuous Redemption? Reflections on the Promises and Perils of the 'Celebritization' of Climate Change." *Geoforum* 40, no. 3 (2009): 395–406.

Brei, V., and S. Bohm. "Corporate Social Responsibility as Cultural Meaning: A Critique of the Marketing of 'Ethical' Bottled Water." *Business Ethics: A European Review* 20, no. 3 (2011): 233–252.

Brockington, D. "The Production and Construction of Celebrity Advocacy in International Development," this issue.

Cameron, J., and A. Haanstra. "Development Made Sexy: How it Happened and What it Means." *Third World Quarterly* 29, no. 8 (2008): 1475–1489.

Cooper, A. F. *Celebrity Diplomacy*. Boulder, CO: Paradigm, 2008.

C.S.R. Europe. Cause Related Marketing. Brussels: CSR Europe, 2000.

Darnton, A., and M. Kirk. *Finding Frames: New Ways to Engage the UK Public in Global Poverty*. London: Bond, 2011.

Daw, J. *Cause Marketing for Nonprofits: Partner for Purpose, Passion and Profits*. Hoboken, NJ: Wiley, 2006.

Einstein, M. *Compassion Inc: How Corporate America Blurs the Line between What We Buy, Who We are, and Those We Help*. Berkeley: University of California Press, 2011.

Flannery, M. "Kiva at Four". *Innovations* (Special issue for the Skoll World Forum 2009) (2009): 29–48 http://media.kiva.org/INNOV-SKOLL-2009_flannery.pdf].

Frumkin, P. *Strategic Giving: The Art and Science of Philanthropy*. Chicago, IL: University of Chicago Press, 2006.

Giardina, M. D. "One Day, One Goal? PUMA, Corporate Philanthropy and the Cultural Politics of Brand 'Africa'." *Sport in Society: Cultures, Commerce, Media, Politics* 13, no. 1 (2010): 130–142.

Goodman, M. K. "The Mirror of Consumption: Celebritization, Developmental Consumption, and the Shifting Cultural Politics of Fair Trade." *Geoforum* 41 (2010): 104–116.

Goodman, M. K., and C. Barnes. "Star/Poverty Space: The Making of the 'Development Celebrity'." *Celebrity Studies* 2, no. 1 (2011): 69–85.

Hawkins, R. "'One Pack = One Vaccine' = One Global Motherhood? A Feminist Analysis of Ethical Consumption." *Gender, Place & Culture: A Journal of Feminist Geography* 18, no. 2 (2011): 235–253.

Hawkins, R. "Shopping to Save Lives: Gender and Environment Theories meet Ethical Consumption." *Geoforum* 43 (2012): 750–759.

Hawkins, R. "A New Frontier in Development? The Use of Cause-related Marketing by International Development Organisations." *Third World Quarterly* 33, no. 10 (2012): 1783–1801.

Hickel, J. "Liberalism and the Politics of Occupy Wall Street." *Anthropology of This Century* no. 4 (2012) http://aotcpress.com/articles/liberalism-politics-occupy-wall-street/.

Himmelman, N., and D. Mupotsa. "(Product) Red: (Re)Branding Africa? Introduction to special issue on RED." *Journal of Pan African Studies* 2, no. 6 (2008): 1–13.

Integer Group "M/A/R/C Research February 2011: The Checkout Study." 2011.

King, S. *Pink Ribbons Inc: Breast Cancer and the Politics of Philanthropy*. Minneapolis: University of Minnesota Press, 2006.

Littler, J. *Radical Consumption: Shopping for Change in Contemporary Culture*. Maidenhead, UK: Open University Press, 2009.

Littler, J. "Introduction: Celebrity and the Transnational." *Celebrity Studies* 2, no. 1 (2011): 1–5.

Littler, J. "'I Feel Your Pain': Cosmopolitan Charity and the Public Fashioning of the Celebrity Soul." *Social Semiotics* 18 (2008): 237–251.

Long, N., and J. D. Van Der Ploeg. "Demythologizing Planned Intervention: An Actor Perspective." *Sociologia Ruralis* 29, no. 3–4 (1989): 226–249.

Marks, M.P., and Z.M. Fischer. "The King's New Bodies: Simulating Consent in the Age of Celebrity." *New Political Science* 24, no. 3 (2002): 371–394.

McGoey, L. "The Philanthropic State: Market–State Hybrids in the Philanthrocapitalist Turn," this issue.

Nickel, P. M., and A. M. Eikenberry. "A Critique of the Discourse of Marketized Philanthropy." *American Behavioural Scientist* 52, no. 7 (2009): 974–989.

Richey, L. A. "Mobilizing for Global AIDS Treatment: Clicking Compassion and Shopping Salvation." *Glocal Times/Nordicom Review* (Special issue on "Mobilizing Communication Globally: For What and For Whom?", edited by K. Wilkinson and F. Enghel), 33 (2012): 29–44.

Richey, L. A., and S. Ponte. "Better (Red)™ than Dead? Celebrities, Consumption and International Aid." *Third World Quarterly* 29, no. 4 (2008): 711–729.

Richey, L. A., and S. Ponte. Brand Aid: Shopping Well to Save the World. Minneapolis: University of Minnesota Press, 2011.

Smith, M., and H. Yanacopulos. "The Public Faces of Development: An Introduction." *Journal of International Development* 16, no. 5 (2004): 657–664.

Street, J. "Do Celebrity Politics and Celebrity Politicians Matter?" *British Journal of Politics and International Relations* 14, no. 3 (2012): 346–356.

Street, J. "Celebrity Politicians: Popular Cultural and Political Representation." *British Journal of Politics and International Relations* 6, no. 4 (2004): 435–452.

Tierney, M. J., D. L. Nielson, D. G. Hawkins, J. T. Roberts, M. G. Findley, R. M. Powers, and B. Parks. "More Dollars than Sense: Refining our Knowledge of Development Finance using AidData." *World Development* 39, no. 11 (2011): 1891–1906.

Turner, G. *Understanding Celebrity*. London: Sage, 2004.

Vanhamme, J., A. Lindgreen, J. Reast, and N. van Popering. "To Do Well by Doing Good: Improving Corporate Image through Cause-related Marketing." *Journal of Business Ethics* 109, no. 3 (2011): 259–274.

Wirgau, J. S., K. W. Farley, and C. Jensen. "Is Business Discourse Colonizing Philanthropy? A Critical Discourse Analysis of (PRODUCT) RED." *Voluntas: International Journal of Voluntary and Nonprofit Organizations* 21, no. 4 (2010): 611–630.

Youde, J. "Ethical Consumerism or Reified Neoliberalism? Product (RED) and Private Funding for Public Goods." *New Political Science* 31, no. 2 (2009): 201–220.

The production and construction of celebrity advocacy in international development

Dan Brockington

Institute for Development Policy and Management, University of Manchester

There has been a proliferation of celebrity within development publicity, media events and representations, which has received little attention from development scholars. This paper charts the rise of celebrity within development, drawing from over 120 interviews conducted with development, media and celebrity professionals. I examine how the presence of celebrity within development is mediated and the political economy of the celebrity–charity–corporate complex which results. I use these findings to interrogate recent writings on the work of celebrity advocacy in development and demonstrate that understanding the production and construction of celebrity development interventions helps substantially in understanding their effects.

Introduction

I must first dispel a common misconception. The study of celebrity is not a shallow or trivial exercise. Critics may bemoan the intellectual content of much celebrity news, but that does not make it off-limits to the academe – quite the opposite. If it is vacuous, then we need to explain its popularity and success. Rubbish may be rubbish, but the study of rubbish is scholarship.[1]

The study of celebrity in fact has an august history. Some of the earliest analyses of celebrity remain landmarks. Daniel Boorstin's *The Image*, defining celebrities as people who are 'famous for being famous', is one such.[2] Horkheimer and Adorno's essay 'The Culture Industry' also provides a standard critique of the intellectual value and contribution of much celebrity culture.[3] Studying celebrity is a challenge to which the academic community is rising.[4] It is now a subgenre of media studies, with its own journal (*Celebrity Studies*) launched in 2010. Articles in all journals in the Web of Science which mention the word celebrity rise steeply in the 1990s with no sign of stalling (Figure 1).

Development studies, however, lags behind: articles mentioning celebrity in the main development journals are few (see Figure 1). Development scholars need to take celebrity more seriously than they do at present. Celebrity is an

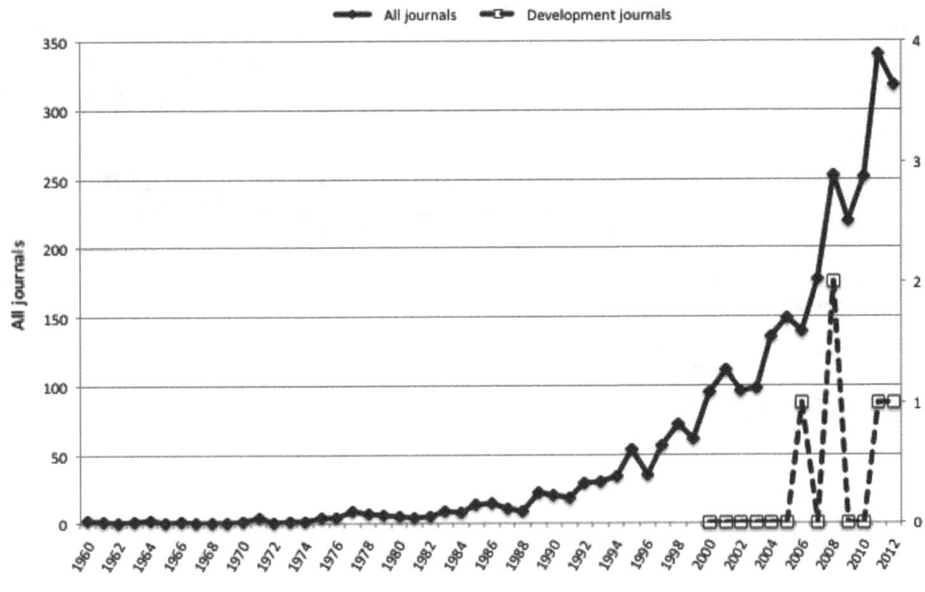

Figure 1. The number of scholarly articles mentioning 'celebrity' in the Web of Science (WOS) across all journals and development studies journals.
Note: Development Studies journals used for the search term were: *Journal of Development Studies*, *World Development*, *Development and Change*, *Third World Quarterly*, *Sustainable Development*, *Development Policy Review*, *Studies in Comparative International Development*, *Economic Development and Cultural Change*, *International Development Planning Review* and *IDS Bulletin*. Results are only shown after 2000 for Development Studies for clarity in the figure above. No articles in these journals mentioning celebrity are reported before this year in WOS.

active force within development affairs. Exploring its presence and influence helps us to understand some of the forces shaping the presentation of development issues in the global North, as well as how different publics are responding to them and how development stories can become, or fail to become, compelling.[5]

Furthermore the importance of celebrity in communicating poverty and development issues is likely to increase. The celebrity industries are expanding into the global South as internet connections, media industries and mobile phones increase their reach. Poverty is expanding in the global North as the global poor come increasingly to be found in the unequal societies of middle-income countries where celebrity industries have been present for longer.[6] In North and South celebrity is likely to become more involved in the communication and mediation of development issues.

In this paper I examine the organisation of relations between the celebrity industries and development NGOs, focusing on those in the UK, and setting the latter within the broader charitable sector of which they are part. This involves examining both how these relationships have developed over time and how they are constructed and mediated on a day-to-day basis. I then examine elements of the political economy of these relationships – how they create and distribute benefit. Here I am interested in benefits beyond those enjoyed by development NGOs.

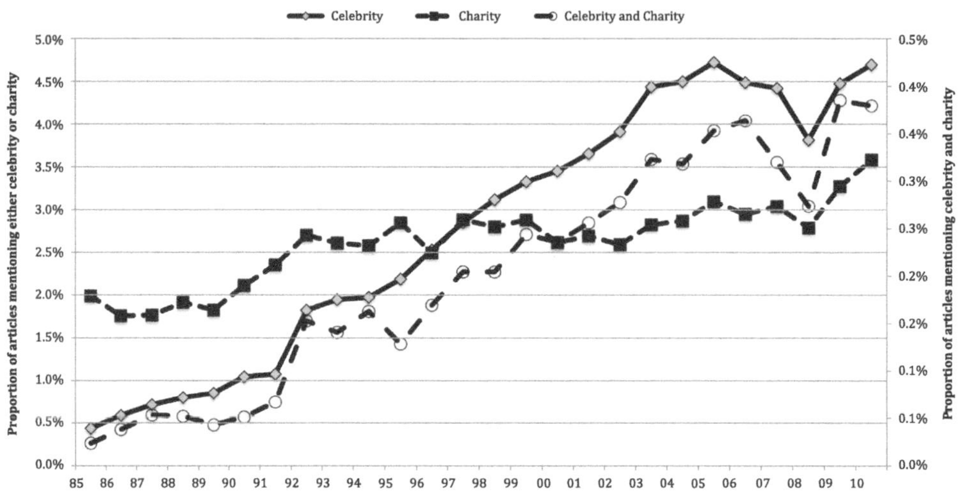

Figure 2. Trends in reporting celebrity, charity and both together.
Source: Lexus Nexus.

I will argue that the work of celebrity in development deserves attention among the new development actors of this special issue.[7] I explore the limitations of this topic and the further research required better to understand it. I also argue that the insights I provide here into the forces, conflicts and structures producing celebrity advocacy improve our understanding of its effects.

The article proceeds thus: first, I review some of the writings on the work, history and functioning of celebrity in (largely Northern) societies and highlight some gaps in writings about celebrity advocacy. Second, I describe the methods used in this study. Third, I highlight recent developments in the history of celebrity and development. Fourth, I explain how the relationships between the celebrity industry and the development sector are forged, examining the key tensions which shape their outcomes. Then I outline the political economy of a 'charity–celebrity–corporate' complex which has been produced by these interactions. Finally, I conclude by considering the implications of these findings for our understanding of the implications of celebrity and development.

Celebrity and development studies

In the public mind there is often a distinction between fame and celebrity.[8] Famous people are credible; celebrities are not, which leads to interesting questions such as 'how can celebrities become famous?'. Turner's definition of celebrity incorporates that distinction. He defines celebrities as those whose private lives attract more attention than their professional lives.[9] Rojek is more inclusive and distinguishes between three forms of celebrity: ascribed greatness (enjoyed by royalty), achieved renown (won by great athletes) and attributed glory (afforded by the media to reality TV stars).[10]

My own definition is not based on how fame was won; it focuses on the commerce and industry that depends on celebrity. Celebrity describes public appearances which are materially beneficial, and where the benefits are enjoyed

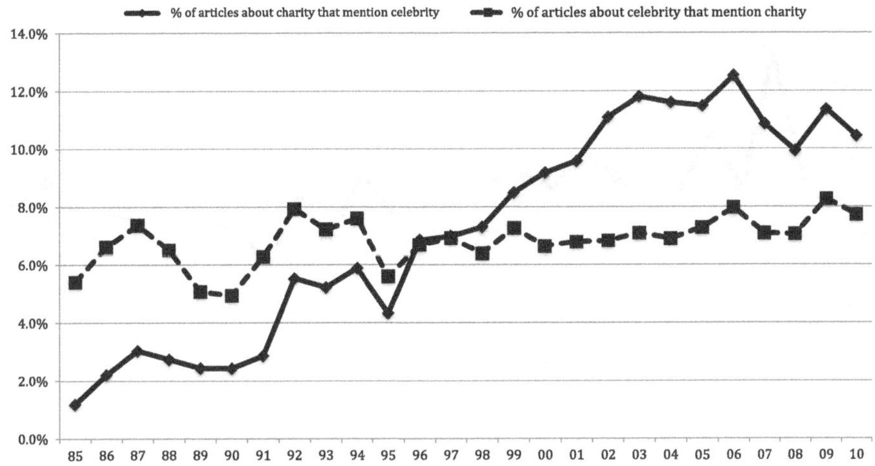

Figure 3. Trends in reporting celebrity and charity.
Source: Lexus Nexus.

by the celebrity themselves and by other stakeholders whose job it is to manage the appearance of that celebrity. According to this definition, members of the public interviewed by roving reporters would not be celebrities. Academics promoting their books in the media would only qualify if those media opportunities were provided by an agent promoting their book. In the account below I use celebrity and fame interchangeably and I refer to celebrities as 'celebrities', 'famous people' or 'public figures'. The term 'celebrity industries' refers to the commercial organisations managing the work of celebrities.

Celebrity can be analysed in three main ways.[11] A political-economy approach examines the political and commercial interests which shape the industry.[12] Celebrity can also be read semiotically, in terms of the signs it represents and finally it can be approached from the point of view of the consumer, and audience identity.[13] There are also analyses which focus more on who has been famous and what they have done, than on the means by which such notice has been acquired.[14] The flaw in this approach is that the result is largely a list of famous names and their activities, with little insight into what drives the attention, or its consequences. If attention to celebrity is to be useful to Development Studies it will need to eschew such an approach. Rather, as I will argue below, if we are to understand the ways in which individuals matter, we need first to explore the machinery around them to be able to gauge the nature of any personal influence.

With respect to the role of celebrity in advocacy John Street has argued that the rise of celebrity-like behaviour among politicians, and of politics among celebrities, reflects the increasing importance of style within politics.[15] Meyer and Gamson and Lester and Hutchins have noted that celebrity advocacy with respect to environmental causes is inherently unstable and weak.[16] For Meyer and Gamson the advocacy is always at risk of being deemed inauthentic, because the celebrity advocates themselves are questioned thus. There is therefore a tendency among celebrity advocates to steer issues towards those causes which will provoke less contention and scrutiny. For Lester and Hutchins the

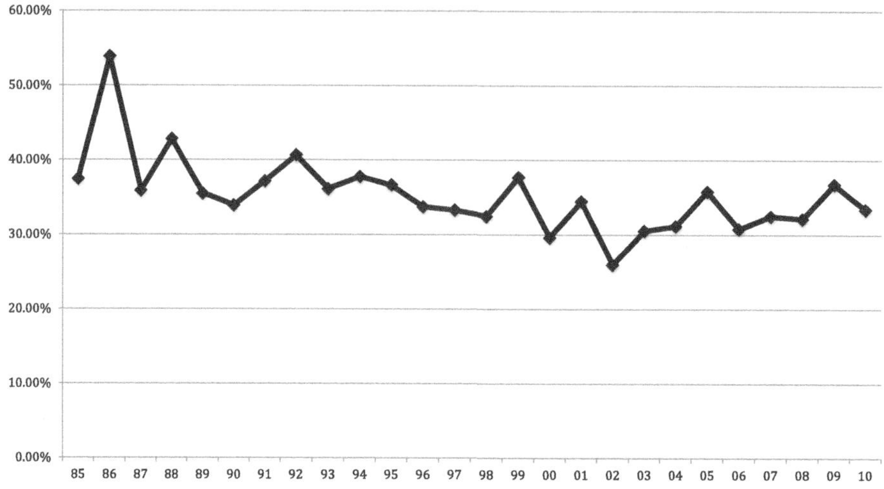

Figure 4. The proportion of articles about celebrity and charity which mention either poverty, international issues or development.
Source: Lexus Nexus.

instability derives from the marginality of environmental causes to the drivers of economic and media power. This makes it harder for environmentalists to present their case, as a sceptical media will question their media events more intensively. Other analysts observe the alignment of celebrity advocacy with hegemonic capitalist power. I have argued elsewhere that the irruption of celebrity within environmental causes is part of a more general mainstreaming of environmental movements within capitalism.[17]

Many authors decry the rise of 'causumerism', with which celebrity can be associated, and the promotion of consumption or 'clicktivism' as a means of tackling global problems but in ways which simply reproduce or leave unquestioned the forces producing poverty or degradation.[18] Others observe that contemporary celebrity interventions in development causes merely focus the attention of Northern publics onto themselves, not towards distant strangers.[19] Similarly Cameron and Haanstra argue that the trend to make development 'sexy' promotes Northern charity rather than an understanding of the structural causes of poverty and inequality.[20]

Within British development NGOs there has been a questioning of the values promoted by relying on celebrity.[21] Within the academe there is a flourishing body of criticism of the role of celebrity in recreating and reproducing hegemonic capitalist inequality.[22] Kapoor adopts the most radical position, arguing that celebrity is part of the forces which create and produce inequality, and that celebrities might in fact be 'sadists' delighting in their position at the top of the pyramid.[23] He further suggests that the only way out of this dilemma is through a Marxist revolution and that following conventional means of tackling poverty (such as supporting NGOs) is no solution – it is better to do nothing.

Finally, some observers embrace the opportunities that celebrity's proximity to power offers. Cooper is the most sycophantic.[24] He celebrates celebrity diplomacy and the ways musicians Bob Geldof and Bono and the actress Angelina Jolie have been able to advance development agendas a little too generously.

Missing thus far from these accounts are three elements necessary to understand the role and consequences of celebrity within development. First, we lack an account of how the celebrity industry and the development sector have become intertwined in recent years. Second, we do not know how relationships between celebrity and development causes are constructed. Third, we need a better understanding of the political economy of these relationships. These are the contributions that this paper provides.

Methods

I present here findings from over 120 interviews conducted between September 2010 and December 2012 with employees of different NGOs, with journalists and with agents, managers and public relations staff, mostly employed in the USA and UK. Interviewees were selected through a mixture of targeted and snowball sampling. I approached the major international development NGOs in the UK using analyses of their income, as well as major talent agencies in the UK and USA.[25] I interviewed staff from NGOs outside the development sector to understand better how changes in that sector fitted into the broader charitable sector. Interviews covered experience in interviewees' current employment and work for previous organisations. I supplemented these interviews with an analysis of articles which mention the words 'celebrity' and 'charity' (and derivatives of both) in the major UK newspapers, using Lexus Nexus.[26]

I will not say who agreed to speak with me, or which organisations they work for, because I insisted on complete anonymity for all my interviewees. Each is represented as a source number below. However, I can report the breakdown of interviews according to the number of organisations in different sectors in which interviewees have worked (Table 1). It was easiest to talk to people in the non-profit and NGO sector but significant minorities were entertainment professionals and journalists.

I believe these data are representative because I have talked to a significant proportion of the important players, including most of the major development NGOs who work with celebrity. It quickly became clear that there was as common story to be told across these interviews, which I presented to my

Table 1. Country and organisation experience of the 123 interviewees consulted in this research.

Region	NGOs	Celebrity industries[1]	Media	Other[2]	Total
Australasia	2				2
Asia	2				2
South America	2				2
North America	14	6		2	22
Africa	13	1			14
Europe excl UK	5				5
UK	109	24	25	14	172
Total	147	31	25	16	219

Notes: [1]Includes intermediary industries negotiating links between celebrities and NGOs.
[2]Includes government officials, researchers and corporate leaders.

interviewees. Their reactions were positive and, crucially, several mistook the anonymised voices of other informants for their own when reading drafts of my work. For these reasons the material below can be taken to represent the experience of diverse actors.

The development of celebrity in development

Let us first survey the variety of celebrity work for development issues. Almost all UN agencies have celebrity ambassadors, although none more than UNICEF, and most development NGOs in the UK have similar programmes.[27] Ambassadors go on publicised field trips (such as singer Beverley Knight's to Malawi for Christian Aid[28]); they design handbags for Haiti (such as actress Scarlett Johansson's for Oxfam[29]); and they facilitate access to powerful people for development activists in the North (for example, when the model Claudia Schiffer lead a lobby of a MPs in Westminster for Make Poverty History) and South (such as former Irish president Mary Robinson's visit to the Presidents of DRC and Rwanda as Honorary President of Oxfam).[30] Some of these engagements promote general awareness, others specific campaigns, others fundraising drives, while others are more about engaging and rewarding existing supporters at particular events (such as musician Tom Yorke's impromptu recital at a Trade Justice Movement event in 2005).[31] In Tanzania actors such as the late Stephen Kanumba conduct public-facing campaigns on the streets to promote awareness of HIV issues and women's rights.[32]

Other celebrities are setting up their own foundations and organisations to pursue their own interests, with variable success. The musician Madonna's foundation in Malawi had radically to reorganise its activities after accusations of inappropriate use of resources, and Wyclef Jean (a musician) was accused of mismanaging funds in Haiti.[33] Conversely actors George Clooney's, Don Cheadle's, Mia Farrow's and John Prenderghast's (an activist) actions around Darfur are alleged to have been too effective, directing attention and activism to inappropriate solutions which may have prolonged the conflict.[34] Groups like the Elders combine the power of celebrity across several different spheres. They are a select group of statesmen and women (including Desmond Tutu, Jimmy Carter and Mary Robinson) who have been brought together by Richard Branson (a businessman) and Peter Gabriel (a musician) under the nominal leadership of former South African president Nelson Mandela to lobby for particularly important development and human rights issues (such as reconciliation in Cyprus).[35] Similarly the Clinton Global Initiative (led by former US president Bill Clinton) seeks to leverage celebrity influence in the political and entertainment fields to encourage philanthropy in the USA.

There is a popular history of the work of celebrity in development issues. We know that the Ethiopian famine in 1984 prompted the Bob Geldof to set up Band Aid and his colleagues in America to set up 'USA for Africa'. The phenomenally successful singles these groups released begat the Live Aid concerts in 1985. Those 'mega-events', combined with Nelson Mandela concerts, the Amnesty International tour, Sun City album and the start of Comic Relief make the late 1980s the moment when humanitarian activism awoke to the power of the celebrity industry.[36] Kofi Anan, the former Secretary General of the United Nations, made substantial use of celebrity within the UN in the

1990s.[37] Since then notable moments combining celebrity with development issues have occurred with the International Campaign to Ban Landmines campaign, during the Jubilee 2000 campaign, the Make Poverty History campaign in 2005, the Save Darfur Coalition (since 2004) and in the Live Earth concerts of 2007.

Many of these episodes have been controversial. The imagery promoted during the early work in Ethiopia prompted a detailed enquiry into African imagery in development.[38] Celebrity in the Make Poverty History campaign was perceived to be associated with over-simplistic messages, and the problematic timing of the Live 8 concerts (clashing with major planned protest marches) produced tension between some NGOs and celebrity advocates.[39] A further tension concerns the Save Darfur Coalition. A number of observers objected to the characterisation of the violence in Darfur by the Coalition and questioned the effectiveness of the measures which the coalition advocated to bring an end to that violence.[40] Partly as a result of these tensions, there is often a reaction against celebrity within the development movement. This is visible in the comments pages of the *Guardian* newspaper whenever Bono's name is mentioned in conjunction with development causes.[41]

However, both the common history of celebrity and development and the reaction against it conceal much. They conceal the fact that what we now call development issues enjoyed the heights of fame many decades ago. Campaigns against slavery and the pursuit of progress in supposedly uncivilised lands produced some of the greatest public figures of the era (David Livingstone, Edward Morrell and William Wilberforce). In the 20th century concern for these issues continued to produce public figures but not noticeably so after Albert Schweitzer won his Nobel Prize in 1952. Between then and the mid-1980s Mother Teresa was the only public figure of any note who emerged to champion development issues.[42]

The common history also conceals the fact that the relationships between the celebrity industry and the development sector have changed substantially quite recently. Since about 2000 they have become formalised, more intensive, competitive (in that charities are competing to get access to celebrities) and systematically organised. Perhaps the most important change is the establishment of a cadre of full-time, dedicated liaison officers working for NGOs. Seventy-five per cent of the 30 largest charities in the UK have such a position.[43] The majority of organisations whose employees I have spoken to had created full-time celebrity liaison posts since 2000. Since 2004 a celebrity liaison officers' forum has been meeting in London monthly to share experience and expertise. A blog (http://charitycelebrity.blogspot.com) set up by one of the more experienced liaison officers in 2010 had over 1000 readers less than a year later; it now has over 500 Twitter followers and forms an occasional column in the *Guardian*'s Voluntary Sector Network. The Media Trust, which exists to promote effective media engagement by charities in the UK, has been organising workshops since 2003 to advise NGOs on how to work with celebrity. The Red Pages, a company selling access contact details of over 25,000 public figures in the UK, began listing celebrity ailments systematically (to facilitate health charities' approaches) in around 2004.

There has been an equivalent shift within the celebrity industry, with three of the four major talent agencies in Hollywood setting up foundations to promote charitable activities to their clients since 2000 (William Morris, 2000; Creative Artists Agency, 2001; United Talent Agency, 2004). These foundations now broker relationships between major international NGOs searching for talent.[44] There are also several specialist liaison companies. The Global Philanthropy Group (begun in 2007) specialises in advising the philanthropy of high net worth and high-profile individuals in the USA. The Cause Effect Agency (also US-based) first began trading in 2005. In the UK Cause Celeb has met less success since starting up in 2004, but Independent Celebrity Liaison (established in 2011) has done relatively well.[45]

There have also been increasing efforts to catalogue all these activities. The *Look to the Stars* website, which documents the work of celebrities for good causes was set up in 2006.[46] The *Ecorazzi* website, concentrating on environmental issues, was set up in the same year. MTV established a website aimed at its activist viewers in 2008. *Third Sector*'s column dedicated to the work of celebrity in NGOs first appeared in 2002; it became weekly in 2005.[47] The Red Page's weekly newsletter detailing deals between celebrities and brands, and celebrities and charities (or all three) first came out in 2007 and went bi-weekly two years later.

Finally, the effects of all this activity are clearly visible in the long-term trends in the reporting of charitable and celebrity activity in British newspapers. There has been an increase in the proportion of articles mentioning celebrity, the proportion mentioning charity, and the proportion mentioning both (Figure 2). The contrasting trends between the proportion of charity articles that mention celebrity, and the proportion of celebrity articles that mention charity, are more interesting (Figure 3). This demonstrates that only a small proportion of celebrity articles include any mention of anything charitable, and mention does not change much over time. There is, however, a marked increase in mention of celebrity in articles about charities. In other words, while the world of celebrity remains little altered by charitable activities, reporting on charities has been markedly reoriented to include the celebrity industry. International development issues have maintained a constant presence within these trends (Figure 4).

In summary, relations between the charitable sector and celebrity industries have become more organised and systematic in the past 10 years. They have become more professional. To understand the consequences of this shift within the development sector, however, we have to appreciate better how these relationships are constructed and nurtured.

Constructing effective relationships

There are doubtless cases where the enthusiasm of the celebrity explains their relationship with development NGOs. But this does not explain all celebrity activism, nor could it explain how any of these desires are brought into the public domain in effective and convincing ways. The interactions between celebrity and development cannot be conceived as merely interactions between individuals. They are encounters between development organisations and celebrity industries.

We will view these interactions from the perspective of the celebrity liaison officers of NGOs who mediate them. There are several elements to their work. First, making the approach; second developing the relationship; third coping with the expectations and demands of colleagues in NGOs; and, fourth, working with agents and managers of celebrities.

When NGOs approach public figures for support (and it is almost always that way round), they have to have worked out how 'their artists [are] going to have credibility and relevance'. Relevance is not given. It has to be recognised, and then realised (ie brought into effect) by the NGOs, the public figures and those surrounding them. In the first instance this may require that liaison officers know the field, who is out there in the public eye, and what they are interested in. This requires exploring people's backgrounds and interests as well as contemporary gossip. As one put it: 'my job is to read everything'. The Red Pages began listing celebrity ailments and charitable interests in the early 2000s precisely in order to improve the value of their list to NGO clients. Tracking people before making an 'ask' (a request for action or assistance) can take longer than a year.[48]

It is one of the continual struggles of the job for all but the most prestigious NGOs that all the work can fall at the first hurdle. Public figures, their agents and contacts, receive hundreds of requests weekly to work for free for good causes. They refuse or ignore the vast majority; a thick skin is required to cope with all the refusals. There are coping strategies. The UN agencies, for example, meet quarterly to ensure that they are not approaching the same people with different requests. The celebrity liaison officer's forum in the UK serves a similar purpose. Avoiding an instant rejection requires 'pitching something that they might be interested in and…that means doing lots of research'. Agents insist that well designed letters, tailored to their client alone, are vital if they are to consider the 'ask'. However they also typically advise their clients to choose up to three organisations with which they would work for up to 12 days a year (or two to three 'asks' per organisation). This makes it easier for the agents to handle, and refuse, 'asks' from other organisations.[49]

The distinguishing feature of professional relations between celebrities and NGOs is the way NGO staff seek to build lasting relationships with celebrity patrons. Some of the liaison officers with whom I spoke were the first to hold their positions; they observed that the first thing they had to do was to turn what had been incidental fragmented encounters between their organisation and public figures into more lasting relationships. As one put it, the liaison officer's role is to 'stay in their lives'.[50] This could involve thank you cards, flowers or gifts donated by corporate partners following appearances, as well birthday cards and bespoke, personalised newsletters. They keep patrons up to date with the outcomes of their actions, reporting the outcome of fundraising ventures, of how funds were used and providing updates on people encountered in field trips.[51]

The 'asks' themselves can be a means of developing relationships. Some organisations deliberately designed publicity events as opportunities to develop relationships with celebrities. One liaison officer was 'working to invent' more domestic events rather than relying on the more taxing commitment of an international field trip. Other liaison officers designed gradations of events specifically to initiate and then deepen relationships.[52]

One of the problems facing smaller organisations is precisely that they are not able to generate the right sort of meetings to enable them to develop relationships with public figures:

> It is difficult when you work for a small charity to provide the range of things to...keep people's interests up...It was easy at [a large charity]...there were always events going on...you wanted someone to keep their involvement...and therefore you could invite them to open something or come to something...at a smaller agency that is much more difficult, you don't have those kind of on-going things...so you are working much harder...to find things which allow you to maintain that relationship with people, which is really important as otherwise they forget you and move on.[53]

For many development organisations a key component of relationship building is the field trip overseas. The field trips serve three purposes. First, for the public figures, the trips can have a dramatic personal impact:

> If we can get someone to the field and work around their interests and availability, without a doubt most people find it's a really moving, engaging and inspiring experience.[54]

The dry statistics of briefings about poverty are replaced by real people in difficult circumstances:

> everything [in the briefings] will be absolutely reinforced in the most simple black and white way when you go on a trip.[55]

Second is the effect of this experience on the relationship between the public figures and the organisation:

> there are just so many examples that I could give you of the difference that a trip like that makes to a celebrity and just in terms of really engaging them and really cementing the relationship.[56]

Field trips allow for quality time spent with the liaison officers and public figures at a time when these figures may also be rapidly changing their world-view.

Third, field trips help celebrities to pass the authenticity test demanded by sceptical publics. Coping with the difficult circumstances of a field trip 'provides huge credibility to the role'. When public figures handle interviews they can speak with more conviction and ease, they are able to tell stories of people they met, adding much more colour.[57]

Field trips can go wrong. The public figure can fail to connect with the people they meet, or cope with the shock of their new circumstances; they can place unreasonable demands on the time of country offices, and they can be poorly portrayed in the press coverage which results. Memories of these trips still echo around the celebrity liaison and press communities, if not in the public mind. Sometimes field trips are conducted in private, to nurture the relationship, but this is rare, for some form of publicity is usually required to justify any trip. Besides, part of the skill is to avoid problematic publicity by getting the trip right – negotiating it with the field staff who will host the visit, inviting the right journalists and communicating effectively with the celebrities themselves.[58]

Ultimately successful relationship building hinges on treating public figures as human beings. The fact that they donate their time, and often cover their own costs, makes them effectively major donors-in-kind and they need to be treated as such by the causes they support. Celebrities want relationships with NGOs which matter and which can be nurtured over time, and which feel authentic to them. [59]

Developing strong relationships requires negotiating three significant constraints. It requires understanding the uncertainty that defines the professions of many celebrities – one can never tell where or when the next job will come up. One interviewee called the effect 'Steven Spielberg': any moment someone more important may call your celebrity in to do a lucrative job.[60]

Second, it requires coping with colleagues with much expectation, but little understanding, of celebrity. These people they are keen to use public figures, do not know how to, but do not realise that. One person found it 'maddening…half of my job, half of my week, is about managing the expectations of my colleagues'. This was a common theme in the interviews.[61]

> They say 'we need a celebrity for this, I'm like no you don't, you don't need a celebrity'. [62]

Part of the skill of celebrity liaison is to promote events when celebrity is *not* used. Publicity events need to stand up creatively without any celebrity presence. Simply adding celebrity to create attention will not work; 'it still has to come back down to being a good story either to get the celebrity or to get the coverage'.[63]

Third, there are the unequal power relations that define interactions between celebrities and charities. Even the most prestigious organisations can find that the top people have 'lots of layers' and are hard to get to. Agents were particularly important because they could control schedules and shut down potential events. Some liaison officers therefore 'treat the agent as well as I treat the celebrity'. It helps that there is a mutual interest in these relationships working successfully for all sides: 'we all know we need something out of this, both parties need something out of this relationship'. Ultimately this should lead to a close, trusted relationship whereby the NGO can become another reliable means of managing the public persona of the celebrity.[64]

> my goal is not to have anything to be approved by a publicist…because quite honestly I don't want you to look bad either…The ideal is for when they have their [organisation M] hat on for me to be their [organisation M] publicist and for that to be enough.[65]

After all, in the long term the celebrities come and go, but the agents remain.[66]

In sum, particular staff within some development NGOs are deeply engaged in working closely with agents, publicists, managers and celebrities. These interactions are, from the point of view of the NGOs, designed to produce deeper and more meaningful relationships between NGOs and celebrities, and the appearance of deeper and more meaningful relationships. We need now to consider how these relationships create and distribute benefit, that is, the political economy of celebrity and development interactions.

The political economy of celebrity advocacy

I want to examine two elements of this political economy: first, the creation of a specific niche element of the celebrity industry now concerned with charitable activities; second, the role of corporate interest in fuelling the celebrity–charity–corporate complex.

The fact that celebrity–charity interactions now constitute a specific niche within the celebrity industry is visible in ways in which the media deliberately seek contacts with charities in order to conduct their business:

> If we have a target list for celebrities…if we are looking for an interview…we definitely might go through a charity if we know that there is something coming up in a campaign…We are often approached by charities about certain [tasks] and we might use that as an excuse to try and get a particular celebrity. So we will look for them to chase a certain celebrity for us.[67]

Television programmes like 'Celebrity who Wants to be a Millionaire' depend upon good links with charities in order to function. The contestants win money for their chosen charity, and celebrity liaison officers' links are required in order to source appropriate talent for the shows.[68]

The niche is also visible in the brand images of certain celebrities. Geldof's role as a chairman of the recently launched 8 Miles private equity fund has credibility and appeal because the fund seeks to invest in African business opportunities.[69] Another example is a recent advertising campaign featuring Bono, his wife Ali Hewson and Angelina Jolie, who all appeared in a series of advertisements for Louis Vuitton bags. Bono and Hewson were pictured leaving a small plane somewhere in Africa, with the caption 'Every Journey Begins in Africa'.[70] Angelina Jolie was pictured in Cambodia with the same campaign.[71] The power of the images depends on the brand values that Bono and Jolie have so strongly cultivated with respect to development philanthropy.[72]

Note, however, that Bono and Hewson earned no fee from their appearance in these advertisements. That was donated to charities, as was a portion of Jolie's. There were fringe benefits (extending Bono's and Jolie's brand, and mention of Hewson's clothing range – Edun – in which Vuitton had a 49% stake) but there is no indication that this was particularly profitable to these celebrities personally. It may well have been most beneficial for Louis Vuitton, which leveraged the brand value of these figures.

Crucial to understanding the political economy of celebrity advocacy is the role of corporate interests. The rise and systematisation of the celebrity–charity–corporate complex is not just an important part of the media industries, it is part of a more general orienting of the corporate sector towards the celebrity sector, for economic as well as more personal reasons. Properly to understand the shift that has taken place through the intertwining of the celebrity industries and charitable sector we have to appreciate the role of corporate interest in both.

One of the strongest and most persistent themes that emerged across all the interviews was the importance of corporate interest in celebrity. Corporate sponsors of NGOs simply have a reputation in the third sector of loving celebrity associations. The corporate teams within NGOs can be those who make the most requests for celebrity involvement. This interest is both a vehicle for driving the presence of celebrity within NGOs and a powerful force shaping the conduct of negotiations between the latter and the celebrity industry.[73]

> It's very expensive for a corporation to get a celebrity spokesperson, so they love it when by doing good works they also get to grab a few photos...or do a joint press conference with a celebrity. It's a big added benefit…They love getting that opportunity to be associated with a celebrity for free.[74]

NGOs cultivate that enthusiasm. Numerous NGOs now seek to cultivate support from businesses, and to be chosen as that business's charity of the year by offering associations with their celebrity supporters on their websites.

Corporate interest in charitable causes can reflect cause-related marketing opportunities. It is good business sense to build relationships with NGOs where that provides access to fashionable events and people:

> in the first instance the draw is going to be that to have [public figure E] associated with their product is highly desirable and to sponsor an event that we do at [location F] which is very elite, which an awful lot of very rich or famous people come to is perfect to their brand.[75]

In one instance the very level of celebrity involvement in a fundraising campaign was determined by the corporate preference for celebrity involvement:

> [We asked] do we in fact even involve celebrities or is it that we have real women…in the ads. We came to the conclusion that actually the corporates like to be associated with the campaign because of the kudos it holds and because of the level of celebrities it has supporting it. Because the majority of the income is raised through corporate partners…we do actually need to have celebrity support to keep them engaged.[76]

Corporate interest in access to talent can be so strong that I have come across instances where NGOs became obliged to deliver public figures to corporate events and resorted to buying in the talent for a day from appropriate agencies.[77]

The interest of businesses in charities' celebrities carries two major risks. First, celebrities will endorse charities without charge, but they do charge companies. When corporates become involved with charitable events there is a risk of free endorsement. This would deprive public figures, and their agents, of their income, and agents would 'have a fit' if that happened. Getting things right here is so important that more than one organisation has produced written guidelines as to how to behave in such circumstances.[78]

The second complication is that public figures' corporate endorsements and general behaviour can threaten the brand of the NGOs with whom they then associate. For the larger NGOs the risks of association with public figures were 'all about the brand', which meant what these figures might do to the NGO brand. For, 'that is the other side of celebrity…if you screw up you screw up in the headlights'. Some undertake careful due diligence on the public figures with whom they build relationships, before they get serious, to prevent any embarrassment. Even then things can go wrong, if public figures subsequently develop relationships with companies who are doing things the NGOs oppose. Or if, for example, they behave in ways which are detrimental to the campaign, such as when Salman Khan shot a protected antelope in India shortly after appearing in a calendar for the WWF, or when Ralph Fiennes was reported to have had casual sex with an air hostess en route to India to promote HIV/AIDS awareness for UNICEF.[79]

Finally, we must note that corporate interest in the celebrity–charity–corporate complex (and the rise of corporate social responsibility more generally) cannot be reduced to profit motives. One of the reasons why corporates are star struck is because corporate elites enjoy meeting publicly desirable figures in person:

> A lot of middle aged men melt at the idea...A lot of middle aged business men, and young ones and older ones actually just kind of fawn at the idea of somebody reasonably well known and reasonably attractive. I'm sure that there are equally a number of business women [who are similar].[80]

Sometimes the value of meeting people is not just about the physical attractiveness of the person, but reflects their enduring influence through decades of media presence.

> [Company G] absolutely loved [public figure H]...she's very special to a group of men of a certain age...She's...lovely and charming and articulate...she delivers both emotionally and rationally and...appeals to the softer side of them.[81]

Similarly, many observers commented on the power of celebrity to give them access to high-level political circles:[82]

> You might be able to meet with someone lower down in the office but suddenly you are meeting with the chief of staff or with the principal instead of a staff member two or three levels below because you are accompanied by a celebrity. You also might be able to get a hearing on Capitol Hill because one of those testifying would be a celebrity...That happens all the time.[83]

In summary, the construction of the celebrity–charity–corporate complex has become a niche element of the celebrity industries. These associations are, however, attractive to corporate sponsors of charities because of the valuable publicity and associations they can create, and because of the personal pleasure the company of the famous affords.

Discussion

Does any of this matter? Have we just emerged from this account with the rubbish of celebrity more deeply engrained beneath our fingernails? I believe that the depth and sophistication of the organisation of relationships between celebrity and the charitable sector described above, the carefully constructed and negotiated relationships and the importance of these relationships with charitable and development causes for the celebrity industries and corporate associations means that the presence of celebrity does need to be taken seriously by the development studies community. These people have become an important set of development actors, of whose presence and influence we need to take better notice.

At the same time we must recognise the limits of this field. Celebrity's increasingly sophisticated association with development issues is often marginal to the way in which these issues are played out in individual countries. Celebrities can be associated with significant fundraising efforts, but these funds themselves are only a minority of the development aid, and the effectiveness and influence of the organisations which wield them are substantially questioned.[84] The proliferation of celebrity associations with development causes in the media is no indication that celebrity matters that much on the ground.

But, in a sense, that is the contribution of this paper. In outlining the history of the celebrity and development intertwining, in explaining how these associations come about, and in plotting the distribution of these benefits, the paper has described a realm which is decidedly marginal to many development activities and issues in the South. The value of this account is that it delineates the limits of interest in the topic for development scholars. The interests outlined above are important, as I have approached them, for understanding the political economy and representation of development issues in the North.

However, we must also recognise that celebrity may well become more important in the future. I have worked mainly in the UK and talked to largely Northern practitioners and professionals. Celebrity cultures, however, vary from country to country, as do their roles and interactions with development causes. The work of celebrity and development in India, Brazil or Nigeria, where there are strong entertainment industries, and development issues, may produce different accounts. When Southern-based NGOs work with their own national celebrities in public-facing campaigns, they do so with figures who will be listened to by the intended beneficiaries of their development activities, not potential funders or Northern-based activists.[85]

But the importance of celebrities' work does not just lie in these mediating roles for Northern audiences. Celebrity works in development because it facilitates access to elites, because the powerful want to meet the famous. Here a different set of interactions may be taking place, which I have not been able to describe. Altogether different methods would be required to do so. The work of celebrity elites with other political elites in shaping economic and social policies important for development issues will require greater scrutiny.

Finally, this contribution creates the space to understand the role of individuals better in celebrified development. Celebrity studies can be vitiated by its individualistic approach, which focuses too much on the celebrity and not enough on the broader structures of which they are part.[86] The same focus on a few individuals, to the detriment of our understanding of the broader processes of which they are part, affects some contributions on celebrity in development, even as they focus on those broader structures.[87] The result is that the academic study of celebrity can be, as Turner observed, rather too similar to popular celebrity culture.[88] We become preoccupied with individual personae, characters and escapades, rather than with the more powerful forces producing them.

However, once we do understand the structures, then the space for individuals opens up. For understanding the structures and industries at work makes it possible to identify domains and occasions where a particular individual's influence and actions have been important. For example, in the 1960s musician Nina Simone's creation of *Mississippi Goddam!* owed little to any celebrity–charity machinery; more recently the outspoken remarks of the Dixie Chicks against President Bush were similarly spontaneous.[89] Likewise, where individuals are involved in promoting less desirable change, so too understanding the structures at play makes it easier to understand the individual role.

My hope therefore is that celebrity will be taken a little bit more seriously by the Development Studies discipline and the way to take it seriously is to engage with the mechanisms producing and constructing celebrity and development interactions. Doing so will make it possible to respond more effectively and intelligently to the associations between famous people and good causes. We may well conclude that these associations are best avoided. Or we may identify certain types of interaction that can be promoted effectively and justly in ways which make the world a better place to live in. Or we may need even to consider the possibility that some celebrities may wish to free themselves from the hegemonic regimes of which they are part. All such responses must be grounded in a deeper understanding of the production of celebrity advocacy.

Acknowledgements

This research has been made possible by virtue of an ESRC Fellowship (070-27-0035) and the kind cooperation of all my interviewees. I am grateful for comments on the text and project from Bram Buscher, Graham Harrison, Jim Igoe, Lisa Richey, Stefano Ponte and an anonymous reviewer.

Notes on Contributor

Daniel Brockington is Professor of Conservation and Development at the Institute for Development Policy and Management, University of Manchester. His research covers diverse aspects of conservation and development, from the social impacts of protected areas to conservation planning, media and celebrity and conservation NGOs. His recent books are *Celebrity and the Environment* (2009) and *Nature Unbound* (2008, with Rosaleen Duffy and Jim Igoe).

Notes

1. I follow here Dreben's paraphrase of Saul Lieberman's introduction to Gershom Scholem's lectures on Merkabah Mysticism in 1957, when Lieberman declared that 'nonsense is nonsense but the study of nonsense is scholarship'. Quoted in Socher, "The History of Nonsense." I am not implying that celebrity is rubbish; my language is addressed to those who think it is.
2. Boorstin, *The Image*.
3. Horkheimer and Adorno, *Dialectic of Enlightenment*. The book first appeared in German in 1944.
4. Beer and Penfold-Mounce, "Researching Glossy Topics."
5. Lewis et al., "The Fiction of Development"; Goodman, "The Mirror of Consumption"; and Richey and Ponte, *Brand Aid*.
6. Sumner, "Where do the Poor Live?"
7. See also Ponte and Richey, this issue.
8. Epstein, "Celebrity Culture."
9. Turner, *Understanding Celebrity*, 3.
10. Rojek, *Celebrity*.
11. *Ibid*; Turner, *Understanding Celebrity*; and Ferris, "The Sociology of Celebrity."
12. Marshall, *Celebrity and Power*; and Turner et al., *Fame Games*.
13. Dyer, *Heavenly Bodies*; Gamson, *Claims to Fame*; and Alexander, "The Celebrity-Icon."
14. Gundle, *Glamour*; and Inglis, *A Short History of Celebrity*.

15. Street, "Celebrity Politicians."
16. Meyer & Gamson, "The Challenge of Cultural Elites." Hutchins & Lester.
17. Brockington, "Powerful Environmentalisms"; and Brockington, *Celebrity and the Environment.*
18. Dieter & Kumar, "The Downside of Celebrity Diplomacy"; Littler, "'I Feel Your Pain'"; Boykoff & Goodman, "Conspicuous Redemption"; Yrjölä, "The Invisible Violence of Celebrity Humanitarianism"; Davis, "Feeding the World a Line?"; Richey & Ponte, *Brand Aid*; Yrjölä, "From Street into the World"; Hawkins, "A New Frontier in Development?"; and Hawkins, "Shopping to Save Lives."
19. Chouliaraki, "The Theatricality of Humanitarianism."
20. Cameron & Haanstra, "Development Made Sexy."
21. Darnton & Kirk, *Finding Frames.*
22. Biccum, "Marketing Development"; Yrjölä, "The Invisible Violence of Celebrity Humanitarianism"; Yrjölä, "From Street into the World"; and Kapoor, *Celebrity Humanitarianism.*
23. Kapoor, *Celebrity Humanitarianism.*
24. Cooper, *Celebrity Diplomacy and the G 8*; Cooper, "Beyond One Image Fits All"; and Cooper, *Celebrity Diplomacy.*
25. Atkinson et al., "Charitable Giving for Overseas Development."
26. Brockington, "Trends in Reporting on Celebrity, Charities and Development and Humanitarian NGOs."
27. Fall & Tang, *Goodwill Ambassadors in the United Nations System.*
28. http://www.mirror.co.uk/3am/celebrity-news/beverley-knights-malawi-mission-275884.
29. http://www.oxfam.org/en/pressroom/pressrelease/2010-02-04/scarlett-johansson-designs-handbag-haiti.
30. Sireau, *Make Poverty History*; and http://www.realizingrights.org/index.php?option=com_content&view=article&id== 400&Itemid=104.
31. http://wn.com/trade_justice_movement?upload_time=all_time&orderby=relevance. Accessed June 3, 2012.
32. Sources 102, 104.
33. http://www.independent.co.uk/news/world/africa/madonna-malawi-and-the-mismanaged-millions-2253507.html. Accessed June 3, 2012; and http://www.guardian.co.uk/music/2010/jan/19/wyclef-jean-haiti.
34. De Waal, "The Humanitarian Carnival"; Flint & De Waal, *Darfur*; and Crilly, *Saving Darfur.*
35. http://www.theelders.org/home.
36. Garofalo, "Understanding Mega-Events."
37. Alleyne, "The United Nations' Celebrity Diplomacy"; and Wheeler, "Celebrity Diplomacy."
38. van der Gaag & Nash, *Images of Africa.*
39. Sireau, *Make Poverty History.*
40. De Waal, "The Humanitarian Carnival"; Flint & De Waal, *Darfur*; and Crilly, *Saving Darfur.*
41. http://www.guardian.co.uk/lifeandstyle/lostinshowbiz/2010/sep/23/bono-one-millennium-development-goals & http://www.guardian.co.uk/commentisfree/2010/sep/27/down-with-bono-bashing. Accessed February 21, 2012.
42. West, "Angelina, Mia and Bono." Brainard & Chollet, *Global Development 2.0* provide an account of interactions after the Second World War and leading up to the 1980s, as does, more humorously, Wolfe, *Radical Chic.*
43. "Celebrity Activists," BBC Radio 4, February 2011.
44. Sources 3 and 85; and Foreman, "How Hollywood finds its Charitable Causes."
45. Sources 21, 55 and 69. This kind of organisation has existed before but its earlier iterations were not always sustainable. One such, Celebrity Outreach Inc., began as a non-profit in 1988 connecting public figures to other non-profits in the USA. In the late 1990s it morphed into a company that acquired signed celebrity memorabilia wholesale for auction by charities. It is struggling now because, as part of the intensification of relations between charities and sports companies, the latter are now themselves selling this sort of memorabilia directly to the NGOs for auction. Source 10.
46. Source 11.
47. *Third Sector is* a trade journal for NGOs in the UK.
48. This paragraph is based on sources 9, 26, 35, 37, 45, 51, 74 and 81.
49. Sources 23, 35, 76, 85, 94 and 108.
50. Sources 45, 65, 71 and 77.
51. Sources 14, 23, 37, 67, 70, 71, 77 and 86.
52. Sources 26 and 37.
53. Source 48.
54. Source 85.
55. Source 74
56. Source 53
57. Sources 53, 74 and 85.
58. Sources 14, 25, 26, 29, 31, 35, 51, 56, 76 and 77.
59. Sources 35, 51, 53, 55, 70 and 71. Cf. http://www.guardian.co.uk/voluntary-sector-network/2012/feb/13/celebrity-supporters-more-than-volunteers. Accessed February 18, 2012.
60. Sources 14, 21, 35, 37, 45, 49 and 86.
61. Source 9, 35, 51, 53, 54 and 77.

62. Source 54.
63. Sources 9, 26, 48, 51, 64, 77, 93.
64. Source 37, 51 and 85.
65. Source 85.
66. Source 35.
67. Source 90.
68. Source 96.
69. http://www.guardian.co.uk/world/2012/mar/01/bob-geldof-africa-private-equity. Accessed June 2, 2012.
70. http://www.dailymail.co.uk/femail/article-1308429/Stuck-Louis-Vuitton-moment-Bono-Ali-Hewson-pose-French-megabrand–clothes-ethical-label.html. Accessed June 2, 2012.
71. http://fashion.telegraph.co.uk/Article.aspx?Id=TMG8572326. Accessed June 2, 2012. The photographs of Jolie and Bono were taken by Annie Leibovitz, who is herself a celebrity photographer of celebrities and who has built her reputation partly on development-focused pictures, including the cover of the 'Africa Issue' of *Vanity Fair* in July 2007. This featured 21 famous faces in an issue guest edited by Bono and dedicated to African development issues. See http://www.vanityfair.com/politics/features/2007/07/onthecover_slideshow200707#intro. Accessed June 2, 2012.
72. The advertisements may not have worked with the public, but that is a different matter. The advertisers thought they would and they thought this because of these figures' brands.
73. Source 35, 48 and 77.
74. Source 55. Similar sentiments were repeated by sources 51, 63 and 76.
75. Source 67.
76. Source 63.
77. Source 34. Corporate pressure explains both the incidents of charities hiring celebrity support mentioned above.
78. Source 51, 61 and 71.
79. Sources 14, 34, 53 and 80. An example of such misalignment between corporate behaviour and NGO work occurred when Oxfam ambassador Kirsten Davies endorsed beauty products made in the Occupied Palestinian Territories by an Israeli firm. See http://codepink.org/blog/2009/08/official-release-oxfam-suspends-ahava-spokeswoman-kristin-davis-from-all-publicity-work/. Accessed February 18, 2012. On Kahn, see Brockington, *Celebrity and the Environment*. On Fiennes, see http://www.dailymail.co.uk/femail/article-436846/Air-stewardess-secrets-mile-high-sex-romp-Ralph-Fiennes.html. Accessed June 3, 2012.
80. Source 75.
81. Source 48.
82. Sources 40, 77, 81 and 93.
83. Source 93.
84. Bebbington et al., *Can NGOs Make a Difference?*.
85. Sources 101, 102, 104, 106 and 107.
86. Gundle, *Glamour*; and Inglis, *A Short History of Celebrity*.
87. Tester, *Humanitarianism and Modern Culture*; Kapoor, *Celebrity Humanitarianism*; and Browne, *The Frontman*.
88. Turner, "Approaching Celebrity Studies."
89. Street, *Rebel Rock*; and Lynskey, *33 Revolutions per Minute*.

Bibliography

Alexander, J. C. "The Celebrity-Icon." *Cultural Sociology* 4, no. 3 (2010): 323–336.

Alleyne, M. D. "The United Nations' Celebrity Diplomacy." *SAIS Review* 250, no. 1 (2005): 175–185.

Atkinson, A. B., P. G. Backus, J. Micklewright, C. Pharoah, and S. Schnepf. "Charitable Giving for Overseas Development: UK Trends over a Quarter Century." *Journal of the Royal Statistical Society, Series A* 175, no. 1 (2012): 167–190.

Bebbington, A. J., S. Hickey, and D. C. Mitlin. *Can NGOs Make a Difference? The Challenge of Development Alternatives*. London: Zed, 2008.

Beer, D., and R. Penfold-Mounce. "Researching Glossy Topics: The Case of the Academic Study of Celebrity." *Celebrity Studies* 1, no. 3 (2010): 360–365.

Biccum, A. "Marketing Development: Live 8 and the Production of the Global Citizen." *Development and Change* 38, no. 6 (2007): 1111–1126.

Boorstin, D. J. *The Image: A Guide to Pseudo-events in America*. New York: Vintage Books, 1992.

Boykoff, M., and M. K. Goodman. "Conspicuous Redemption: Promises and Perils of Celebrity Involvement in Climate Change." *Geoforum* 40 (2009): 395–406.

Brainard, L., and D. Chollet, eds. *Global Development 2.0: Can Philanthropists, the Public and the Poor Make Poverty History*. Washington, DC: Brookings Institution Press, 2008.

Brockington, D. "Powerful Environmentalisms: Conservation, Celebrity and Capitalism." *Media Culture & Society* 30, no. 4 (2008): 551–568.

Brockington, D. *Celebrity and the Environment: Fame, Wealth and Power in Conservation*. London: Zed, 2009.

Brockington, D. "Trends in Reporting on Celebrity, Charities and Development and Humanitarian NGOs in UK Newspapers." Research report 2 (2011). http://celebrityanddevelopment.files.wordpress.com/2011/09/trends-in-reporting-on-celebrity-and-charity-in-uk-newspapers-5.pdf. Accessed January 7, 2014.

Browne, H. *The Frontman: Bono (In the Name of Power)*. London: Verso, 2013.

Cameron, J., and A. Haanstra. "Development Made Sexy: How it Happened and What it Means." *Third World Quarterly* 29, no. 8 (2008): 1475–1489.

Chouliaraki, L. "The Theatricality of Humanitarianism: A Critique of Celebrity Advocacy." *Communication and Critical/Cultural Studies* 9, no. 1 (2012): 1–21.

Cooper, A. F. "Celebrity Diplomacy and the G8: Bono and Bob as Legitimate International Actors." Working Paper 26. Waterloo: Centre for International Governance Innovation, University of Waterloo, 2007.

Cooper, A. F. "Beyond One Image Fits All: Bono and the Complexity of Celebrity Diplomacy." *Global Governance* 14 (2008): 265–272.

Cooper, A. F. *Celebrity Diplomacy*. Boulder, CO: Paradigm, 2008.

Crilly, R. *Saving Darfur: Everyone's Favourite African War*. London: Reportage Press, 2010.

Darnton, A., and M. Kirk. *Finding Frames: New Ways to Engage the UK Public in Global Poverty*. London: Bond, 2011.

Davis, H. L. "Feeding the World a Line? Celebrity Activism and Ethical Consumer Practices from Live Aid to Product Red." *Nordic Journal of English Studies* 9, no. 3 (2010): 89–118.

De Waal, A. "The Humanitarian Carnival: A Celebrity Vogue." World Affairs Fall (2008). http://www.worldaffairsjournal.org/articles/2008-Fall/full-DeWaal.html.

Dieter, H., and R. Kumar. "The Downside of Celebrity Diplomacy: The Neglected Complexity of Development." *Global Governance* 14 (2008): 259–264.

Dyer, R. *Heavenly Bodies: Film Stars and Society*. Basingstoke: Macmillan, 1987.

Epstein, J. "Celebrity Culture." *Hedgehog Review* 7, no. 1 (2005): 7–20.

Fall, P.L., and G. Tang. *Goodwill Ambassadors in the United Nations System*. Geneva: Joint Inspection Unit, 2006. https://www.unjiu.org/en/reports-notes/archive/JIU_NOTE_2006_1_English.pdf.

Ferris, K. O. "The Sociology of Celebrity." *Sociology Compass* 1, no. 1 (2007): 371–384.

Flint, J., and A. De Waal. *Darfur: A New History of a Long War*. London: Zed Books, 2008.

Foreman, J. "How Hollywood Finds its Charitable Causes." *The Sunday Times*, October 4, 2009.

Gamson, J. *Claims to Fame: Celebrity in Contemporary America*. Berkeley: University of California Press, 1994.

Garofalo, R. "Understanding Mega-Events: If We are the World, then How do We Change It?" In *Rockin' the Boat: Mass Music and Mass Movements*, edited by R. Garofalo, 15–35. Boston, MA: South End Press, 1992.

Goodman, M. K. "The Mirror of Consumption: Celebritization, Developmental Consumption and the Shifting Cultural Politics of Fair Trade." *Geoforum* 41, no. 1 (2010): 104–116.

Gundle, S. *Glamour: A History*. Oxford: Oxford University Press, 2008.

Hawkins, R. "A New Frontier in Development? The Use of Cause-related Marketing by International Development Organisations." *Third World Quarterly* 33, no. 10 (2012): 1783–1801.

Hawkins, R. "Shopping to Save Lives: Gender and Environment Theories meet Ethical Consumption." *Geoforum* 43 (2012): 750–759.

Horkheimer, M., and T. Adorno. *Dialectic of Enlightenment*. New York: Herder and Herder, 1972.

Hutchins, B., and Lester, L.. "Environmental Protest and Tap-dancing with the Media in the Information Age." *Media, Culture & Society* 28, no. 3 (2006): 433–451.

Inglis, F. *A Short History of Celebrity*. Princeton, NJ: Princeton University Press, 2010.

Kapoor, I. *Celebrity Humanitarianism: The Ideology of Global Charity*. London: Routledge, 2012.

Lewis, D., D. Rodgers, and M. Woolcock. "The Fiction of Development: Literary Representation as a Source of Authoritative Knowledge." *Journal of Development Studies* 44, no. 2 (2008): 198–216.

Littler, J. "I Feel Your Pain': Cosmopolitan Charity and the Public Fashioning of the Celebrity Soul." *Social Semiotics* 18, no. 2 (2008): 237–251.

Lynskey, D. *33 Revolutions per Minute: A History of Protest Songs*. London: Faber and Faber, 2010.

Marshall, D. P. *Celebrity and Power: Fame in Contemporary Culture*. Minneapolis: University of Minnesota Press, 1997.

Meyer, D. S., and J. Gamson. "The Challenge of Cultural Elites: Celebrities and Social Movements." *Sociological Inquiry* 65, no. 2 (1995): 181–206.

Richey, L. A., and S. Ponte. *Brand Aid: Shopping Well to Save the World*. Minneapolis: University of Minnesota Press, 2011.

Rojek, C. *Celebrity*. London: Reaktion Books, 2001.

Sireau, N. *Make Poverty History: Political Communication in Action*. London: Palgrave Macmillan, 2008.

Socher, A. "The History of Nonsense." *Assocation for Jewish Studies* Fall (2006): 32–33.

Street, J. *Rebel Rock: The Politics of Popular Music*. Oxford: Basil Blackwell, 1986.

Street, J. "Celebrity Politicians: Popular Culture and Political Representation." *British Journal of Politics and International Relations* 6 (2004): 435–452.

Sumner, A. "Where do the Poor Live." *World Development* 40, no. 5 (2012): 865–877.

Tester, K. *Humanitarianism and Modern Culture*. University Park, PA: Pennsylvania State University Press, 2010.
Turner, G. *Understanding Celebrity*. London: Sage, 2004.
Turner, G. "Approaching Celebrity Studies." *Celebrity Studies* 1, no. 1 (2010): 11–20.
Turner, G., F Bonner, and D. P. Marshall. *Fame Games: The Production of Celebrity in Australia*. Cambridge: Cambridge University Press, 2000.
van der Gaag, N., and C. Nash. *Images of Africa*. Rome: fao, 1987.
West, D. M. "Angelina, Mia and Bono: Celebrties and International Development." In *Global Development 2.0. Can Philanthropists, the Public and the Poor Make Poverty History?*, edited by L. Brainard and D. Chollet, 74–84. Washington, DC: Brookings Institution Press, 2008.
Wheeler, M. "Celebrity diplomacy: United Nations' Goodwil Ambassadors and Messengers of Peace." *Celebrity Studies*. 2, no. 1 (2011): 6–18.
Wolfe, T. *Radical Chic and Mau-Mauing the Flak Catchers*. New York: Farrar, Straus & Giroux, 1970.
Yrjölä, R. "The Invisible Violence of Celebrity Humanitarianism: Soft Images and Hard Words in the Making and Unmaking of Africa." *World Political Science Review* 5, no. 1 (2009).
Yrjölä, R. "From Street into the World: Towards a Politicised Reading of Celebrity Humanitarianism." *British Journal of Politics and International Relations* 14, no. 3 (2011): 357–374.

The philanthropic state: market–state hybrids in the philanthrocapitalist turn

Linsey McGoey

Department of Sociology, University of Essex, Colchester, UK

Over the past decade a new form of philanthropy has emerged, termed 'philanthrocapitalism'. Champions of philanthrocapitalism suggest that private giving can fill the void left by diminished government spending on social and development programmes. Critics suggest that philanthropy is no substitute for strong governmental support for social welfare. Both arguments perpetuate a dichotomy between the public and the private, implying that philanthrocapitalism operates in a vacuum largely divorced from governmental interventions. In this article I challenge that assumption, exploring how new philanthropic initiatives have compelled increased financial support from governments toward the private sector. Drawing on three cases – advanced market commitments (AMCs) in drug development; impact investing; and direct philanthropic and governmental grants to corporate entities – I illustrate the ways that governments remain one of the most powerful – if not the most powerful – philanthropic actors in the philanthrocapitalist turn.

Introduction

While he was building Microsoft into one of the most profitable businesses in history, Bill Gates had little time for charity. In 1997 Microsoft staff grappled with the worry that the internet might derail Windows's market strength. At one stage Gates was presented with a proposal by employees to write for the web rather than simply for Windows. Gates was incensed, shouting, 'Why don't you just give up your options and join the Peace Corps?'[1]

In 2008 Gates decamped to the world of philanthropy, leaving his day-to-day role at Microsoft to run the Bill and Melinda Gates Foundation full-time. The Gates Foundation is currently the largest transparently operated philanthropic foundation in the world, spending more annually on global health than the

World Health Organization (WHO), and reshaping governmental priorities in the area of domestic US education, global agriculture and global health. Today there is no area of global development that is not affected by Gates Foundation policies, whether through direct grants, or through the indirect impact of efforts by foundation staff to rally governments and non-governmental actors to fund causes which the foundation aims to prioritise. Has Gates been converted to the voluntary ethos underpinning institutions such as the Peace Corps? The short answer is obviously yes. Gates has devoted an astonishing amount of money and time to charitable activities in a transformation that *Forbes* recently dubbed 'the most productive midlife crisis in history'.[2]

The longer answer is more complex. Gates has not so much departed from Microsoft as embraced the chance to make his foundation run more like Microsoft, applying management techniques refined at the latter to foundation operations. By modelling philanthropic activities on Microsoft, Gates is at the forefront of a new movement dubbed 'philanthrocapitalism', the effort to transform philanthropy into a more efficient and lucrative industry in itself (see Blowfield and Dolan in this issue). A number of trends underpins the new philanthropy: an emphasis on strategic investing to realise measurable objectives; the increased visibility of individual philanthropists as policy drivers; and the growing effort to enrol private sector actors in development and welfare programmes.[3]

In exploring the rise of philanthrocapitalism, this paper has three main aims. First, drawing parallels between new organisations such as the Gates Foundation and earlier foundations such as Rockefeller and Ford, I suggest that philanthrocapitalism is simultaneously far less novel and more novel than proponents suggest. Second, I suggest that a neglected actor within discussions of philanthrocapitalism is the state itself. Just as legislative change and governmental subsidies were crucial to the 19th- and 20th-century development of global economic markets, state support is vital to the rise of 'new' philanthropic movements. Governments are, somewhat ironically, instrumental to the success of philanthropic movements strengthened by proclaiming the ineptitude and waning influence of government policies. Third, I suggest that recent work in economics on what Lazonick and Mazzucato call the 'risk–reward nexus' can help development scholars better theorise the relationship between private and state actors in development projects.

The article draws on three case studies. The first is of the growth of direct governmental grants to financially robust companies such as Vodafone, both through direct grants and through tax waivers to philanthropic entities offering grants to corporations. The second is of increased governmental support for a trend termed 'impact investing'. The third is of the role of governments in financing the first advanced market commitment (AMC), a mechanism to encourage the development of drugs and vaccines for underfunded diseases. The paper concludes with a brief discussion of the paradoxes at root in the image of the lone philanthrocapitalist 'entrepreneur' reshaping development policies.

Methodologically the article draws on 50 semi-structured interviews carried out between 2009 and 2013 with policy experts in global health and global philanthropy at institutions such as the WHO, the Global Alliance for Vaccines and Immunization (GAVI) and Médecins Sans Frontières (MSF).

The new empire of giving

The term 'philanthrocapitalism was coined in 2006 in an article in *The Economist*. Matthew Bishop, an editor at *The Economist*, and Michael Green, a former policy maker at the UK's Department for International Development (DFID), later developed the concept in a 2008 book, *Philanthrocapitalism: How the Rich can Save the World*.[4] Championed by entrepreneurs, who had often made fortunes in the finance and tech industries, philanthrocapitalism is driven by the desire to bring 'hard-nosed' strategy, performance metrics, innovative financing models and increased control of grantee decision making to philanthropy. The movement encompasses dozens of foundations and advisory groups advocating a new, aggressive, muscular philanthropy that aims to (1) make philanthropy more effective; and (2) make it a more lucrative industry in itself.[5]

Turning a sceptical gaze on the 'new' philanthropy movements, the historian Stanley Katz has suggested that the objective to render philanthropy more cost-effective and results-oriented has a far longer historical heritage than most proponents of philanthrocapitalism appear to realise.[6] Both John D Rockefeller and Andrew Carnegie aimed, as Nicolas Guilhot writes, 'to apply the rational methods of business to the administration of charitable deeds, which they considered to be outdated and deficient'. These early philanthropists explicitly claimed to separate their practices from acts of alms giving prevalent within Christian religious orders, which viewed charity as valuable in itself, regardless of whether a donation produced any observable benefits.[7]

William Schambra, director of the Washington, DC-based Hudson Institute's Bradley Center for Philanthropy and Civic Renewal, emphasised this heritage to me in an interview in January 2012. He stated: 'The notion that we should organise our philanthropies the way we organise our corporations – that was John D Rockefeller's original idea…[Philanthrocapitalism] is just more of that.'[8]

What *is* new about the new philanthropy is the unprecedented scale of philanthropic spending. As outlets such as *Forbes* have reported each year since the onset of the recent financial crisis, the net worth of the world's richest individuals is growing larger even as economies are shrinking. Wealth concentration has reached unprecedented levels. Worldwide the number of billionaires more than tripled from 2000 to 2010, growing to 1011 from 306. Nearly half of the 75,000 private foundations in the USA alone were created in the past 10 years. Some 5000 more philanthropic foundations are set up each year.[9]

The state–corporate nexus

The explosion of new philanthropic trusts comes at a time when governments are facing public demand to reduce overseas development assistance, something that already comprises a miniscule portion of most states' gross national income (GNI). At the UN General Assembly in 1970 donor governments pledged to spend 0.7% of GNI on official development assistance. This pledge has been renewed at international forums since. Despite such commitments, the majority of rich nations have regularly failed to meet the 0.7% target. In some years aid falls to between 0.2% and 0.4% of GNI – a shortfall amounting to hundreds of billions.[10]

The fact that private philanthropic giving is *increasing* at the same time that, proportionately, the amount spent by Western governments as a ratio of their GNI is *decreasing*, has led to the growing public perception that private actors are taking a strong, even a leading role in development financing. This is not, in fact, the case. Take the example of the Gates Foundation and global health. When it comes to financial investment the Gates Foundation outpaces any other private philanthropic foundation in the world, donating over $15.3 billion to global health programmes to date.[11]

While that figure is significant, it is not nearly as much as rich nations spend collectively on global health initiatives each year. From 2004 to 2008, for example, the President's Emergency Plan for AIDS Relief (PEPFAR), spent over $18.1 billion on global HIV/AIDS programmes – more than the Gates Foundation's total spending on global health since its inception. In recent years the Gates Foundation has spent more annually on global health than individual nations such as Canada and Germany, but less than the UK and USA. In 2012 Canada contributed roughly $379 million to overseas health programmes. Its annual spending on development aid in general – including funds earmarked for health – tends to hover around the $1.5 billion mark. Germany spent $307 million on health aid in that year, while the UK contributed $1.3 billion – a rise of 2.3% over the earlier year. The Gates Foundation, in comparison, spent $899 million on global health in 2012. US spending on global health amounted to more than that of the Gates Foundation, Canada, Germany and the UK combined: its outlay in 2012 was $7 billion.[12]

Although governmental overseas development assistance exceeds the amount spent by private foundations on international development, foundations are rich in political influence. The visibility of the Gates Foundation enables it to leverage its own resources in order to rally partners to the causes it aims to prioritise. Gates has been a high-profile speaker at recent G20 meetings, while at the WHO today there are, as the eminent global health scholar Laurie Garrett writes, virtually no major policy decisions that take place without being 'casually, unofficially vetted by Gates Foundation staff'.[13]

The visibility of the Gates Foundation helps to galvanise state funders in areas which the Gates Foundation aims to prioritise, while simultaneously helping to entrench the questionable perception that states are increasingly deferring their own commitments to the philanthropic and corporate sectors. Many states are not, in fact, deflecting commitments to the private sector. They are channelling more aid directly to it.

Increasingly governments are championing market-based solutions to health and development in order to (1) remedy market failures; (2) ostensibly reduce debt burdens in the North and South; (3) increase financial liquidity in developing regions; and (4) invigorate entrepreneurship at the local and global level. Governments are extending themselves in new directions in a semblance of surrendering control to private entities which are, in many ways, *less* entrepreneurial than governments themselves.

In 2003, for example, DFID provided just under £1 million in a one-off, non-repayable donation to Vodafone to establish M-Pesa, a system allowing villagers in Kenya to pay bills through text message on their mobile phones. By 2007 Vodafone and Saraficom, a Kenyan company partly owned by Vodafone, had M-Pesa up and running. Within two years more than 20% of Kenya's population was registered for the service, and the M-Pesa scheme accounted for a significant portion of Safaricom's £150 million annual profits. By 2008 Safaricom was Kenya's (and also East Africa's) largest and most profitable company.[14] In 2007 Vodafone partnered with Citibank to extend the M-Pesa scheme worldwide. In 2010 the Gates Foundation offered a non-repayable grant of $4.8 million to Vodacom, a Vodafone subsidiary, to enable the company to roll out M-Pesa in Tanzania.[15]

As of December 2011 Vodafone, the second-largest mobile operator in the world, had a market capitalisation of £89.4 billion. In September 2010 the British-based company was criticised for tax avoidance schemes that enabled it to save some £6 billion in revenue by routing the acquisition of a German corporation through a Luxembourg subsidiary. Despite its ample resources, the company has stated that seed funding from the UK government was necessary to expanding operations in less-developed markets. Nick Hughes, the global head of international mobile payment solutions at Vodafone, stated that, without the £1 million from DFID towards the development of M-Pesa, he could not have persuaded Vodafone to invest in the venture.[16]

DFID's support for Vodafone is regularly touted as an example of the benefits of providing governmental support to finance or corporate ventures. It is pointed to by DFID officials as an example of mutual gain: Vodafone expands its market reach, while domestic users benefit from enhanced technology. Cases such as the Vodafone example are underpinning the 'market' turn in development, characterised by the recent explosion of public–private partnerships intended to combat persistent market failures in the provision of basic services or treatments.[17]

Interestingly, in most public–private partnerships, the private sector is often seen as bring market 'efficiency', as well as financial resources and know-how, to the relationship. But often, as in the case of the grant to Vodafone and in the case below of AMCs, is it governments that provide a financial subsidy or grant to industry, not the reverse. Despite the role played by governments in funding a development initiative, the ability of a private actor to capitalise on a project at the point of market access means that many casual observers are unaware that governments were involved at all. Most popular press articles on M-Pesa celebrate the entrepreneurial acumen of Vodafone and Safaricom, despite the fact that Hughes is on record attesting to the fact that his colleagues at Vodafone refused to invest in the initiative without a government grant (see above). A recent article in *Wired*, for example, hails M-Pesa as a 'non-governmental, cashless system', calling it a 'rare example of Africa successfully leapfrogging the developed world's legacy infrastructure and moving straight into a mobile system'.[18]

Governments to the Rescue

Public ignorance of DFID's direct grant to Vodafone helps to entrench a widely held fallacy: the notion that private actors are *inherently* more innovative or entrepreneurial than public ones. Recently a handful of influential economists has sought to challenge this notion, questioning the idea that the private sector is necessarily more risk-prone than state actors in creating new economic markets.

The economists Mariana Mazzucato and William Lazonick have been at the forefront of research examining the role of the public sector in driving innovation in the private sector. They suggest there is a growing disconnect between the economic actors driving innovation, including governments, and those reaping the financial rewards of public-sector investment. 'While risk-taking has become more collective – leading to much discussion about *open* innovation and *innovation* ecosystems', they write, 'the reward system has become dominated by individuals who, inserting themselves strategically between the business organization and the product market…lay claim to disproportionate share of the rewards of the innovation process'.[19]

Mazzucato points out that the algorithm that led to Google's success was funded by a US National Science Foundation grant, and that the UK's Medical Research Council financed the early discovery of molecular antibodies instrumental to the develop of biotechnology, something that attracted venture capital only after government-funded research showed signs of promise.[20] Governmental willingness to invest in the most uncertain phase of a fledgling sector's development suggests that states don't simply regulate or 'fix' markets, they actively create and shape new market opportunities. While that insight is not particularly new or enlightening to sociologists familiar with work by scholars such as Karl Polanyi or Giovanni Arrighi on the 'embedded' nature of economic markets in social networks and political policies, most literature in mainstream neoclassical economics, as Mazzucato and Lazonick point out, remains largely indifferent or blind to the role of the state in financially underwriting new innovations. As they note, while there is widespread recognition of the import of Keynes' insight on the value of state investment during economic *downturns*, the fundamental role of the state in driving innovation in economic *upswings* is often ignored. Similarly, while many economists recognise the strong role played by states in creating new markets in developing regions, very few economists 'have focused on the state as a leading actor even in the most developed regions of the world, such as Silicon Valley'.[21]

Because the state's early investments in innovation are often capitalised upon by private investors, it is difficult to measure the financial returns directly generated *through* state investment. In other words, it is hard to measure who is the *most* innovative – the state or the private sector. As Lazonick and Mazzocato write, the 'failure to recognize the State's risk-taking role, and the 'bumpy' landscape on which it invests, makes it almost impossible to measure its success'. Despite this difficulty, it is incontestable that government investment has been the genesis of many of the most successful and profitable innovations in recent decades, including the development of the internet.

One factor increasing the reliance of profitable firms on government subsidies or direct grants is the recent growth of financialisation, defined, as Milberg writes, in three key ways. First, a greater share of the net worth in industrialised companies is accounted for by the financial sector. Second, gross international capital flows have grown at a faster rate than trade in goods and services. Third, non-financial firms (eg Nike or Ford) increasingly rely on finance rather than production as a source of funds and a preferred channel for the reinvestment of surpluses.[22] As sociologists such as Greta Krippner and Robin Blackburn have shown, financialisation, chimed with the explosion of stock-based executive compensation schemes, and have weakened the corporate incentive for investing in human capital or infrastructural development through increased jobs, skills training or capital expansion. In Krippner's words, 'confronted with labour militancy at home and increased international competition from abroad, non-financial firms responded to falling returns on investment by withdrawing capital from production and diverting it to financial markets'.[23]

In line with Krippner and Blackburn Lazonick and Mazzucato emphasise that the growth of financialisation has increased a company's incentive to retreat from human capital expansion or investment in R&D, where rewards are uncertain. Their novel claim is that there is a direct link between increased financialisation and growing state support for industry. The government's own philanthropic role – its direct donations to research-intensive industries such as the pharmaceutical and telecoms sectors – is increasing alongside the growing divestment of non-financial firms from their traditional core competences. In blunt language, Lazonick and Mazzucato suggest that increased state subsidies 'permit companies to get off the hook of making these risky investments themselves even as their executives deliberately make no mention of State support. Indeed they invoke "free market" ideology to claim that, having taken all the risks, "private enterprise" needs to reap all the rewards'.[24]

The misguided tendency to see private actors as *inherently* more innovative than governments underscores a degree of rhetorical confusion within the philanthrocapitalism movement. Often, words such as 'entrepreneurial' and 'innovative' are used interchangeably to describe the purportedly novel approach of new philanthropic initiatives, with little empirical support for whether these 'new' approaches do actually represent substantive changes over earlier business models.

As Ruth McCambridge, editor of *Non-profit Quarterly*, writes in an article questioning the increased vogue for words such as innovation and entrepreneurship, in reality these things are often are very distinct, if not incompatible:

> You do not necessarily need a new idea to be an entrepreneur – you just need to figure out the packaging that will sell a product to the buyer in a way that builds an institution. The most common definition of an entrepreneur is 'one who organizes, manages, and assumes the risks of a business or enterprise'...entrepreneurs open up pizza places and spas, and build carpeting emporiums – none of which is especially innovative.[25]

Defined in this way, it becomes clear that very few of the 'new' development initiatives touted by the new philanthropists, such as microfinance, could be called either innovative or entrepreneurial. The first modern microfinance institution (MFI), the Grameen Bank, founded in 1983 by Muhammad Yunus, who later won a Nobel Peace Prize for his work, was indeed innovative – providing financial services to populations shunned by high-street lenders on a non-profit basis. But imitators since have been mostly derivative. Those that *have* innovated, such as by charging increased interest rates, have done so at the expense of Yunus' initial vision. Many MFIs today operate on a for-profit rather than non-profit basis. Some charge interest rates exceeding 100%, eliciting Yunus's censure for the explosion of MFIs that increase indebtedness rather than its reverse. An analysis of the much-hyped realm of impact investing helps to expand on this point.

The new déjà vu: impact investing as market opportunity

Part of the popular appeal of the new philanthrocapitalism is the idea that philanthropy is ceasing to be, in effect, charity. Philanthropy is upheld as an increasingly lucrative business opportunity in itself. By earning a return on investments aimed at improving services and the welfare of marginalised populations, the new philanthropists can 'do good by doing well'.

Thus far, rhetorical enthusiasm over the potential profitability of the new philanthropy exceeds reality. Although Bishop and Green assert that a marked feature of philanthrocapitalism is the realisation and embrace of the fact that philanthropy can be personally profitable, only a small segment of the field called 'impact investing' enables individuals to make a tangible financial profit from investing in projects aimed at providing goods or services to people who lack them.[26]

Impact investing is the idea that individuals can earn 'market-rate' financial returns for investing in projects geared at providing environmental and social benefit. A recent report from Monitor, a consultancy firm founded by the management scholar Michael Porter, provides a comprehensive overview of impact investing. The report states that investor excitement over impact investment has been fuelled by a 2010 study from J.P Morgan, the Rockefeller Foundation and the Global Impact Investing Network, which predicted that potential profits for investors could range from $183 billion to $667 billion, with invested capital ranging from $400 billion to $1 trillion.

Attracted by the capacity for profit, investors flocked to this space. Since then, as the Monitor report notes, investors have been dealt a 'reality check'. There are not enough financially promising companies for impact investors to invest in. Organisations abound that appear to offer *social* benefit – but whether they can offer market-based returns is questionable. The experience of the Acumen Fund, a non-profit group that funds market-based solutions to development challenges, illustrates this problem. After considering 5000 potential companies over 10 years, it invested in just 65 of them. Quoting a candid comment from Andrew Carnegie, 'pioneering don't pay', the Monitor report acknowledges that most for-profit investors are reluctant to invest in areas where the financial pay-off is uncertain. The authors conclude that, because for-profit investors are uneasy about investing in risky financial ventures, 'truly realizing the impact in impact investing will require more, not less, philanthropy'.[27]

The Monitor report draws on the case of microfinance to support its call for increased philanthropic support for impact investing. The authors note that, before microfinance became financially profitable, the microfinance sector received roughly $20 billion in subsidies from philanthropies and governmental aid. 'It is easy to forget', the report notes, 'that the microfinance business model was promising but unprofitable for many years, long before it burst into the public consciousness. In those unprofitable years, subsidies in the form of grants, soft loans and guarantees from philanthropists and aid donors' enabled the field to flourish.

The report emphasises that microfinance is now a financially robust impact investment area. While still underperforming in comparison to some market-based sectors, 'internal rates of return for debt-based microfinance investment vehicles (MIVs) averaged 4.9 percent through 2008, while riskier equity-based MIVs achieved 12.5 percent'. Two leading proponents of social entrepreneurship, Jed Emerson and Antony Bugg-Levine share this favourable view. In a recent online interview, they point out that, even during the recent economic downturn, 'impact investors in microfinance bonds received a consistent 6 percent return… not a bad financial return at all'.[28]

In other words, after billions in government subsidies, microfinance initiatives are finally starting to turn a handsome profit for investors in the North. But are they actually helping loan recipients in the South? The answer appears, so far, to be no. Neither the Monitor report nor Emerson and Bugg-Levine acknowledge that there is growing doubt over the benefits of microcredit for loan recipients. There is considerable literature on the adverse effects of microfinance, detailing the ways that both for-profit and non-profit microfinance lending often saddle loan recipients with crippling debt. There is currently no evidence that microfinance is playing any significant role in poverty reduction.[29]

The cases of impact investing and microfinance underscore an unresolved question surrounding the new philanthrocapitalism: what is the evidence that recent philanthropic initiatives are, on par, helping rather that harming the global poor? Take the example of the Gates Foundation. Its endowment has two main revenue sources: Gates's personal fortune and stock in Berkshire Hathaway, Warren Buffett's conglomerate holding company. The foundation invests 5% of its endowment in McDonalds, and 7% in Coca-Cola, companies which are seen as exacerbating health epidemics such as obesity. Coca-Cola has been linked to human rights abuses in a number of countries, leading sales of the drink to be banned on some US campuses. When shares of Berkshire Hathaway are fully transferred to the endowment as part of Buffett's 2006 donation, the Gates Foundation is poised to become the largest shareholder of Coca-Cola in the world.[30] Although Bill and Melinda Gates initially indicated a willingness to divest from companies shown to have negative health effects, the foundation later confirmed previous polices would stand. The foundation continues to invest in companies that maximise financial return regardless of the adverse health or environmental effects.

In 2013 The Gates Foundation announced a grant of $100,000 to Ogilvy PR, a public relations firms, for a project called 'Aid is working: tell the world'. Ogilvy PR is part of Ogilvy and Mather, one of the largest marketing companies in the world. That Ogilvy is a benefactor of Gates Foundation largesse raises uncomfortable questions. Corporations receive sizeable tax breaks in the USA. Is a gift from the Gates Foundation to Ogilvy, or its $4.8 million grant to Vodacom, really the best use of money which, if it had been taxed as income rather than placed in a philanthropic trust, would have benefitted government relief programmes? It is incontestable that M-Pesa has created benefits for local communities in Kenya and elsewhere. But given the financial windfall the programme has generated for Vodafone, should the company not have borne the cost of its investment? Why are taxpayers increasingly helping to subsidise the returns of for-profit companies that have healthy profit margins, as the Vodafone and Ogilvy examples indicate?

These questions are at the heart of a recent controversy over the value of AMCs, a type of financial mechanism whereby manufacturers are guaranteed a market for new products at a set price in exchange for developing treatments for diseases such as malaria and tuberculosis. Contracts such as AMCs aim to correct the disconnect between demand for treatments for diseases such as HIV/AIDS, malaria, tuberculosis and neglected tropical diseases and the willingness of manufacturers to generate and supply treatments at a price sufferers can afford. Despite governmental and industry acclaim for AMCs, critics suggest the first and sole AMCs to date – a vaccine against pneumococcal disease – has not been as cost-effective as it could have been, profiting industry at the expense of taxpayers.

Below, I explore recent debates over the first AMC. My aim is to emphasise the following point: by partnering with the private sector through a public–private partnership such as the pneumococcal vaccine, governments often surrender both the ability to generate revenue from products and the legal ability to determine the cost-effectiveness of existent or future projects. Both knowledge and income are sacrificed in the name of purported increases in efficiency.

Advanced market commitments: hype or hope?

For decades health and development scholars have called attention to an intractable problem in global health: the lack of new drugs for diseases which afflict the world's poor proportionately more than the world's rich. In 2002 Trouiller and colleagues found that, of the 1393 new chemical entities marketed between 1975 and 1999, only 16 were for tropical diseases and tuberculosis. They noted a 13-fold greater chance of a drug being developed for central nervous system disorders or for cancer than for a 'neglected disease', a broad term used to describe afflictions that have high mortality rates in developing regions, but which have long been neglected by industry because there is little financial incentive in developing products as R&D costs might not be recouped through sales.[31]

Since the early 2000s there has been a groundswell of political and public support for financing and legal initiatives intended to combat this problem by incentivising multinationals to invest in research and development for diseases which primarily afflict the poor. Such initiatives tend to fall into two interrelated and often overlapping categories: 'push' mechanisms (the provisions of early stage seed funding), and 'pull' mechanisms (regulatory or financial incentives that help to guarantee markets for available treatments). Forms of patent restructuring, which reconfigure existent intellectual property structures in order to induce innovation and reward drug and vaccine discovery, are generally seen as 'pull' factors.

Proposals include, to name a few, the establishment of an international biomedical R&D treaty; 'prize funds', which would serve as a large monetary reward in exchange for product development; the creation of patent pools to enable multiple organisations to share and profit from early stage scientific findings; and regulatory incentives, such as priority review vouchers, which expedite regulatory processing times for a company aiming to market a treatment for a neglected disease.[32]

The AMC is a pull mechanism. It is a model of vaccine and drug development first proposed in the 1990s by Michael Kremer, Gates Professor of Developing Societies at Harvard University. One of Kremer's aims was to battle the shortage of vaccines in developing regions.[33] After a burst in increasing vaccination rates in the 1970s and 1980s, vaccinations fell throughout the 1990s for basic diseases in developing countries. Often vaccines for diseases in developed countries become affordable in low-to-middle income countries only 10 or 15 years after distribution in wealthier regions.[34]

To tackle this, Kremer's initial idea was fairly simple: a donor makes a legally binding commitment to purchase a particular amount of a vaccine or drug if that product is successfully developed and made available in developing regions. The win-win is apparent: if no vaccine is produced, donor organisations are not liable to meet costs; if one is produced, manufacturers are guaranteed a financial reward. The appeal is easily apparent: usually much early research seed funding fails to yield viable products. Donors are left with few end results for vast investments. AMCs reward concrete results rather than simply signs of early promise.

In 2004 the Bill and Melinda Gates Foundation funded a working group to examine the viability of AMCs. This led to *Making Markets for Vaccines*, a 2005 report from the Centre from Global Development (CGD) spearheaded by the Centre's Ruth Levine.[35] The report spurred a flurry of political interest: in December 2005 the UK government announced its intention to fund an AMC for malaria; other EU countries stated that they might consider the same move in 2006. By June 2009 plans for the first AMC had crystallised. Working with GAVI, the governments of Italy, Norway, Canada, Russia and the UK, together with the Gates Foundation, committed a total of $1.5 billion towards the development of a vaccine against pneumococcal disease, which kills an estimated 1.6 million people each year, most of them children.

In 2010 Pfizer and GlaxoSmithKline responded to a tender to distribute the vaccines, committing to supply 30 million doses of vaccines, which each manufacturer had previously developed: Synflolix, in GSK's case, and Pfizer's Prevenar-13. Although each vaccines command a market price of about US$70 per injection in developed regions, the companies agreed to distribute them for an initial price of $7, then $3.50 for the next 10 years, with local governments committing 15 cents of the $3.50, and the rest covered by pledges from Northern governments and the Gates Foundation, via contributions to AMC.

A first roll-out of the AMC-funded pneumococcal vaccine took place in December 2010, with doses distributed in Nicaragua, Honduras and Guyana, followed by Mali and Sierra Leone.[36] In a press release for the Nicaraguan launch GAVI commended both the speed and the scale of the roll-out, noting that the vaccine reached Nicaraguan children less than a year after hitting US markets, a huge advance on the 10–15 year delay facing earlier vaccines. 'By rapidly scaling up the roll out of the pneumococcal vaccine to more than 40 countries', GAVI stated, 'the GAVI Alliance and its partners, including PAHO,

WHO and UNICEF, can avert approximately 700,000 deaths by 2015 and up to seven million deaths by 2030'.[37]

Despite fanfare greeting the Nicaraguan launch, the development of the first AMC faced persistent criticism. Health economists and health activists suggested that the vaccines might have been purchased more cheaply by regular UNICEF procurement procedures; that GAVI lacked transparency in deciding how much to reimburse manufacturers for each vaccine; and that the creative possibilities first envisioned by Kremer, such as patent flexibilities, were eclipsed from deliberations as the model became a reality.

Concerns centred on the high costs of the first AMC. Part of the challenge of the AMC model is generating a figure that would ensure that industry manufacturing costs in rolling-out the vaccine are reimbursed, while convincing donors that tax dollars have been spent effectively. In May 2008, at one of the final meetings of the CGD expert working group convened by Ruth Levine, the group recommended a payment of $10 per dose. Donor countries, led by Norway, argued that the cost was too high and had been set, as an article in the *Lancet* noted, 'by industry premises'. Norway insisted the cost should be no higher than $7.[38]

The health economist and sociologist Donald Light argued that the size of the advance purchase suggested by Levine's group was based on much-debated industry figures of how much it costs to bring a new drug to market, a sum often priced very differently by industry and by independent researchers. This difference is crucial to industry calls for stringent patent rights and freedom from price controls; claims of high R&D costs help to cement political support for high drug costs.[39] The economist Andrew Farlow has suggested that champions of AMCs promote 'advance purchase commitments in much the same way that some pharmaceutical companies promote "wonder drugs": emphasising the positives, burying the negatives, and ending up suggesting that we now have all the answers – or rather just the one answer – that we need'.[40]

GAVI eventually finalised the price at $7 per initial dose – considerably less than initial estimates. Rather than alleviate concerns, the arbitrary price drop simply compounded the controversy over AMCs because the price drop was just that: arbitrary. Nobody could say why GSK and Pfizer should receive $15 per dose, or $10 or $7, because the companies refused to release information on their own manufacturing costs. In 2008 Tido Von Schoen-Angerer, then acting as executive director of MSF's Access to Essential Medicines programme, asked for the baseline data on which the AMC was modelled. GAVI promised to release the data, but failed to follow through.[41]

During an interview in May 2010 a representative from GAVI told me that she would have liked to have been able to share more data with MSF and other organisations, but emphasised that legally GAVI was not permitted to. 'One of the biggest challenges we have is how big is this incentive…the criticism is, "you're overpaying." And you say, "no, we're not overpaying," but how can you share it when you can't share the cost information?'

NGOs such as MSF remain concerned that, in the absence of data on manufacturing costs, it is hard to gauge whether GAVI – and the governments that help to fund it – have been overpaying GSK and Pfizer for distributing the vaccines. In 2010 MSF and Oxfam International released a report questioning whether AMCs were 'an appropriate mechanism for stimulating development of new vaccines, as originally hoped'. The unanswered question of exactly *how much* the pneumococcal AMC financially profited GSK and Pfizer is particularly important, given budget reductions at UN bodies such as the WHO. In recent years the WHO has seen significant reductions in voluntary contributions from states. As Garrett reports, the current budget crisis at the WHO has seen over 12% of the agency's staff let go in the past four years.[42]

During a period of diminished contributions to the WHO, governments such as those of the UK, Italy and Canada have increased contributions to new public–private partnerships such as GAVI. In many ways the money for GAVI is to be much welcomed. Increased childhood vaccinations are considerable health improvement of the past decade. But an outstanding question is whether payments to industry could have been lower, ensuring that government grants to the private sector are spent in a cost-effective way. The more fundamental question is whether state development aid should be subsidising the pharmaceutical industry, currently one of the most profitable industries in the world, at all.

Public health scholars Anne-Emanuelle Birn and Joel Lexchin have suggested that, as a long-term strategy, GAVI should support the development of public, parastatal companies for vaccine research and production. Cuba and Brazil are two states that have adopted such a model. Since focusing on local capacity building in the 1980s, Brazil has become self-sufficient in producing eight vaccines, including for polio and hepatitis B. Embracing a public model may avoid the detriment detailed above: the inability to access commercial production costs.[43]

Conclusion: lionising the wrong Schumpeter

As the examples above demonstrate, recent years have seen an explosion of new financing and investment initiatives such as AMCs, impact investing and microfinance that are routinely held up as evidence that for-profit industries are playing an increased role in global development. My main aim in this article has been to illuminate the ways that governmental support has been vital to ensuring the sustainability and profitability of 'market-based' health reforms. A defining feature of the new philanthrocapitalism is the idea that lone entrepreneurs have the best tools to solve persistent social problems. The new philanthrocapitalists, in Bishop and Green's words, 'see a world full of big problems that they, and perhaps *only* they, can and must put right'.[44] It is a belief repeated often in rhetoric surrounding new philanthropic movements. Jeffrey Skoll, the first president of eBay and the founder of the Skoll Foundation, a leading organisation for social entrepreneurship, has suggested that 'at the world's great foundations, universities and charitable institutions, social entrepreneurship has rapidly become the most influential idea of our time…social entrepreneurs have a vision of the future and will stop at nothing to see that future come true'.[45]

Management scholar Roger Martin and Skoll Foundation president Sally Osberg suggest that the new philanthropists and social innovators are inspired by 'Schumpeter's entrepreneurial spirit, who identifies a commercial opportunity – whether a material, product, service or business – and organizes a venture to… propagate the innovation to the point of "creative destruction," a state at which the new venture and all its related ventures effectively render existing products, service and business models obsolete'.[46]

In this paper I have sketched some preliminary challenges to the assumption that lone entrepreneurs and philanthrocapitalists represent a radical break from earlier efforts to court capital investment from traditional lenders such as governments and philanthropic foundations. Within the 'new' philanthrocapitalism movement state aid to for-profit organisations continues to be a key source of support for business ventures which, as the microfinance case illustrates, tend to benefit wealthy investors at the expense of loan recipients. In *Capitalism, Socialism, and Democracy*, Schumpeter extensively detailed the ways that corporations rely on legally favourable institutional arrangements, including patents, in order to ensure returns on investment.[47] 'Long-range investing under rapidly changing conditions…is like shooting at a target that is not only indistinct but moving – and moving jerkily at that', Schumpeter wrote. 'Hence it becomes necessary to resort to such protecting device as patents'.[48] He emphasised the importance of government aid and intellectual property protections to economic growth.

Today's philanthrocapitalists are valorising a convenient caricature of Schumpeter, neglecting his analyses of ways that, through patents, subsidies and competition legislation, governmental support is instrumental to sustaining economic prosperity. Through such selective valorisation philanthrocapitalists have helped to perpetuate a dubious belief: the idea that corporations and private entrepreneurs are subsidising gaps in development financing created by increasingly non-interventionist states. In reality, it is often governments subsidising the philanthrocapitalists.

Acknowledgements

This paper benefited from comments from Troy Cochrane, William Davies and participants at the 2012 annual British International Studies Association (BISA) conference in Edinburgh. Thanks also for helpful comments from Lisa Ann Richey and Stefano Ponte.

Notes on Contributor

Linsey McGoey is Lecturer in Sociology, University of Essex. Her articles have been published in the *British Journal of Sociology, Economy and Society*, the *Lancet*, the *Journal of Medical Ethics*, *Science as Culture*, and *History of the Human Sciences*. She recently co-edited a special issue of *BioSocieties* focused on global health governance, and a special issue of *Economy and Society*: 'Strategic Unknowns: Towards a Sociology of Ignorance'.

Notes

1. The incident is reported in Bank, *Breaking Windows*.
2. "Midlife Crisis," quoted in Perlroth and Noer, "World's Most Powerful People." On the growing influence of the Gates Foundation on policy setting, see Stuckler et al., "Global Health Philanthropy."
3. See Richey and Ponte, *Brand Aid*.
4. Bishop and Green, *Philanthrocapitalism*.
5. On the role of hedge funds in the new philanthropic movement, see Jenkins, "Who's Afraid of Philanthrocapitalism?" For a discussion of increased rhetoric surrounding market-based, 'innovative' approaches to global health, see Harman, "Innovation."

6. Katz, "What does it Mean to Say that Philanthropy is Effective?"
7. Guilhot, "Reforming the World," 451. See also Bornstein, "The Impulse of Philanthropy"; Zunz, *Philanthropy in America*; Villadsen, "The Emergence of 'Neo-philanthropy'"; Edwards, *Small Change*; and McGoey, "Philanthrocapitalism and its Critics."
8. Interview with author, January 2012.
9. Crutchfield et al., *Do More than Give*. See also Moran, *Private Foundations and Development Partnerships*.
10. Shah, "Foreign Aid for Development Assistance."
11. Youde, "The Rockefeller and Gates Foundations."
12. Institute for Health Metrics and Evaluation, *Financing Global Health 2012*. See also McCoy et al., "The Bill and Melinda Gates Foundation."
13. Garrett, "Money or Die."
14. See http://fletcher.tufts.edu/CEME/publications/~/media/Fletcher/Microsites/CEME/newpdfs/SafaricomFinal112010.ashx.
15. Koh et al., "From Blueprint to Scale," 16.
16. Whitehead, "Africa," fourth para.
17. On public–private partnerships, see Buse and Harmer, "Power to the Partners?" and Buse and Walt, Part I and Part II, "Global Public–Private Partnerships." On changing forms of reason and accountability generated through the emergence of novel state–market–NGO relationships, see Krause, *The Good Project*; and Watkins et al., "Outsourcing Social Transformation."
18. Collins, "Africa's First Bitcoin Wallet," fourth para.
19. Lazonick and Mazzucato, "The Risk–Reward Nexus," 1095. Emphasis in the original.
20. Mazzucato, "The Entrepreneurial State."
21. Lazonick and Mazzucato, "The Risk–Reward Nexus," 1099.
22. See Milberg, "Shifting Sources and Uses of Profit"; and Palley, "Financialization," 3.
23. Krippner, "The Financialization of the American Economy," 182.
24. Lazonick and Mazzucato, "The Risk–Reward Nexus," 1097.
25. McCambridge, "Social Entrepreneurship," fifth para.
26. Nicholls, "The Institutionalization of Social Investment."
27. Koh et al., "From Blueprint to Scale," 10.
28. Emerson and Bugg-Levine's comment is available in an online interview at http://www.good.is/post/social-impact-investing-it-s-not-wall-street-as-usual.
29. See Banerjee et al., *The Miracle of Microfinance?* and Sinclair, *Confessions of a Microfinance Heretic*.
30. Stuckler et al., "Global Health Philanthropy."
31. Trouiller et al., "Drug Development"; and McGoey et al., "Global Health Complex."
32. On a research and development treaty and prize funds, see Love, "Assessment of Additional Global Partnerships." On a version of prize funds diverging from Love's earlier proposal, see Hollis, "The Health Impact Fund." On patent pools, see Lexchin, "One Step Forward, One Step Sideways?" On priority vouchers, see Ridley et al., "Developing Drugs for Developing Countries."
33. Kremer and Glennerster, *Strong Medicine*.
34. Guari and Khaleghian, "Immunization in Developing Countries."
35. See Usher, 2009.
36. Scudellari, "Are Advance Market Committments for Drugs a Real Advance?"
37. See http://www.gavialliance.org/media_centre/press_releases/nicaragua_pneumococcal.php.
38. Usher, "Dispute over Pneumococcal Vaccine."
39. Light, "Making Practice Markets for Vaccines"; and Light and Warburton,"Demythologizing the High Costs of Pharmaceutical Research."
40. Farlow, "Over the Rainbow," 2011.
41. Usher, "Dispute over Pneumococcal Vaccine."
42. Garrett, "Money or Die."
43. Birn and Lexchin, "Beyond Patents."
44. Bishop and Green, Philathrocapitalism, 3. Author's emphasis..
45. Skoll, "Preface," vi.
46. Martin and Osberg, "Social Entrepreneurship," 31.
47. Brenner, "The Economics of Global Turbulence," 31. See also Palmås, "Re-assessing Schumpeterian Assumptions"; and Schumpeter, *Capitalism, Socialism and Democracy*, particularly 80–88.
48. Schumpeter, *Capitalism, Socialism and Democracy*, 88.

Bibliography

Banerjee, A., E. Duflo, R. Glennester, and C. Kinnan. *The Miracle of Microfinance? Evidence from a Randomized Evaluation*. Poverty Action Lab Working Paper. 2009. http://economics.mit.edu/files/4162.

Bank, D. *Breaking Windows: How Bill Gates Fumbled the Future of Microsoft*. New York: Free Press, 2001.

Birn, A.-E., and J. Lexchin. "Beyond Patents." *Human Vaccines* 7, no. 3 (2011): 1–2.

Bishop, M., and M. Green. *Philanthrocapitalism: How the Rich can Save the World*. London: Bloomsbury Press, 2008.
Blackburn, R. "Finance and the Fourth Dimension." *New Left Review* 39, May/June (2006): 39–70.
Bornstein, E. "The Impulse of Philanthropy." *Cultural Anthropology* 24, no. 4 (2009): 622–651.
Brenner, R. "The Economics of Global Turbulence: A Special Report on the World Economy, 1950–98." *New Left Review* 229, May/June (1998): 1–265.
Buse, K., and A. Harmer. "Power to the Partners? The Politics of Public–Private Health Partnerships." *Development* 47, no. 1 (2004): 49–56.
Buse, K., and G. Walt. "Global Public–Private Partnerships: Part I – A New Development in Health?" *Bulletin of the World Health Organization* 78, no. 4 (2000): 549–561.
Buse, K., and G. Walt. "Global Public–Private Partnerships: Part II – A New Development in Health?" *Bulletin of the World Health Organization* 78, no. 5 (2000): 699–709.
Collins, K. "Africa's First Bitcoin Wallet Launches in Kenya." *Wired*, July 9, 2013. Crutchfield, L., J. Kania, and M. Kramer. *Do More than Give: The Six Practices of Donors Who Change the World*. San Francisco: Jossey-Bass, 2011.
Edwards, M. *Small Change: Why Business won't Change the World*. New York: Demos, 2010.
Farlow, A. "Over the Rainbow: The Pot of Gold for Neglected Diseases." *Lancet* 364 (2004): 2011–2012.
Garrett, L. "Money or Die: A Watershed Moment for Global Public Health." *Foreign Affairs*, March 6, 2012.
Guilhot, N. "Reforming the World: George Soros, Global Capitalism and the Philanthropic Management of the Social Sciences." *Critical Sociology* 33 (2007): 447–477.
Guari, V., and P. Khaleghian. "Immunization in Developing Countries: Its Political and Organizational Determinants." *World Development* 30, no. 12 (2002): 2109–2132.
Harman, S. "Innovation and the Perils of Rebranded Privatisation: The Case of Neoliberal Global Health." In *Handbook of the International Political Economy of Governance*, eds. A. Payne, and N. Phillips. Cheltenham: Edward Elgar, 2014.
Hollis, A. "The Health Impact Fund: A Useful Supplement to the Patent System?" *Public Health Ethics* 1 (2008): 124–133.
Institute for Health Metrics and Evaluation (IHME). *Financing Global Health 2012: The End of the Golden Era?* Seattle, WA: IHME, 2012.
Jenkins, G. "Who's Afraid of Philanthrocapitalism?" *Case Western Reserve Law Review* 61, no. 3 (2011): 753–821.
Katz, S. "What does it Mean to Say that Philanthropy is 'Effective?' The Philanthropists' New Clothes." *Proceedings of the American Philosophical Society* 149, no. 2 (2005): 123–131.
Koh, H., A. Karamchandani, and R. Katz, *From Blueprint to Scale: The Case for Philanthropy in Impact Investing*. Monitor Group, April 2012. http://www.mim.monitor.com/blueprinttoscale.html.
Krause, M. *The Good Project: Humanitarian Relief NGOs and the Fragmentation of Reason*. Chicago, IL: University of Chicago Press, 2014.
Kremer, M., and R. Glennerster. *Strong Medicine: Creating Incentives for Pharmaceutical Research on Neglected Diseases*. Princeton, NJ: Princeton University Press, 2004.
Krippner, G. "The Financialization of the American Economy." *Socio-Economic Review* 3 (2005): 173–208.
Lazonick, W., and M. Mazzucato. "The Risk–Reward Nexus in the Innovation–Inequality Relationship: Who Takes the Risks? Who Gets the Rewards?" *Industrial and Corporate Change* 22, no. 4 (2013): 1093–1128.
Lexchin, J. "One Step Forward, One Step Sideways? Expanding Research Capacity of Neglected Diseases." *BMC International Health and Human Rights* 10 (2010). doi:10.1186/1472-698X-10-20.
Light, D. "Making Practice Markets for Vaccines." *PLOS [Public Library of Science] Medicine*. 10 (2005): 0934–0938.
Light, D., and R. Warburton. "Demythologizing the High Costs of Pharmaceutical Research." *Biosocieties* 6 (2011): 34–50.
Love, J. "Assessment of Additional Global Partnerships in the Areas of Access to Essential Medicines, Debt Relief and Transfer of Technology," Presentation on the Global Fund and TDR. Report to the Human Rights Council. United Nations, Geneva, April 1–9, 2009.
Martin, R., and S. Osberg. "Social Entrepreneurship: The Case for Definition." *Stanford Social Innovation Review Spring* (2007): 27–39.
Mazzucato, M. The Entrepreneurial State: Debunking Public vs Private Sector Myths. London: Anthem Press, 2013.
McCambridge, R. "Social Entrepreneurship and Social Innovation: Are They Potentially in Conflict?" *Non-profit Quarterly* 25 December 2011.
McCoy, D., G. Kembhavi, J. Patel, and A. Luintel. "The Bill and Melinda Gates Foundation's Grant-making Programme for Global Health." *Lancet* 373 (2009): 1645–1653.
McGoey, L., J. Reiss, and A. Wahlberg. "The Global Health Complex." *Biosocieties* 6, no. 1 (2011): 1–9.
McGoey, L. "Philanthrocapitalism and its Critics." *Poetics* 40, no. 2 (2012): 185–199.
Milberg, W. "Shifting Sources and Uses of Profits: Sustaining US Financialization with Global Value Chains." *Economy and Society* 37, no. 3 (2008): 420–451.

Moran, M. *Private Foundations and Development Partnerships: American Philanthropy and Global Development Agendas*. London: Routledge, 2013.
Nicholls, A. "The Institutionalization of Social Investment: The Interplay of Investment Logics and Investor Rationalities." *Journal of Social Entrepreneurship* 1, no. 1 (2010): 70–100.
Palmås, K. "Re-assessing Schumpeterian Assumptions Regarding Entrepreneurship and the Social." *Social Enterprise Journal* 8, no. 2 (2012): 141–155.
Palley, T. Financialization: What it is and Why it Matters." Working Paper 525. Levy Economics Institute, 2007. http://www.levyinstitute.org/pubs/wp_525.pdf
Perlroth, N., and M. Noer, eds. "World's Most Powerful People." *Forbes* November 2, 2011.
Richey, L., and S. Ponte. *Brand Aid: Shopping Well to Save the World*. Minneapolis: University of Minnesota Press, 2011.
Ridley, D., H. Grabowski, and J. Moe "Developing Drugs for Developing Countries." *Health Affairs* 25 (2006): 313–324.
Schumpeter, J. *Capitalism, Socialism and Democracy*. 1962. Reprint, New York: Harper & Row, 1975.
Scudellari, M. "Are Advance Market Committments for Drugs a Real Advance?" *Nature Medicine* 17 (2011): 139.
Shah, A. "Foreign Aid for Development Assistance." Globalissues.org. Accessed April 8, 2012. http://www.globalissues.org/print/article/35.
Sinclair, H. *Confessions of a Microfinance Heretic: How Microlending Lost Its Way and Betrayed the Poor*. San Francisco: Berrett-Koehler Publishers, 2012.
Skoll, J. "Preface." In Nicholls, A., ed. *Social Entrepreneurship: New Models of Sustainable Social Change*. Oxford: Oxford University Press, 2006.
Stuckler, D., S. Basu, and M. McKee. "Global Health Philanthropy and Institutional Relationships: How Should Conflicts of Interest be Addressed?" *PLOS Medicine* 8 (2011): c1001020.
Trouiller, P., P. Olliaro, E. Torreele, J. Orbinski, R. Laing, and N. Ford. "Drug Development for Neglected Diseases: A Deficient Market and Public-health Policy Failure." *Lancet* 359 (2002): 2188–2194.
Usher, A. D. "Dispute over Pneumococcal Vaccine Initiative." *Lancet* 374 (2009): 1879–1880.
Villadsen, K. "The Emergence of 'Neo-philanthropy': A New Discursive Space in Welfare Policy?" *Acta Sociologica* 50 (2007): 309–323.
Watkins, S., A. Swidler, and T. Hannan. "Outsourcing Social Transformation: Development NGOs as Organizations." *Annual Review of Sociology* 38 (2012): 285–315.
Whitehead, E. "Africa: Aiding Business." *All Africa*, January 5, 2012.
Youde, J. "The Rockefeller and Gates Foundations in Global Health Governance." *Global Society* 27, no. 2 (2013): 139–158.
Zunz, O. *Philanthropy in America: A History*. Princeton, NJ: Princeton University Press, 2011.

The politics of industrial policy: ruling elites and their alliances

Lindsay Whitfield[a] and Lars Buur[b]

[a]*Department of Society and Globalization, Roskilde University, Denmark;* [b]*Danish Institute for International Studies, Copenhagen and Department of Society and Globalization, Roskilde University, Denmark*

Economic transformation is driven by successfully implemented industrial policy, but industrial policy is inherently political. We cannot understand why some governments pursue and implement industrial policy better than others without understanding its politics. This article addresses the conditions under which industrial policies are successfully implemented. It presents an analytical approach to understanding why some ruling elite-capitalist alliances lead to better economic outcomes than others. Sub-Saharan African countries present a particular puzzle, given their low productive capabilities and the relatively small number of successful productive sectors. The article examines the most successful productive sectors in Mozambique and in Ghana in order to illuminate the conditions under which such alliances occur and their specific characteristics and outcomes.

Introduction

Economic development is fundamentally a process of structural transformation. It involves the reallocation of assets and resources from unproductive, subsistence and low-productivity economic activities into high productivity economic activities in agriculture, manufacturing and services. It involves diversifying into new areas of production, strengthening economic linkages and increasing domestic technological capabilities.[1]

Such transformation does not emerge spontaneously from the interplay of market forces, but rather requires concerted state interventions that not only ensure macroeconomic stability and provide infrastructure and utilities but also include selective industrial policies. We use the term 'industrial policy' to refer to any government initiative that tries to stimulate specific economic activities in productive sectors. The issue of industrial policy has caused heated debates over the past decades, but the importance of industrial policy in stimulating economic transformation is increasingly recognised.[2]

At the heart of industrial policy are issues of resource allocation, institutional change and the enforcement of new rules in institutions governing land, labour and capital as well as learning rents.[3] Industrial policy necessarily requires changing the distribution of economic benefits and prioritising among economic activities, which are often contested. Governments not only have to create the institutions required for implementation, but also have to be willing and able to enforce implementation of socially contested decisions.

This article presents an analytical framework for understanding the conditions under which governments pursue and successfully implement industrial policy. We then use this framework to examine success in productive sectors in two African countries by looking at how alliances between ruling elites, industry actors and state bureaucrats work out (or not), under what conditions, and leading to what kind of development outcomes. Mozambique and Ghana were selected because they are part of a research project examining industrial policies in four African countries.[4] Literature on the politics of industrial policy is based on empirical evidence that has not typically included African cases or sought to explain African experiences, and this project sought to rectify that. The cases presented here are of the most successful sectors in Ghana and Mozambique. The case material comes from interviews with relevant industry actors, state bureaucrats and ruling elites, combined with official government reports, donor and consultancy reports, and published and unpublished secondary sources.

The politics of industrial policy

A significant body of literature has debated the conditions under which industrial policies are successfully implemented, largely with reference to East Asian countries. Three general approaches can be discerned.[5] The developmental state approach argued that success owed to a group of technocratic elites in the bureaucracy who devised and implemented visionary long-term industrial policy under conditions where they were isolated from distributional pressures within society and from political interference from political elites. However, this body of literature did not satisfactorily answer the question 'what motivated the state?'. Critics argued that the empirical studies had 'thin politics' and downplayed the agency of business.

These criticisms led to two further approaches. The second can be called the business–state relations approach. This argues that business has played an important role in driving state actions and policy design. This literature branches in several directions but a large part of it focuses on explaining why some business–state relations are more developmental than others. It focuses on determining the factors that shape whether collaborative or collusive business–state relations emerge, where 'collusive' is often used synonymously with 'rent-seeking'. The empirical work tends to focus on formal institutionalised relations through business associations, at the national and sector level.

The third approach, which we call the political survival of ruling elites approach, emphasises that government's policy choices and its ability to implement them, as well as its interactions with businesses, are shaped by incentives arising from the imperatives of ruling elites to remain in power and thus build and maintain political support. It argues that the state is never completely insulated, and no set of ruling elites is completely autonomous. Rather, what matters is how coalitional pressures shape the political costs of certain policies and the ability to implement them, given the resistance or support from factions and individuals within the ruling coalition and those financing it. This literature focuses on explaining why some forms of rent-seeking support productivity improvements and learning, while others do not.

We find the political survival of ruling elites approach the most convincing. However, there have been few attempts to move beyond specific country experiences and create a general framework explaining the conditions for industrial policies to be successfully implemented, and the politics that make those conditions possible. We do this by synthesising the existing literature and incorporating insights from new empirical research on African countries. Here we present a short version of our politics of industrial policy framework.[6]

Successful industrial policy requires that (a faction of) ruling elites have incentives, through mutual interests, to address the key productivity-constraining problems in particular industries. Furthermore, the faction of ruling elites driving the industrial policy must be able to fend off distributional demands from other individuals and factions within the ruling coalition, as well as to overcome resistance from societal groups to changes in institutions and rules which govern economic benefits. This situation gives state bureaucrats the political support to implement the policy, but state bureaucrats must be trusted by the ruling elites, have technical expertise of the industry, and have close relations with the relevant capitalists in order to understand their specific needs. Relations with the relevant capitalists cannot be too close, as state bureaucrats must be able to ensure learning among capitalists in return for policy-created rents. We refer to these conditions as mutual interests, pockets of efficiency and learning for productivity. Whether or not these conditions emerge depends on a country's specific political settlement and how it shapes the interests and alliances of actors with regard to the particular productive sector.[7] The conditions necessary for successfully implementing industrial policy are graphically illustrated in Figure 1.

The key factor that makes industrial policy successful is whether it addresses the concerns of capitalists about their ability to profit in the future from investment decisions.[8] This is true regardless of whether the objective is to promote investment from domestic or foreign private firms, state-owned firms, public–private joint ventures, or party-owned firms. Capitalists may not pursue new economic activities, because the risk of not becoming competitive and thus losing the investment is high.[9] The uncertainty of the return on investment must be low enough for capitalists to risk investing; but of course the threshold varies by the individual capitalist firm or farm, depending on its technological capabilities. Political support can reduce uncertainty, and state support can be provided in many ways. This kind of predictability and credible commitment can occur even when the overall business environment is poor. What it does require is that ruling elites and capitalists have mutual interests: ruling elites must need the relevant capitalists, and vice versa.[10] For example, capitalists typically need the government to provide physical infrastructure and access to low-cost capital, to subsidize the costs of training labour and of research and development, to help them obtain access to scarce land or natural resources, and to negotiate preferential trade agreements.[11]

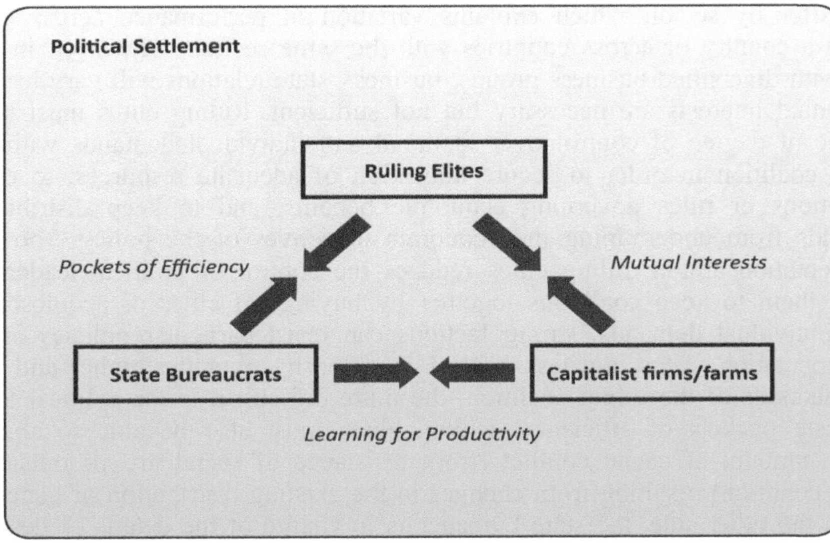

Figure 1. The politics of industrial policy.

Whether (a faction of) ruling elites have mutual interests with a particular group of capitalists depends on whether they need those capitalists for their primary objective of political survival through building and maintaining their ruling coalition in order to remain in power.[12] In democratic political systems that includes winning elections. With or without elections building and maintaining ruling coalitions always require financing. In short, political survival means accommodating powerful groups, which can include financiers of political parties; firms or families who dominate key sectors in the economy; political elite factions with strength derived from their organisational capabilities; and lower levels whose support is needed to mobilise votes.

Ruling elites generally pursue the easiest avenues for generating resources.[13] If alternatives to developing new productive sectors or upgrading old ones are available, ruling elites will use them. Such alternatives include extractive natural resources, official foreign aid and agricultural primary commodity exports. Agricultural exports in sectors that have existed for a long time are often important sources of foreign exchange and dominant pillars of the economy in many sub-Saharan African countries. It is also easier for ruling elites to continue relying on the export of such raw materials than to turn them into higher value exports or to become competitive in non-traditional exports. Thus, firms and economic sectors providing major sources of state revenues and foreign exchange are given attention by ruling elites when formulating economic policy.

We argue that the size and type of financing that ruling elites have access to, combined with the characteristics of domestic capitalists, determine whether ruling elites have an interest in working with domestic capitalists. Where there are mutual interests with a faction of domestic capitalists, the policy direction depends to a significant degree on the type of economic activity in which those capitalists are engaged. Political relations between ruling elites and businesses can differ by sector, which explains variation in performance across sectors within a country or across countries with the same sector.[14] However, in countries with diversified business groups, business–state relations will vary less.[15]

Mutual interests are necessary but not sufficient. Ruling elites must have a significant degree of control over factional and individual demands within the ruling coalition in order to secure allocation of adequate resources, to change institutions or rules governing economic benefits, and to keep distributional demands from undermining the economic objectives of the policy. Too much fragmentation among ruling elites reduces the control of political leaders.[16] It forces them to keep coalitions together by buying off elites or acquiescing to their individual demands; strong factions can resist particular policies or their implementation. Thus, the less control or authority over the higher and lower level factions of the ruling coalition, the more difficult it is for political leaders to create pockets of efficiency. Ruling elites must also be able to absorb a certain amount of social conflict (from resistance of social groups outside the ruling coalition) resulting from changes in the existing distribution of benefits.

On the other side, the state bureaucrats in charge of the details of designing and implementing the industrial policy must be trusted by the ruling elites but also knowledgeable of the targeted industry. State bureaucrats must have technical knowledge of the industry as well as practical knowledge of the actually existing industry in the country – the constraints facing individual firms, segments of the industry and the industry as a whole.[17] And they need to be able to mediate between the political and economic objectives of ruling elites in ways that create industrial policies that promote increasing productivity and learning within the industry. A pocket of efficiency emerges when the faction of ruling elites driving the industrial policy can fend off demands from within the ruling coalition and overcome resistance from societal groups, giving state bureaucrats with the relevant technical expertise and knowledge of the industry's needs the political support to implement the policy. It is this situation that lends the impression of strong 'state capabilities'.[18]

Lastly, state bureaucrats must be able to enforce the new rules or conditions attached to rents for the relevant capitalists, which requires that capitalists are not able to use political connections and influence to undermine enforcement. When these conditions emerge, learning for productivity takes place. Capitalists pursue profits above all else, so rents have to have the conditions for increasing productivity and upgrading. State bureaucrats must be embedded in order for them to know the productivity constraints facing individual firms and the industry as a whole, and then be able to translate those needs into effective industrial policy by mediating the political objectives of ruling elites and the economic needs of the industry.

This is the ideal situation. In reality the degree of alliances varies and leads to variations in outcomes, as the cases of sugar in Mozambique and cocoa in Ghana illustrate. In the conclusion, we draw out the key differences explaining variation in performance between the two sectors.

Rehabilitation of the sugar industry in Mozambique[19]

At Mozambique's independence in 1975 six sugar estates and industrial plants were in operation. Sugar production was the third largest export sector, and the sugar sector had the largest private firm in the whole of Mozambique. Before independence sugar production had begun to decline because of the rapidly intensifying independence war, the flight of capital and skilled labour of all types, and falling global market prices. After independence production fell further as the destabilisation war with South Africa turned into a civil war during the 1980s. From the mid-1990s onwards the government decided to revive the sugar sector and implemented a strategy that targeted four out of the six sugar estates.

With implementation of the rehabilitation strategy the area under cultivation rose from 7266 hectares in 1998 to 42,703 hectares in 2011. Sugar production increased to 389,425 tons in 2011, of which 198,181 tons were exported. Around 32,000 full time jobs were created. The industry also led to the creation of independent producers and to jobs in outsourced service functions in land preparation, planting, maintenance and transport, as well as to other jobs along the value chain. The sugar industry is once again the largest formal non-state employer.

This outcome is astonishing in a country that has seen relatively little economic transformation, and where the government is seen as corrupt and simultaneously characterised by too much state intervention and a lack of state capacity. We explain the government's success in implementing the sugar rehabilitation strategy as resulting from the sustained political support from a faction of Frelimo ruling elites who had mutual interests with a group of foreign sugar companies; from the ability of that faction of ruling elites to overcome resistance to implementation inside and outside the ruling coalition; and from the ability of the state agency implementing the strategy to enforce the rules structuring the sugar companies' access to rents.

Drivers of ruling elite support

The Frelimo ruling coalition provided sustained political support for rehabilitating the sugar industry over 15 years, which was important, as rehabilitating an industry cannot be done quickly. One of the most striking features of the organisation of power in Mozambique is that the same party, and more or less the same group of top Frelimo Party leaders, has been in charge since independence. Despite being a dominant party, Frelimo was (and still is) significantly fragmented, and tensions between different factions within the Frelimo ruling elite are important. The sugar strategy was successfully implemented because it was driven by a faction among the ruling elite that remained in power and was able to overcome conflicting interests within the party.

The sugar rehabilitation strategy was led by a faction of ruling elites around President Joaquim Chissano, whose presidency lasted from 1986 to 2004 (thus including the introduction of multiparty democracy in 1994), with key government people staying during the first years of Emilio Amado Guebuza's administration until 2008. This faction of ruling elites pursued industrial policies to develop several productive sectors after the General Peace Agreement was signed in 1992 as a result of severe pressures, which included a completely decimated economy, a bankrupt government budget and threats to its control over the country's territory and population. They could not stay in power through a purely redistributive strategy, but rather had to revitalise productive sectors that in turn could provide jobs, rural infrastructure and services, and revenue for the state.

At independence Frelimo's control over the population and territory was rather fragile. The move from destabilisation war to civil war with Renamo turned increasingly into contests, in which both parties tried to conquer as much territory and rein in as much of the population as possible before the peace accord in 1992. In negotiations leading up to the transition to multiparty democracy, the Frelimo administration secured a form of 'winner takes all' political system where the president had the power to appoint province governors, district administrators, and so on. Frelimo won the presidency in the first national elections in 1994 but lost in a majority of provinces, yet it was able to exclude the opposition party Renamo from taking up political positions. However, Frelimo needed to do something to increase its political support in rural areas, particularly in Renamo strongholds.

The sugar sector was identified based on its superior track record as an export commodity, as well as its capacity to industrialise and 'urbanise' the rural areas. Furthermore, the rehabilitated sugar estates were situated in areas that were either controlled or strongly influenced by Renamo, or where Frelimo needed to realign itself to key constituencies. In some of these areas Frelimo lost the 1994, 1999 and 2004 elections. The sugar industry allowed the Frelimo government to create job opportunities, support the extension of services and rebuild destroyed infrastructure and communication networks, which provided income for demobilised soldiers and forged new relationships with formerly 'hostile' populations. It also created employment opportunities for lower-level factions of the Frelimo Party. Whereas the majority of sugar estates did not become profitable until after 2008, there were immediate benefits in the surrounding rural areas. By 2008 and 2009 Frelimo had won both local and national elections in former Renamo areas.

The interests of the Chissano faction of ruling elites driving the sugar strategy were well aligned with the interests of the investing companies. The Mauritian and South African sugar companies were looking to access new markets and faced constraints on expanding production at home because of land constraints. The companies needed the Frelimo government to access finance for them (through concessional loans at various multilateral and commercial credit facilities), to create a protected domestic market, to negotiate preferential access to export markets, and to provide stability and assistance in overcoming obstacles that emerged during the rehabilitation process. From the perspective of the Chissano faction, the foreign companies brought in expertise, and their involvement ensured that Renamo elites did not benefit or have opportunities to accumulate.

Emergence of a pocket of efficiency

The Chissano faction was able to overcome resistance within the ruling coalition because it garnered the support of other ruling elite factions; in short, the factions supporting the sugar strategy were greater than those opposing it. The factions supporting it included the younger generation of Frelimo leaders and technocrats in charge of the ongoing economic reforms in customs, tax, investments, privatisation and the financial sector. They also included the trade unions, the old ideological faction of Frelimo who were for national industries and state-led development, and left-aligned intellectuals who were against the increasing influence of the World Bank Group. The group that opposed the sugar strategy, particularly a sugar tariff, included individuals who imported sugar, legally and illegally, and owners of transport companies used to transport illicit sugar imports. Individuals having companies in these businesses included top Frelimo leaders, as well as financiers of the party. The ruling elite factions supporting the sugar strategy and their mutual interests with foreign sugar companies convinced downstream users of sugar, such as the beverage companies, to go along, and this gave them the political leverage to ignore criticism from the World Bank Group. It also meant that the Chissano faction was able to provide state bureaucrats in the National Sugar Institute with resources and political back-up needed to enforce the sugar tariff and curb smuggling, as well as the room to mediate between the political imperatives of the party and the economic interests of the investing firms.

State bureaucrats in the National Sugar Institute could play this mediating role because they had technical and practical knowledge of the sugar industry *and* the trust of the Chissano faction. The former resulted from the state bureaucrats' past experience in the industry and from people moving in and out of industry and state positions, both of which meant that state bureaucrats understood what was needed to rehabilitate the industry. The latter resulted from the overlap between Frelimo Party members and state bureaucrats, thanks to the history of the one-party state and the rotation between political office and bureaucratic office. Many of the state bureaucrats had worked in relation to the sugar industry in private, bureaucratic and political positions since the 1970s and were involved in running (down) productive enterprises in the past while also gaining valuable trial-and-error lessons that could be used in the future. They had considerable knowledge about how to get politically sensitive, bureaucratically complicated and highly legal issues through the political system without compromising the industrial needs and requirements to such an extent that it would have brought the industry to a standstill.

The sugar sector is known for highly volatile markets, where the free world market price can often be lower than production costs as a result of overproduction and price speculation. For the same reason all the top sugar producers in the world protect their sugar industries through different forms of tariff regimes. A protected internal market was necessary in order to create a favourable milieu that could stimulate new investments promoting efficient production to mitigate the effects of the world market. Furthermore, the internal market was necessary while negotiations for preferential market access were ongoing. In the 2000s developments around the European market and mechanisms such as the Economic Partnership Agreement and Everything but Arms Agreement created favourable conditions that allowed unlimited access to the European market.

Establishing a protected market for sugar had implications for the distribution of benefits and resources in several ways. First, it challenged trade monopolies and the informal (contraband) sugar trade. By the time sufficient sugar had become available, the tariff had become an important political issue and created substantial public discussion. The industry pressed for its implementation, while different Frelimo and government factions and individuals lined up to either support or resist it. Implementation involved a number of ministries and regional coordination of harbour and border control entities, leading eventually to a major overhaul of customs and immigration structures and affecting existing investment policies, as well as curbing Indian family trade houses. Challenging trade monopolies, which often spanned several continents and had strong internal cohesion (besides paying generously for protection to the Frelimo Party and individuals) required considerable political support for the national sugar industry and continual and skilful liaison, both within the governing party and with external actors, particularly the World Bank Group, which feared the resurrection of inefficient state-run businesses.

Moving from imported sugar to nationally produced sugar also had implications for the beverage sector. The beverage sector had been the site of considerable investments by big multinational companies, as well as by members of the newly created Mozambican economic elite, which became an important constituency of Frelimo after waves of privatisation in the 1980s and 1990s. The tariff increased the price for refined sugar two-fold and even more. Some beverage industry actors protected the need for importation by requiring a certain refinement level for the sugar used in soft drink production, which was not available at that time in Mozambique at a reasonable price. A compromise was struck where upstream industries bought sugar from the sugar industry at a favourable price that was considerably lower than the reference price used for defining the tariff, and white sugar was provided for the local beverage industry after a 'tollgate refining', where brown sugar was exchanged for white sugar from South Africa and the price difference was paid by the sugar industry.[20]

The steep price increase was passed directly to urban consumers. This happened during Chissano's last elected period from 1999 until the national elections in 2004. The Chissano-run ruling elite carried through the sugar policy despite being close to losing the 1999 general elections and despite its unpopularity among urban voters, because supporting the sugar sector allowed the government to fashion new links to rural electoral constituencies in areas where it had struggled to assert itself before.

Underpinnings of incentives for productivity

State bureaucrats in the Sugar Institute supported bringing in foreign firms to rehabilitate the sugar estates and worked with them to meet the industry's needs. Incentives for productivity were created because the foreign firms needed the state to provide infrastructure, the internally protected market and government-guaranteed loans, while state bureaucrats in the Sugar Institute could credibly threaten to withhold support if the firms did not deliver theirs: investing and upgrading production and processing to become profitable and produce a surplus to export. But, importantly, the foreign firms investing in the sugar estates also had the technological capabilities to become profitable and thus had the incentive to use rents productively.

An important requirement for both engaging with the Sugar Institute and implementing key parts of the sugar strategy was the creation of new organisations within the sugar industry. The first organisation to emerge was the national sugar-producing organisation, which emerged after 1998 to take care of the sugar producers' interests. It was the organisational centre for the tripartite minimum salary negotiations and the organisation that acted as a mediator between the state and industry when necessary. The second important organisation was the industry-owned National Sugar Distributor, which was created to market all sugar internally as well as externally, which hugely cut down transactions costs.

The Frelimo government pressured sugar producers to organise themselves in branch organisations, or what we could call 'rent sharing organisations'. The enforcement was done by cutting communication until an organisation was created with the mandate to speak on behalf of the industry regarding sugar marketing and distribution. Intra-industry collective action crystallised around the sharing of rents: rents generated by the protected market pricing policy (both revenues and taxes); rents generated from first preferential export quotas to the USA and later from export access to the European and other markets as they became available; and rents created by preferential treatment of the beverage sector. The sugar industry also managed to develop mechanisms for coordinating marketing strategies that allowed it to avoid having to dump sugar onto world markets. The existence of relatively few investing firms and their collective organisation made mitigation and reconciliation of conflicting interest relatively easy.

Rehabilitating cocoa bean exports in Ghana

The cocoa sector is Ghana's most successful productive sector, and the only one to have received sustained political support since the 1980s across four different ruling coalitions. When the Provisional National Defence Council government led by J.J. Rawlings took over the country in 1982, the economy was decimated. When economic reforms began in the mid-1980s, the government chose the rehabilitation of cocoa bean exports as the centre of the reform strategy because of the cocoa sector's history as the dominant pillar of the colonial and postcolonial economy: as the main export, a key source of government revenue, and an important source of income in rural areas. The rehabilitation of cocoa bean exports involved restructuring the state marketing board, the Ghana Cocoa Board (Cocobod, for short). The key policies included liberalising the internal marketing of cocoa beans to bring in private, licensed buying agents, increasing the producer price, restructuring Cocobod to focus on quality control and external marketing, and increasing the productivity of cocoa farms. In the 2000s incentives were introduced to attract foreign investment in cocoa processing.

These policies were relatively well implemented and had impressive results, although non-policy factors also contributed to the success, such as increases in the international price of cocoa beans from the mid-2000s. Cocoa bean production increased from an all-time low of 159,000 tons in the 1982–83 season, slowly recovering to 350,000 tons by 2000–01, booming to 740,000 tons in 2005–06, and was estimated to have reached 900,000 tons in the 2010–11 season.[21] Ghana exports the finest quality cocoa beans in the world, which fetch a premium on the world market, about 10% over standard bean price.[22] New cocoa processing factories were established in the late 2000s, resulting in increasing exports of processed cocoa products.

Drivers of ruling elite support

Compared with Mozambique, Ghana has a very different distribution of power within society and thus ruling coalitions have a different structure and retain power for shorter periods of time. Since 1982 Ghana has had four ruling coalitions. The Provisional National Defence Council (PNDC) took over in a military revolt led by J.J. Rawlings. The PNDC created a political party, the National Democratic Congress (NDC), in order to contest elections in late 1992, which it won and Rawlings became president for two terms. The NDC contained many PNDC ruling elites, but its composition of the ruling coalition changed over time to become quite different. The NDC lost power to the other major political party, the New Patriotic Party (NPP), in the 2000 elections. The NPP government, led by President J.A. Kufuor, took two terms, before being defeated at the polls in 2008 by the NDC. And the NDC government held on for a second term in the 2012 elections. Since the return to multiparty rule the political landscape has been dominated by the NDC and NPP political parties, which are umbrellas of political elite factions and patron–client networks.[23]

Ruling elites' focus on immediate political survival, both in terms of jockeying for power within their political party as well as winning national elections, has meant that few industrial policies are pursued and even fewer are successful. The cocoa sector is an exception. Ruling elites across the different governments supported cocoa bean exports. This sustained political support was based on mutual interests between the ruling political elites and cocoa bean producers. The cocoa farmers were not generally characterised by capitalist production, but rather represented a hybrid of capitalist and pre-capitalist modes of production. These smallholder cocoa farmers shared a common interest in keeping producer prices high in a well functioning export system and in distributive initiatives. For their part, ruling elites faced incentives to keep farm gate prices high in order to encourage production. These incentives stemmed from the fact that ruling elites depended on the cocoa sector both to finance the state and to provide foreign exchange. This is a different type of mutual interest than in the sugar case in Mozambique, in that the smallholder cocoa farmers did not constitute a well organised group of capitalists with high technological capabilities, which accounts for why increasing productivity and moving into cocoa processing was difficult, as explained below.

The small group that took power as the PNDC had incentives to revive the cocoa sector because it was the single easiest way to revive production and exports. It was also a way to revive state finances, because the cocoa export tax was easy to collect when the state had a monopoly on exports. The PNDC and NDC governments implemented sector-specific reforms in collaboration with Cocobod technocrats and through negotiations with the World Bank. The PNDC ruling elites and Cocobod technocrats negotiated hard to shape the reform process, creating a more efficient marketing board and internal buying process but refusing to completely liberalise and privatise.[24] Other West African countries that completely liberalised their cocoa sectors experienced a declining quality of exports. Cocobod officials used this argument in negotiations, with the international cocoa grinders and chocolate manufacturers on their side.[25]

The cocoa sector accounted for almost 10% of GDP at the end of the 1980s, dropped in the 1990s to around 5% but rose again to reach 8% of GDP by the end of the 2000s.[26] Cocoa also accounted for a large proportion of export earnings, as high as 60% in 1983 and then hovering between 20% and 40% in the 1990s and 2000s.[27] Foreign exchange earnings from cocoa bean exports pass through the state marketing board, Cocobod. The cocoa sector was also the single biggest source of government revenue until the late 1990s, as a result of a cocoa export tax.

When the NPP came to power, the new ruling elites continued to support the cocoa sector, perhaps even more vigorously, partly because its electoral strongholds were located in key cocoa producing regions. But it was also because, by the 2000s, 80% of cocoa bean production came from about 720,000 smallholder farmers (producing on farms smaller than 12 acres) across six out of the 10 regions in the country and affecting the livelihoods of about 30% of the population. Supporting the cocoa sector made sense in terms of electoral calculations.

Emergence of a pocket of efficiency

The exceptional performance of cocoa bean exports was a result of the organisation of the sector from production to marketing as a result of the role played by the state-run Cocobod. The emergence of Cocobod as a pocket of efficiency and its continuation as such after the return to multiparty democracy in 1993 was the outcome of a combination of several factors. General ruling elite support for the cocoa sector because of its economic importance, and the availability of sources other than cocoa export tax revenue to fund the state, created a 'pocket' in which Cocobod officials could operate without political interference undermining its economic performance. The 'efficiency' side emerged as the result of the unique history of Cocobod in Ghana's economy, which gave it technical expertise that was not lost during the years of economic decline and then structural adjustment in the 1980s.

Cocobod consists of five public companies: (1) the Cocoa Marketing Company (CMC), with a de facto monopoly on the export of cocoa beans; (2) the Produce Buying Company, which purchases, stores and distributes cocoa to designated takeover centres agreed by CMC, in competition with other private licensed buying companies;[28] (3) the Cocoa Research Institute of Ghana, which carries out research and development activities; (4) the Quality Control Division, which is responsible for quality assurance and undertakes checks at the farm level and before export; and (5) the Cocoa Processing Company, which processes raw cocoa beans into semi-finished products for export and also manufactures finished products for the domestic market. The CMC is the most efficient of the subsidiaries of Cocobod.[29] Thanks to its monopoly on external marketing, CMC benefits from economies of scale when negotiating prices with international buyers, raising finance, and arranging transport.

Each set of actors involved in the domestic cocoa value chain receives a margin of the export value of cocoa beans based on the projected free on board (FOB) price, and the Ministry of Finance receives a cocoa export duty. Cocobod gradually increased the producer price from the low of 40% of the FOB price in 1983 to reach 52% in 1998–99, and then 70% in the 2000s as part of the Cocoa Sector Strategy. The producer price increase was achieved by increasing the efficiency of Cocobod, and later by reducing the export duty. The buying agents' margin hovered between 8% and 12%, and Cocobod companies received the remaining share of the FOB price to cover domestic transport, storage and shipping, disinfection and crop finance. Notably, CMC receives an 'extra margin' in terms of the difference between the FOB price and the actual export value, because its sales are usually made on a cost, insurance and freight (CIF) basis.[30] Cocobod reinvests the gains from this 'extra margin' in productivity-enhancing initiatives in the cocoa sector such as research and development and disease control programmes, as well as in more re-distributional initiatives such as building roads, and cocoa farmer pension and housing programmes that encourage farmers to stay in cocoa.[31]

State involvement in cocoa marketing existed from the late colonial period and persisted through the post-independence period. While the Ghanaian state bureaucracy as a whole suffered from politicisation and patronage appointments, resulting in under-qualified staff being hired, the quality control and export management functions of the cocoa marketing system always functioned relatively well.[32] The CMC, which controlled the system, had an institutional history of recruiting based on merit and providing extensive training to its employees, and its officials interacted primarily with international buyers and maintained a great deal of autonomy from the rest of the state bureaucracy.[33] Reforms in the 1980s did not gut the state agency, but rather made it more efficient: reducing low-skilled staff and raising pay for the remaining staff. Another key source of Cocobod's efficiency was its financial autonomy. CMC began borrowing from abroad in 1993, and by 1998 international banks were competing to lend funds to it because of its reputation.[34] Thus, it did not depend on transfers from the unpredictable government budget or foreign aid.

Limits to incentives for productivity

However, weaknesses in Cocobod and the large number of unorganised smallholder cocoa farmers made it difficult to implement productivity-enhancing initiatives. It would require a large state agency to implement initiatives to increase productivity of such a large number of smallholder cocoa farmers. Nevertheless, as a result of the reforms, Cocobod had become a buying and marketing organisation, with good research and development facilities, but insufficient organisational means to improve production practices.

Cocobod attempted productivity-enhancing initiatives in the 1990s and 2000s, with mixed success. The productivity of smallholder cocoa producers increased but are low compared with other cocoa-producing countries and compared with what is achievable in Ghana.[35] Here we focus on the initiatives tried in the 2000s, which involved supplying fertiliser and other inputs on credit, as well as pesticide.[36] The credit facility failed because farmers did not repay the loans, and Cocobod did not have the means or the political backing to enforce repayment. The programme was hived off to a private company, which had more success but on a small scale. The pesticide programme was partially successful as only just over half of surveyed farmers indicated they received the minimum number of sprayings, and farmers did not have equal access to the programme. Implementation was hampered by social hierarchy and conflicts within communities, by ineffective monitoring by Cocobod, and by the challenges of poor infrastructure.

The NPP government pushed for increasing the percentage of the annual cocoa crop processed locally.[37] It created incentives that led to a wave of investments in processing factories. But the motivations and alliances that had produced relative success for cocoa bean exports were not supportive of a shift into processing. Before the 2000s cocoa processing was undertaken only by the Cocoa Processing Company and its joint ventures with a small German processor after privatisation of two state-owned factories in the 1990s.[38] These factories encountered operational problems almost from the beginning as a result of disagreements with Cocobod over the pricing of beans.[39]

Cocoa grinding traditionally took place in the dominant end-markets of Europe and the USA but in the 2000s things began to change.[40] International cocoa processing companies were expanding cocoa processing capacity in cocoa producing countries, as part of integrating trading and processing, especially in light of the falling quality of beans in most countries. The three leading multinational corporations already had factories in the Ivory Coast. Some NPP ruling elites actively sought out the international cocoa processors and encouraged them to set up processing facilities in Ghana, promising companies access to adequate volumes of beans and at a discount.[41] Callebaut established a full processing factory in 2004, and the others followed suit, with Cargill becoming operational by 2008 and ADM by 2009. This trend spurred investments by Ghanaians, often in joint ventures with foreign capital and expertise.

The discount on beans is interpreted as the key reason why the multinational corporations set up in Ghana and explains the wave of Ghanaian investors.[42] Ghanaian beans command a premium price on the world market, building a -factory is a large investment, and other ingredients for making chocolate have to be bought at world market prices. Processors were promised a 20% discount on light crop beans based on the projected price for main crop beans. 'Light crop' beans are produced from a second harvest and are smaller in size than the beans that fetch a premium on the international market.[43]

Incentives created for investing in processing were sufficient for starting up, but they are now under strain.[44] Processing capacity rose from around 100,000 tons in 2000 to nearly 350,000 tons in 2012, and more factories were being built. The amount of light crop beans varies with each crop season, but during the 2000s they constituted barely 20% of the annual crop which, during a good harvest, is 100,000–200,000 tons. Cocobod could not fulfil processors' contracts because of the limited amount of light crop beans, and sometimes Cocobod used light crop beans to fulfil its own export contracts. Cocobod tabled a proposal to end the processors' discount in 2010, in advance of producing a new cocoa sector strategy. The processing companies mobilised to lobby NDC ruling elites to oppose it. This situation resulted in a stalemate.

Cocobod was against the discount and generally not interested in expanding processing for several reasons. Exporting a large volume of beans is essential to maintaining the existing production system and to maintaining Cocobod's powerful position. CMC sells the majority of the cocoa harvest in forward contracts, which allows it to stabilise the producer price and provides collateral for foreign loans, which in turn finance Cocobod operations as well as its ability to make loans to licensed buying agents. Thus, if half of the cocoa beans went to local processing, the finances of Cocobod would be reduced, potentially undermining the existing quality control and internal buying system in place. Furthermore, the discount results in another set of actors making a claim for a margin of the cocoa export value that must come at the expense of some existing actor, namely the cocoa producer, through the reduced producer price.[45] In the absence of more effective means of increasing productivity, Cocobod wanted to keep the producer price as high as possible as an incentive to increase production.

In sum, Cocobod's interests were not aligned with the move into processing, so while the processors were more organised in expressing their interests than smallholder cocoa farmers, they did not find a receptive bureaucracy nor a group of politicians ready to go against the interests of smallholders. Ruling elites had mutual interests with the processors, which stemmed from ideas embedded in economic nationalism about moving into processing and from the perceptions that international processing corporations were necessary to expand processing in Ghana. In one way this put the ruling elites at odds with Cocobod officials. But ruling elites also had an incentive *not* to change the distribution of economic benefits in favour of a small number of processors. The 2008 national election had been extremely close. The presidency was determined in a second round of voting, which saw the incumbent NPP party lose by 40,000 votes, and the NPP lost its majority in parliament by a small number of seats. It would be a very risky strategy to change the distribution of benefits substantially. The only way out is to increase productivity of cocoa producers, but this too would require focusing on a smaller number of producers, where it is feasible for producers to organise and for Cocobod to implement productivity-enhancing initiatives, something that is very difficult for ruling elites to do, given the configuration of political power.

Conclusions

The two sector case studies examined in this paper provide real experiences regarding the conditions necessary for successfully implementing industrial policies, and the politics that makes them possible. But they also provide additional nuance in how we think about ruling elites and their alliances with capitalists and state bureaucrats, especially in African countries that are still largely agrarian and have few capitalists with significant technological capabilities.

In Mozambique the interest of the Frelimo ruling elite (or a significant portion of the factions that comprise it) in supporting the rehabilitation of the sugar industry was to use the industry to mobilise political support. We argue that Frelimo ruling elites chose this kind of political survival strategy, because in the mid-1990s they lacked resources with which to make easy side payments but were pressured to do something as they were concluding a civil war and faced limited political support within large parts of the population. The Frelimo government of Chissano actively sought foreign sugar companies with the technological capabilities to revive the Mozambican industry, who were at the same time searching for opportunities to invest abroad. The small number of companies investing in the sugar industry made it easier for them to organise themselves and their strong capabilities gave them considerable political power with the ruling elites. The interests of both sides were aligned, leading to a mutual dependence.

In Ghana the dispersion and low capabilities of cocoa producers meant that the state had to take a lead role in organising the sector. Patterns of smallholder production of cocoa beans were in place before the move into cocoa processing began, and processors were entirely dependent on smallholder production via the state agency for their supply of beans; they did not establish nucleus farms (and could not because of challenges in accessing land). In contrast, when sugar processing was re-established in Mozambique, production of sugar cane by smallholders did not exist and production became an activity vertically integrated into the sugar estates. Thus, the state in Mozambique did not need to play a dominant role in organising production, but rather one of just facilitating industry actors. As the sugar industry grew, sugar companies ran into problems accessing more land. It was only at that point that small and medium-scale cane producers were brought into the industry in order to expand production. This change also allowed the Frelimo ruling elites to meet demands within the ruling coalition to provide more economic opportunities to party supporters. Notably, the involvement of small and medium-scale cane producers primarily took place *after* the establishment of efficient sugar companies.

But alliances are not static; they are transformed as a result of changes in the configuration of political power or the power of capitalists. For example, in Mozambique under President Guebuza from 2004 onwards, support for the sugar industry waned. All the key players from the National Sugar Institute and Frelimo left the sector or were redeployed elsewhere, and the Institute was merged into a larger organisation responsible for agriculture, which slowly undermined capacity and longstanding relationships between the different actors. Staff of the Institute was hired by the sugar companies. Currently the state bureaucracy only monitors the sugar industry. Alliances evolved when strong state intervention was no longer necessary. Presently, there is no longer a state agency that can mitigate and reconcile conflicts emerging from new alliances. Furthermore, alliances that drive good economic outcomes at one stage can later become stumbling blocks for furthering economic transformation. Alliances that led Ghana to become the producer of the best cocoa beans in the world were not able to solve the challenges encountered in upgrading and creating a national processing industry.

Acknowledgements

The authors thank the anonymous reviewer for very helpful comments on an earlier version of the article. They also wish to thank Rasmus Ludvigsen for access to his empirical data on cocoa processing in Ghana, and to acknowledge that the framework presented in this article was produced in collaborative work with Ole Therkildsen and Anne Mette Kjær.

Notes on Contributors

Lindsay Whitfield is Associate Professor of Global Studies, Roskilde University. She has just completed a four-year collaborative research programme called 'Elites, Production and Poverty' (2008–11), which was based at the Danish Institute for International Studies. Her previous work includes *The Politics of Aid: African Strategies for Dealing with Donors* (co-authored, 2009) and the edited volume, *Turning Points in African Democracy* (2009). Her work has also been published in *African Affairs*, *Third World Quarterly*, *Journal of Development Studies*, *Oxford Development Studies*, and *Development Policy Review*.

Lars Buur is Senior Researcher at the Danish Institute for International Studies and from February 2014 Associate Professor of International Development Studies, Roskilde University. His recent research focuses on the politics of industrial policy and the new extractive developing economies in East Africa, and conflicts over land, rights and economic opportunities.

Notes

1. See Whitfield, "How Countries Become Rich."
2. For recent arguments in favour of industrial policy in the sense used here, see Hausmann and Rodrik, "Doomed to Choose"; Rodrik, *One Economics, Many Recipes*; Cimoli et al., *Industrial Policy and Development*; and the debate between Ha-Joon Chang and Justin Lin reproduced in Lin, *New Structural Economics*.
3. On learning rents, see Khan, *Learning, Technology Acquisition and Governance Challenges*. For a broader discussion of the term rent, as it is used in this article, see Khan, "Rents, Efficiency and Growth".
4. The research project is the Elites, Production and Poverty research programme, which ran from 2008 to 2011, based at the Danish Institute for International Studies, Copenhagen. see www.diis.dk/epp.
5. This argument about the three approaches is based on a large literature review presented in Whitfield and Therkildsen, *What Drives States*?
6. The full framework is presented in Whitfield et al., *The Politics of Production*.
7. For further discussion of the concept of political settlement, see Khan, *Political Settlements*.
8. Moore and Schmitz, *Idealism, Realism and the Investment Climate*.
9. Khan, *Learning, Technology Acquisition and Governance Challenges*.
10. In using the term 'mutual interests', we were inspired by Moore and Schmitz, "Idealism, Realism and the Investment Climate," but our conceptualisation of the factors and relations giving rise to mutual interests go beyond the arguments presented by them, by drawing on the works of other authors such as Kang, *Crony Capitalism*; Khan, *Political Settlements*; and Geddes, *Politician's Dilemma*.
11. See Maxfield and Schneider, "Business, the State and Economic Performance"; and Doner and Schneider, "Business Associations and Economic Development."
12. Geddes, *Politician's Dilemma*; and Khan, *Political Settlements*.
13. Doner et al., "Systemic Vulnerability."
14. For example, see Doner, *The Politics of Uneven Development*; and Cammett, *Globalization and Business Politics*.
15. For example, see Kang, *Crony Capitalism*; and Schneider, "Review."
16. Geddes, *Politician's Dilemma*; and Khan, *Political Settlements*.
17. Evans, "State Structures."
18. The term 'pocket of efficiency' has been used in the literature in many ways. See Leonard, '"Pockets" of Effective Agencies" for the origins of the term. However, the argument presented here on what gives rise to a pocket of efficiency is not based on that literature, but rather draws inspiration from other sources, such as the discussion of the bifurcated state in South Korea in Kang, *Crony Capitalism* and of pockets of state capabilities in Thailand in Doner, *The Politics of Uneven Development*.
19. The following analysis of the sugar industry in Mozambique draws on some unpublished studies in English and Portuguese and on government documents. A full list can be found in Buur et al., "Strategic Privatisation"; and 'Buur et al., "The White Gold."
20. The surcharge underwent adjustments after the first period of implementation and was downsized in 2003 for raw sugar and 2004 for refined sugar.
21. Kolavalli and Vigneri, "Cocoa in Ghana." Output in 2010–11 received an artificial boost as a result of smuggling Ivorian cocoa to Ghana to avoid international sanctions imposed on exports of the Gbagbo government.
22. Barrientos et al., "Mapping Sustainable Production."
23. For further details on the political settlement in Ghana, see Whitfield, *Competitive Clientelism*.
24. For a good summary, see Williams, *An African Success Story*.
25. Fold, "Lead Firms and Competition."
26. Calculated by the authors from data obtained from the Ministry of Finance in 2012.

27. Data obtained from the Ministry of Finance in 2012.
28. The Produce Buying Company acts as a buyer of last resort, penetrating difficult areas of the country to make sure that all cocoa farmers are reached, despite the higher costs of doing so.
29. Hubbard, "Reforming the Role of Government"; and Williams, *An African Success Story*.
30. FOB price means that the seller only pays for transport to bring the goods to the departure port. There is another price in the international market: CIF, which means that the seller is responsible for the goods and transport costs all the way to the receiving port.
31. Laven, "The Risk of Inclusions." Laven notes a lack of transparency concerning how this money is spent.
32. Williams, *An African Success Story*.
33. Shepherd and Onumah, "Changing Role of Government."
34. Williams, *An African Success Story*.
35. Kolavalli and Vigneri, "Cocoa in Ghana." The main factor behind the massive expansion in production volumes was the clearing of virgin forest land. Planting cocoa in newly cleared forest land delivers what is called a 'forest rent', because the yield of cocoa trees is higher, with no extra costs to the farmer. See Fold, "Spilling the Beans."
36. This analysis draws on empirical material presented in Barrientos et al., "Mapping Sustainable Production"; and Laven, "The Risk of Inclusions."
37. The NPP 2000 electoral manifesto states the goal of increasing processing of the annual cocoa crop from 20% to at least 30%. The 2002 budget statement states 40% and the 2007 budget statement raises the goal to 50%. The 2001 budget statement says that a team will be put together to recommend incentives to attract local and foreign investors into value added processing of cocoa.
38. Ghana Cocoa Sector Development Strategy, Ministry of Finance, April 1999.
39. International Centre for Settlement of Investment Disputes, Gustav Hamester (Claimant) v. Republic of Ghana (Respondent), June 18, 2010. www. icsid.worldbank.org.
40. See Fold, "Lead Firms and Competition."
41. Laven, "The Risk of Inclusions"; and Ludvigsen, "Global Value Chains."
42. Laven, "The Risk of Inclusions"; and Ludvigsen, "Global Value Chains."
43. Light crop beans are sold on the world market at a discount of about 12%–15%, so the real discount for processors is more like 5%–7%.
44. Ludvigsen, "Global Value Chains."
45. Producers lose out from the processor discount because the discount factors into the average FOB price, on the basis of which the producer price is determined.

Bibliography

Barrientos, S. , K. Asenso-Okyere, S. Asuming-Brempong, D. Sarpong, N. A. Anyidoho, Kaplinsky R., and Leavy J.. "Mapping Sustainable Production in Ghanaian Cocoa. Report to Cadbury." Institute of Development Studies and the University of Ghana, 2008.

Buur, L., with C. Mondlane, and O. Baloi. "Strategic Privatisation: Rehabilitating the Mozambican Sugar Industry." *Review of African Political Economy* 38, no. 128 (2011): 235–256.

Buur, L., C. Mondlane, and O. Baloi. "The White Gold: The Role of Government and State in Rehabilitating the Sugar Industry in Mozambique." *Journal of Development Studies* 48, no. 3 (2012): 349–362.

Cammett, M. *Globalization and Business Politics in Arab North Africa: A Comparative Perspective*. Cambridge: Cambridge University Press, 2007.

Cimoli, M., G. Dosi, and J. Stiglitz (eds.). *Industrial Policy and Development: The Political Economy of Capabilities Accumulation*. Oxford: Oxford University Press, 2009.

Doner, R. *The Politics of Uneven Development: Thailand's Economic Growth in Comparative Perspective*. Cambridge: Cambridge University Press, 2009.

Doner, R., and B. Schneider. "Business Associations and Economic Development: Why some Associations Contribute More than Others." *Business and Politics* 2, no. 3 (2000): 261–288.

Doner, R., B. Ritchie, and D. Slater. "Systemic Vulnerability and the Origins of the Developmental States: Northeast and Southeast Asia in Comparative Perspective." *International Organization* 59, Spring (2005): 327–361.

Evans, P. "State Structures, Government–Business Relations, and Economic Transformation." In *Business–State Relations in Developing Countries*, edited by. S. Maxfield, and B.R. Schneider, 63–87. Ithaca: Cornell University Press, 1997.

Fold, N. "Lead Firms and Competition in 'Bi-polar' Commodity Chains: Grinders and Branders in the Global Cocoa–Chocolate Industry." *Journal of Agrarian Change* 2, no. 2 (2002): 228–247.

Fold, N. "Spilling the Beans on a Tough Nut: Liberalisation and Local Supply System Changes in Ghana's Cocoa and Shea Chains." In *Geographies of Commodity Chains*, edited by A. Hughes, and S. Reimer, 63–80. London: Routledge, 2004.

Geddes, B. *Politician's Dilemma: Building State Capacity in Latin America*. Berkeley: University of California Press, 1994.

Hausmann, R., and D. Rodrik. "Doomed to Choose: Industrial Policy as Predicament". Paper presented at the Center for International Development: Harvard University, 2006.

Hubbard, M. "Reforming the Role of Government in Agricultural Markets." In *Developing Agricultural Trade: New Roles of Government in Poor Countries*, edited by M. Hubbard, 120–142. Basingstoke: Palgrave Macmillan, 2003.

Kang, D. *Crony Capitalism: Corruption and Development in South Korea and the Philippines*. Cambridge: Cambridge University Press, 2002.

Khan, M. "Rents, Efficiency and Growth." In *Rents, Rent-Seeking and Economic Development: Theory and Evidence in Asia*, edited by M. Khan, and K. S. Jomo, 21–69. Cambridge: Cambridge University Press, 2000.

Khan, M. *Learning, Technology Acquisition and Governance Challenges in Developing Countries*. Research Paper Series on Governance for Growth. London: School of Oriental and African Studies, 2009. http://mercury.soas.ac.uk.

Khan, M. *Political Settlements and the Governance of Growth-enhancing Institutions*. Research Paper Series on Governance for Growth. London: School of Oriental and African Studies, 2010. http://mercury.soas.ac.uk.

Kolavalli, S., and M. Vigneri. "Cocoa in Ghana: Shaping the Success of an Economy." In *Yes Africa Can: Success Stories from a Dynamic Continent*, edited by P. Chuhan-Pole, and M. Angwafo, 201–217. Washington, DC: World Bank, 2011.

Laven, A. "*The Risk of Inclusions: Shifts in Governance Processes and Upgrading Opportunities for Small-scale Cocoa Farmers in Ghana*". Published doctoral dissertation. Amsterdam: Royal Tropical Institute (KIT) Publishers, 2010.

Leonard, D. "'Pockets' of Effective Agencies in Weak Governance States: Where are They Likely and Why does it Matter?" *Public Administration and Development* 30 (2010): 91–101.

Lin, J. Y. "*New Structural Economics: A Framework for Rethinking Development and Policy*". Washington, DC: World Bank, 2012.

Ludvigsen, R. "*Global Value Chains and Cocoa Processing in Ghana*". Master's thesis: Aalborg University, 2012.

Maxfield, S., and B. R. Schneider. "Business, the State, and Economic Performance in Developing Countries." In *Business and the State in Developing Countries*, edited by S. Maxfield, and B. R. Schneider, 3–35. Ithaca, NY: Cornell University Press, 1997.

Moore, M., and H. Schmitz. *Idealism, Realism and the Investment Climate in Developing Countries*. Working Paper 307. Brighton: Institute of Development Studies, 2008.

Rodrik, D. *One Economics, Many Recipes: Globalization, Institutions and Economic Growth*. Princeton, NJ: Princeton University Press, 2007.

Schneider, B. R. "Review: Elusive Synergy – Business–Government Relations and Development." *Comparative Politics* 31, no. 1 (1998): 101–122.

Shepherd, A., and G. Onumah. "Changing Role of Government in Agricultural Trade in Ghana." In *Developing Agricultural Trade: New Roles of Government in Poor Countries*, edited by M. Hubbard, 65–76. Basingstoke: Palgrave Macmillan, 2003.

Whitfield, L. *Competitive Clientelism, Easy Financing and Weak Capitalists: The Contemporary Political Settlement in Ghana*. Working Paper 2011:27. Copenhagen: Danish Institute for International Studies, 2011.

Whitfield, L. "How Countries become Rich and Reduce Poverty: A Review of Heterodox Explanations of Economic Development." *Development Policy Review* 30, no. 3 (2012): 239–260.

Whitfield, L., and O. Therkildsen. *What Drives States to Support the Development of Productive Sectors? Strategies Ruling Elites Pursue for Political Survival and their Policy Implications*. Working Paper 2011:15. Copenhagen: Danish Institute for International Studies, 2011.

Whitfield, L., O. Therkildsen, L. Buur, and A. M. Kjær. *The Politics of Production: African Experiences in Comparative Perspective*. Forthcoming. Cambridge: Cambridge University Press.

Williams, T. *An African Success Story: Ghana's Cocoa Marketing System*. Working Paper 318. Brighton: Institute of Development Studies, 2009.

'Donors go home': non-traditional state actors and the creation of development space in Zambia

Peter Kragelund

Department of Society and Globalisation, Roskilde University, Denmark

The international development arena is currently subject to major changes in the geographies of power. In this article I analyse how and to what extent the (re)entry on the development scene of China, India and Brazil, together with increasing prices for primary commodities and improved access to international finance, has affected Zambia's political leverage to set, implement and fund its own developmental policies. I argue that, while real changes in external financial flows comparable to aid from these non-traditional state actors are still small, these actors' experience is providing Zambia with an alternative development model that combines purposive state intervention with market-based economic growth and integration into world markets. While Zambia may be taking the first steps in strengthening its 'sovereign frontier', the extent of this movement is still small and its development outcomes are far from assured.

Introduction

The international development arena is the home of major changes in the geographies of power. It consists, among other things, of a combination of the emergence of a number of global and regional powers such as Brazil, India and China, the (re)entry on the development scene of these non-traditional state actors (NTSA),[1] and the relative decline in economic power of long-term established development partners organised in the Development Assistance Committee (DAC) of the OECD. At the centre of this transformation are resource-rich African economies, which are currently benefiting from a combination of booming commodity prices, reduced debt burdens, improved credit ratings and the presence of NTSAs. In this paper, through the case study of Zambia, I examine whether this mix of tendencies brings additional development finance,[2] and whether it increases these economies' political leverage to set, implement and fund their own developmental policies as more actors vie for their favour, and thus whether it opens space for new ideas.

A growing body of literature has analysed constituent parts of this transformation, including the effects of the upsurge in demand for primary commodities on the growth prospects of least developed countries, how the present net value of African countries' debt has been greatly reduced, how and to what extent the rejuvenation of NTSAs' Africa engagement differs qualitatively from that of 'traditional' actors, and how NTSAs affect global governance.[3] Hence we have reached a better understanding of the dynamics of each of the components, but hardly any research has been conducted on the relationship between these components and even less on how this relationship plays out on the ground. This article targets this knowledge gap in the literature by scrutinising how booming commodity prices, reduced debt burdens, improved credit ratings, and the presence of NTSAs affect the Zambian government's possibility of setting, implementing and funding its own policies and thereby create development space. It argues that NTSAs are indeed a contributing factor in explaining the creation of development space in Zambia, but that current changes are incremental and episodic. Furthermore, in order to fully comprehend the mechanisms of development space creation, we have to move beyond conventional concepts in the aid and development literature and pay more attention to insights from the literature on African International Relations.

Zambia is a critical case for understanding current changes in development space for African economies: for two decades it was 'identified as an emblematic case of a country dominated by its donors',[4] but recently copper prices have increased tremendously, making more finance available to the Zambian government to lessen its dependence on traditional partners. Simultaneously Zambia has been courted by a number of NTSAs. The conclusions brought forward here are therefore suggestive of how China, India and Brazil affect the development space in Africa – directly through their presence and finance, and indirectly through increased demand for primary commodities.

These issues are addressed drawing on the author's fieldwork in Zambia, which encompasses interviews with Zambian government officials, stakeholders in Zambian civil society and academia, and representatives of both NTSAs and traditional partners operating in Zambia.[5] Archival studies at the main Zambian newspapers were also conducted to map the flows of funds from NTSAs to the country. These are often misrepresented by analysts, who seem to conflate 'economic cooperation' with aid, official development assistance (ODA) with Other Official Flows, pledges with disbursements, and multiyear commitments with annual flows. Further, a specific loophole in Zambian law results in a situation where 'external loans are not subjected to the scrutiny of Parliament before they are obtained, nor is the Auditor-General supplied with all loan documentation'.[6]

The article is structured as follows: the next section sets out to provide a better understanding of how and why development space can change. The following two sections analyse how and to what extent the sovereign frontier for Zambia has been strengthened by: (1) the availability of development finance from China, India and Brazil; and (2) increasing prices for primary commodities and access to international finance. Section five analyses the extent to which these factors have translated into 'development space' for the Zambian government. A final section draws some conclusions.

Enlarging the development space: insights from the ownership and sovereignty literature

The development arena is filled with terms that seek to grasp a government's development space to define and implement its own policies. The aid literature often uses the term 'ownership' to describe this space. Ownership is broadly perceived as the ability to control policy making and act accordingly. Nonetheless, it is poorly defined and may refer to a situation where executive offices of the state have information about a programme, to a situation where these offices identify politically with the programme, or to a situation where they have designed and funded the programme.[7] In this context ownership is not always differentiated from development space and the concept is often linked to 'self-determination', indicating that what is at stake is the degree of autonomy available to countries and leaders to define and implement policies that affect social and economic development.[8]

Nonetheless, this literature does not help us understand how or to what extent this space is reduced or enlarged. The concept of sovereignty may bring us closer to such an understanding. Sovereignty is a central – though often unstated – concept in the literature on ownership and policy space. In fact, sovereignty is a key concept in studies of African international relations. African state sovereignty is generally perceived as a legal principle that exists above all because of the international legitimacy given to it. Essentially, the concept may refer to the right to rule or to the ability to control policy making. In an African context sovereignty is seen either as a condition that does not fully exist, something that shapes African countries' external relations, or as a strategic choice African ruling elites can make use of to carve out room for manoeuvre *vis-à-vis* external actors. Sovereignty seems to be shaped by interstate relations as well as relations between individual states and their societies and is closely associated with changing norms and ideas.[9]

However, a perception of sovereignty as a legal principle only is constraining if we are to further our understanding of the relationship between aid and sovereignty. Rather, to determine how and to what extent aid affects sovereignty, we have to distinguish between sovereignty as a right to rule and sovereignty as national control over policy outcomes. In essence, aid does not affect the right to rule. In contrast, aid contributes to upholding the state's right to rule over a given territory, but it may to varying degrees influence the development space directly through aid conditionality and aid negotiation and indirectly through donors' position as role models for economic and social development, thereby affecting norms and ideas.[10]

What is of interest here is how development finance and the rejuvenation of NTSAS' Africa engagement interact with African states to strengthen their capacity to control policy outcomes. This is at the core of what Graham Harrison terms the 'sovereign frontier'[11] – a metaphor that seeks to go beyond the traditional discussion of whether or not African states are indeed sovereign (or of how sovereignty is maintained in relations with the international community) to a discussion of how a variety of domestic and international actors interact to shape the (changing) development space.

The sovereign frontier is thus a zone of contestation. It is fluid and dynamic; shaped by the performance and the economic and political power of the actors involved in shaping the frontier. The notion of the sovereign frontier thus helps us understand changing development space by highlighting the contestation for autonomy to define and implement policies that affect social and economic development. Harrison does not provide a crystal clear answer as to which factors affect the sovereign frontier, but his account of historical changes in the sovereign frontier of three African countries informs us that the following aspects matter: the power of the political discourse; economic reliance on external funding; indebtedness; number of external actors involved; issues of security; and changes in the global economy.

In other words, the sovereign frontier is affected by the will and ability to present and implement an alternative policy (to that of important external actors) and the relative economic strength of external actors *vis-à-vis* the potential to fund policies internally. In aggregate terms the rejuvenation of NTSAs' interest in Africa is often highlighted as being the factor that will trigger a change in power relations between African countries and their traditional partners and thus strengthen the capacity to control policy outcomes; however, the specific mechanisms whereby NTSAs affect these power relations have not been systematically analysed.

The sovereign frontier, then, supplements the growing body of literature on 'African agency', which rejects the implicit claim in most China–Africa literature that African elites are merely passive recipients of finance and technical advice from China, and instead demonstrates how these elites and other social actors have used their growing economic and political interest to exert power over international and domestic politics.[12] African agency is most prominent in Angola, where vast oil resources, rapid economic growth and a reduction of the debt burden have meant that the country is perceived as a strategic partner by a growing number of other countries. The Angolan state, for its part, has made a virtue of maintaining its sovereignty by diversifying its development partners.[13] But African agency is not limited to Angola. In Ethiopia the presence of China and its readiness to provide development finance for infrastructural projects has provided the government with development space to strengthen its energy sector – in contrast to the recommendations of the traditional partners. And in Rwanda China's growing interest has fuelled elite agency and helped the country manage its traditional donors.[14]

The next section sets out to analyse the extent to which development finance from NTSAs is in fact additional to the existing finance while simultaneously examining whether the presence of NTSAs offers an alternative to the (post-) Washington Consensus. This is done through an analysis of the flow and modality of development finance from China, India and Brazil to Zambia. Although development finance is only one vector of these three countries' engagement with Zambia, which also comprises trade, investment, migration and cultural encounters, it is the only one that is purely state-driven.

Financing and ideas for development: China, India and Brazil in Zambia

In March 2010 former Zambian Minister of Commerce, Felix Mutati, announced that Zambia had secured a US$ 1 billion concessional loan from China. This was meant to ease budgetary constraints and to finance key infrastructural developments. The loan, which was to be extended 'over a period', would be the equivalent of 40% of Zambia's total public external debt stock at the time. Later that year a $2 billion deal was signed between the Zambian state-owned power utility company, Zezco, a Chinese company and the China Africa Development Fund to develop a hydroelectric power station in Kafue Gorge Lower. In August 2010 another loan of $350 million – this time from China ExIm Bank – was secured to finance an expansion of the Kariba North Bank power station.[15]

Meanwhile Zambia's dependence on aid – and thus, on its traditional partners – had changed drastically. In 2001 the country's aid dependence was remarkable, with aid contributing some 53% of the budget. Although aid's contribution fell slightly thereafter, it still accounted for an average of 43% of the state budget from 2000 to 2005, but it dropped to almost 30% in 2009.[16] According to the 2011 budget speech, the budget will see a drastic reduction in the role of donors, with their support to the national budget cut from 14.5% in 2010 to 7.7% in 2011. Of late this dramatic change has been reinforced by the fact that a number of its traditional partners have withdrawn funds from Zambia, a fact which is connected to a combination of a perceived increase in corruption in the country and to changing interests in donor countries. This has resulted in Canada, Denmark and The Netherlands suspending their aid to Zambia and several others changing the terms of their engagement to reflect greater self-interest.

The combination of the continuous announcements in Zambian and international media of pledges of development finance from China and the diminishing role of traditional partners for the Zambian government makes it unsurprising that Lisa Rakner has stated: 'perhaps the most significant change to the development aid debate in Zambia...is...the enhanced importance of non-traditional donors, most notably China'.[17]

The problem is that the three financial transfers described above are not directly comparable to aid.[18] They generally do not follow the guidelines regarding definitions and disclosure of aid volumes set by the DAC, and hardly any of the financial flows from NTSAs show up on the radar of the Ministry of Finance and National Planning (MOFNP): Data from the MONFP show that, of the three most visible NTSAs in Zambia (China, India and Brazil), China is the only one that provided grants to the country between 2006 and 2009. In total the ministry registered Chinese grants worth $12.3 million over the four years. In terms of loans it registered $68.3 million from China and $4.1 million from India.[19]

If we take these figures at face value, NTSAs' financial transfers for development in Zambia are insignificant. Total aid and loan figures from all donors for the four year period added up to $2971 million; in other words, NTSAs' disbursements made up only 2.9% of the total flow. However, these figures underestimate the magnitude of the relationship. The main reason for this discrepancy is that NTSAs tend to engage directly with State House, which is not obliged to disclose information regarding the scope and magnitude of grants to the ministries.[20] Notwithstanding the lack of accuracy of these data, they do show us that China is by far the most important development partner for Zambia among the NTSAs, followed by India and Brazil.

Chinese engagement in Zambia

China's development cooperation with Zambia is by no means new. China supported Zambia's liberation movement and, as early as three years after the country's independence in 1964, provided its first grants and loans to the country. The most famous project was the construction of the Tazara railway, connecting Zambia and Tanzania. In the years that followed Chinese aid financed the building of the Ministry of Defence, the Mulugushi textiles factory, the Chingola maize mills, roads throughout the country, a new government complex, food relief, and new trains, spare parts and technical assistance for the Tazara.

Chinese engagement in Zambia has recently been rejuvenated. Unfortunately all Zambian agreements with China are confidential, but a comparison between official announcements of grants and loans with the data obtained by the MOFNP clearly shows that the latter's figures do not add up. In 2006 the MOFNP registered grants worth \$4.3 million but the state-owned newspaper reported grants worth \$7.2 million. In 2008 again there were discrepancies in the recorded grant figures: MOFNP did not register any grants at all, while the media announced grants worth \$6.2 million from China. A \$39 million loan to purchase Chinese capital equipment to repair infrastructure was not registered either.[21]

Although these figures portray a more accurate – if by no means full – picture of Chinese aid to Zambia, they still depict aid flows as small compared with the flows from Zambia's traditional partners. We cannot therefore expect them to strengthen the sovereign frontier *vis-à-vis* the traditional partners radically. The three big loans described above may, however, strengthen it, as they may provide the Zambian government with the possibility of funding policies not supported by traditional partners. The specific conditions for these loans are unfortunately not in the public domain and, as a chief economist in the MOFNP puts it, 'China doesn't divulge information...Thus the grants from China are not necessarily recorded by the Treasury. Loans are of course recorded but we are not able to verify the various components of the loan.'[22] We do know, however, that these loans are normally provided at competitive interest rates, but are not concessional.[23]

The definition of debt sustainability in these loans differs from that of the International Financial Institutions (IFIS): while the Chinese development banks assess it as development sustainability, the IFIS perceive it as prudent debt management. In other words, loans for huge infrastructural projects like the Kafue Gorge Lower are perceived by the Chinese as being sustainable, because they bring about economic development and thus enhance the ability to repay the loans, whereas the IFIS look more strictly at a country's repayment ability – not taking potential economic growth into consideration. These conflicting views on debt sustainability sometimes lead to conflicts between traditional partners and China. In the words of a representative of a multilateral donor institution in Zambia:

> What annoys us as donors is that we try to impose discipline in the Zambian government especially in terms of public finance management. At the same time the government is running after the Chinese. They have just signed an MOU for a loan of US\$350 million for the road sector [with the Chinese]...Zambia will drop out of the Poverty Reduction and Growth Facility if they borrow more money...

> I'm not worried by the Kafue Lower Gorge...The problem is the roads...There is no revenue model for that. How will Zambia pay back the money? And what about the stadium in Ndola? You can't eat the stadium.[24]

In addition, the bureaucratic procedures linked to the loans differ. This may affect the Zambian government's loan decisions and thereby the movement of the sovereign frontier. In the words of a representative of another multilateral institution: 'Money from traditional donors is associated with high transaction costs and potentially lots of hassle. The IFIs were about to settle a US$1 billion deal with the government to construct the second stage of the Kafue Gorge Lower. Then the Chinese came along and offered a loan of US$1.5 billion. The Chinese are happy to do anything...The government, however, puts pressure on us to include road projects in the deal.'[25]

It is important to bear in mind that smaller financial transfers may have similar impacts on the sovereign frontier because they affect the modus operandi of the relationship between Zambia and its external partners. For example, this was the case with a $3 million loan from the China ExIm Bank to procure nine mobile hospitals. This project was settled without any involvement of the Ministry of Health. Only after the decision had been made was the ministry informed.[26] In the words of a representative of the donor community in Zambia: 'These mobile hospitals were not even on the horizon. I don't know who came up with the idea. Banda met with the Chinese ambassador to Zambia in January 2009 at Rupiah Banda's farm and a few days later it was announced.'[27] The political settlement of this deal is by no means accidental. China emphasises juridical sovereignty in international relations and sees development finance as a central part of its relationship with Zambia. Development finance is thus provided to the president for his or her discretion. Although these loans should be distinguished from aid as they are not concessional and their aim is not first and foremost developmental but to help Chinese companies access the African market,[28] their specific characteristics are providing Zambia with more development space.

Indian engagement in Zambia

Like China's India's bilateral relations date back to Zambia's independence. Thereafter high-level visits between the two countries have taken place on several occasions, leading to agreements on cooperation, avoidance of double taxation, debt relief, credit lines and investments, but financial transfers resembling aid have been small. They have included a few grants, such as the $100,000 grant for medicine and the $500,000 donation for agricultural equipment given in 2003, $60,000 for two Lusaka schools and $250,000 for flood relief in 2008. Moreover, India provides Zambia with an increasing number of 'aid slots' (up from 30 per year in 2002–03 to 86 in 2010–11) in its Indian Technical and Economic Co-operation Programme.[29] These slots may be exchanged for training of personnel, study trips, humanitarian assistance and project aid. On top of this the Indian government waived $3 million worth of debt in 2003.[30]

Of far bigger importance are Indian Lines of Credit (LOCs) extended by the Export–Import Bank of India. Historically India has offered few LOCs to Zambia, but lately it has boosted this part of its engagement and announced an $80 million LOC to Zambia in 2010. This was followed by a $50 million LOC to finance the Itezhi-Tezhi hydro-power project and by another $50 million LOC to finance pre-fabricated health posts in Zambia.[31] Although Indian LOCs carry a grant element of more than 25% and thus could qualify as ODA, they are not. What is important are the costs of the loan for the donor – not the grant element per se.[32] Further, the aim of these LOCs is first and foremost to boost Indian exports. For example, a minimum of 85% of the value of the contract for the hydro-power project and the total value of the contract for the health posts will be used to source goods and services from India.[33]

Moreover, India's ExIm Bank aims to facilitate Indian companies' investments in Zambia through finance for Indian companies. Although Indian investments have yet to reach the heights of the pledges made (the Indian High Commissioner in Zambia stated that the country planned to invest $5.4 billion in Zambia in 2009), Indian investments worth $3 billion were registered in 2007–09.[34]

Financial transfers comparable to ODA from India to Zambia are very small and thus have hardly any direct effect on the sovereign frontier. A combination of the India–Africa summits held every three years, high-profile projects like the Pan African E-network, LOCs and large-scale investments nevertheless make India highly visible in Zambia; thus the perceived importance of these flows is likely to outweigh their real significance. Therefore Indian financial transfers contribute to strengthening the sovereign frontier as they assist the formulation of an alternative policy to that of the traditional partners.

Brazilian engagement in Zambia

Brazil provides neither grants nor loans to Zambia. Instead, it offers technical cooperation in the form of capacity-building courses and on-site technical assistance. Even though Brazilian technical cooperation with Zambia is still quite small, it has in fact a long history, beginning with the signing of the Treaty of Friendship, Cooperation and Commerce in 1980, which led to a few Zambians being trained in Brazil. It lapsed for many years, however, and has only been rejuvenated lately.

Following a number of Brazilian delegations to Zambia, several agreements were signed during an official state visit in 2010. Some of these agreements resemble aid, others look more like investment. Among the most important was a trilateral agreement entitled 'Zero hunger Zambia' focusing on nutritional security. This is the only project where Brazil has contributed actual funds – $200,000 – and this only if the Zambian government and the trilateral partner did the same.[35] It also included capacity-building programmes in the fields of sports and health, experience sharing in biofuel production, and cultural cooperation.

In addition, the MOFNP is working with representatives from Brazil to cancel Zambia's bilateral debt to Brazil, which at the end of 2001 stood at $70.5 million – some 2.6% of the total debt stock to the Paris Club creditors.[36] More important in the long run, however, is the work that is conducted by Embrapa, the state-owned Brazilian Agricultural Research Corporation. It opened its first Africa office in 2008 and has since then facilitated the transfer of agricultural technologies from Brazil to African countries, especially in the biofuel sector. In Zambia Embrapa currently runs three different projects focusing on capacity building and biotechnology. Embrapa's interest in African agriculture is partly explained by its own development experience, and partly by the opportunities this opens for Brazilian exporters of ethanol and for providers of biofuel feed-stock and processing technology.

Brazilian development relations with Zambia are still in their infancy and, according to representatives of the traditional donor community in Zambia, they currently do not affect Zambia's relations with other actors – at most they operate as an additional source of knowledge and inspiration.[37] But Brazil also acts both as a role model and a development alternative for Zambia: Brazil has been very successful in advancing economic growth while simultaneously reducing poverty. Moreover, during his 2010 visit to Zambia President Lula voiced criticism of the neoliberal model and argued that the global financial crisis was an opportunity to follow a new path.[38] It was exactly this criticism that was voiced regarding the traditional donors a year later (see below).

Moving the sovereign frontier by improving the economy

It is clear that, although NTSAs are increasingly paying attention to Zambia, financial flows comparable with aid from these actors have been relatively unimportant in terms of financing the recurrent costs of Zambia's budget. There are signs, however, that this situation is about to change and, if we include all development finance, they do make up a sizeable part of the total flows to Zambia and thus are one of the pieces that may strengthen its sovereign frontier. Zambia's economic latitude, however, is not only affected by direct transfers to government coffers but also by its ability to generate revenues and access external non-concessional financing. Hence, what also matters is booming commodity prices, a relatively stable economy and the resultant improved credit ratings.

After two and a half decades of economic decline Zambia saw a gradual recovery, beginning shortly after the turn of the millennium. Although improving growth rates span a broad spectrum of the Zambian economy, one of the key factors has been increased demand for copper: from a historical low in 2002 copper prices had risen six times when the global financial crisis hit in 2008. Although prices took a short but drastic downturn in 2008, copper prices are once again increasing. In fact, they rose almost 50% in 2010. This demand, led by the NTSAs (combined with a slow supply response) drove up prices tremendously.[39]

This steep rise is directly seen in export earnings, which rose roughly five times from 2002 to 2008, meaning that mineral exports earnings went from being twice as important as aid in 2002 to being seven times as important in 2008, and in copper production, which almost doubled from 403,000 metric tonnes in 2004 to 720,000 in 2010 (indicating that export revenues not only stemmed from a rise in commodity prices but also from an expansion of production). Notwithstanding these buoyant mineral prices, the Zambian government did not benefit proportionally from the boom: because of an inefficient tax regime the government has been unable to extract large-scale revenues from the mining sector.[40] Despite copper exports making up some 70% of all of Zambia's exports, when in 2007 prices were close to their 2008 high, the sector only contributed 18% of total tax income in Zambia.[41]

In spite of the recent slowdown in demand for copper and the inefficient tax regime, export earnings are expected to continue to rise. Combined with tax arrears from the mines, this is expected to increase tax revenues, which are projected to more than double from the third quarter of 2009 to 2013, thereby increasing copper's contribution to GDP from 12.5% in 2009 to 17.9% in 2013.[42]

Moreover, liberalisation and the relatively stable macroeconomic environment have led to the cancellation of bi- and multilateral debts. In March 2011 this very combination led to Zambia's first sovereign credit rating (B+) from an independent international provider of credit ratings (later followed by another rating). These ratings allow the government to tap into international bond markets to finance public sector investments and thus to reduce dependency on its traditional partners. In the immediate aftermath of the positive credit rating, the Zambian government announced a $500 million sovereign bond to finance key infrastructure developments. As a result of the eurozone debt crisis, however, the launch was postponed to September 2012, when Zambia issued a $750 Eurobond, which has mostly been used to finance infrastructure (railways and hydro power).

Tentative signs of development space creation in Zambia

At the time of independence Zambia was classified as a middle-income country and therefore had easy access to non-concessional loans. It received very little aid and relied instead on incomes from copper, export credits, and equity and portfolio investments. Copper prices quickly fell and in the quest for 'modernisation' government expenditures continued to rise – largely financed by external borrowing. The result was that, two decades later, in 1984, Zambia had become the most indebted country in the world relative to the size of its economy.[43]

Most of these loans came from the IFIs and by the mid-1980s these institutions had laid down a series of economic conditions that needed to be met to receive loans, which limited the development space for the Zambian government. The 1991 multiparty presidential elections marked a further reduction of the sovereign frontier. Zambia's debt burden stood at $7.1 billion,[44] and the ruling party 'concluded that the only way to get the shattered economy back on track was to do everything possible to attract foreign aid and capital…Aid money poured in and the budget became more than 40 percent donor-dependent.'[45]

The frontier, however, was not static. Both Zambia and the 'traditional' partners constantly sought to move it. The Zambian government for its part sought to strengthen it by showing a reluctance to implement key policies, while the traditional partners pressed for constitutional reforms to reduce it. As the power relations were about to tip towards Zambia, the Highly Indebted Poor Countries initiative was introduced. From 1996 to 2006 this was the main instrument through which traditional partners controlled the behaviour of the Zambian government. It linked eligibility to the Initiative, and thus large-scale debt reduction, to the development of a Poverty Reduction Strategy Paper (PRSP) and demonstration of a track record of neoliberal reform. Moreover, it linked full and irrevocable debt reduction to the adoption of the PRSP. Two other key developments shrank the frontier: the introduction of the Harmonization in

Practice initiative in 2003 and the signing of the Joint Assistance Strategy for Zambia (JASZ) in 2007. While the former – a coalition of seven of Zambia's development partners – in theory aimed at harmonising practices and aligning them to Zambia's development priorities, thereby shifting the balance of power towards the Zambian government, in practice it dramatically reduced the government's possibility of playing off one partner against another. The signing of the JASZ did not change this. The idea was to align partners' policies closer to those of the Zambian government but, thanks to its design, it failed to change the power balance.

During the past two decades traditional partners have come to dominate entire sectors of the Zambian economy through far-reaching interventions and policies such as the PRSP, sector-wide approaches and budget support. In this way they have come to control more – not less – of the development process. However, recent events point towards a reversal of this tendency. The first of these is the publication in May 2007 by the MOFNP of an 'Aid Policy and Strategy for Zambia' intended to give the Zambian government a means to manage incoming aid and create a division of labour among donors. According to Fraser, the draft version of this policy contained 'strong assertions of Zambian sovereignty…[and included] a threat to refuse aid that does not conform to Zambia's preferred priorities', as well as proposing to set up a department to appraise 'all donor plans prior to accepting the funding'.[46] Central aspects of the policy, however, were removed from the final version and the Aid Policy never came to signal a real change in the sovereign frontier.

The second key development is the Sixth National Development Plan, 2011–2015, which follows the Fifth National Development Plan, 2006–2010. Although the process of drawing these plans mirrors that of the PRSP, and the priority areas to a large extent follow the fashion in the international development arena, the first draft version of the Sixth Plan was written without the involvement of donors. Only after the draft had been finalised did the MOFNP bring the donors on board for them to select the interventions they intended to finance.[47] The idea of a national plan is to 'manage and harmonise arrangements with donors', but most of the plans laid out in the Fifth Plan were never implemented. It was grossly underfinanced and ended up being a wish list donors could pick and choose from. In fact, the distribution of donor commitment to the 17 sectors singled out in this plan depicts a high degree of concentration in areas perceived relevant for the donors and an almost total absence of donors in areas low on the aid agenda. The Fifth Plan thus ended up being side-tracked by the traditional partners for a lack of government's own resources. Although the Sixth Plan is more detailed in terms of planning and monitoring, key areas such as infrastructure and higher-level education may end up facing the same lack of interest. Thus, although the terminology used in the plan and the genesis of the plan point towards more sovereignty, lack of human and financial capacity may undermine national control.

The third key development is the drafting of the JASZ II, which points to incremental changes in policy autonomy for the Zambian government. In the words of a civil servant from the MOFNP: 'In the JASZ the donors called the shots. In the JASZ II it is going to be different. Now, the government will drive the process and decide the division of labour among the donors.'[48] While the

Sixth Plan and the JASZ II suggest incremental changes in the development space for the Zambian government, the combination of availability of additional development finance and traditional partners' growing fatigue has also led to several confrontations between the former government of Zambia and said partners – indicating a movement of the sovereign frontier.

In response to the donors' reactions to misappropriation of funds in Zambia (see above) key political figures openly stated their anger over what they perceived as traditional partners' interference in internal affairs and encouraged donors to pack their bags. These criticisms include former president Rupiah Banda's charge in June 2010 that 'nobody asked the donors to help Zambia… [hence] we should not allow donors to feel that they can interfere in our internal affairs'.[49] A couple of days later Banda made another outburst at donors, saying that they should stop blackmailing Zambians: 'If somebody [the donors] is fed up with us, they should pack their bags and go'. His lashing out was a response to what he perceived as donor interference in internal affairs.[50] Only a few days later, Vice-President George Kunda reiterated Rupiah Banda's statement saying that donors should stop treating Zambia as if it was still a colony.[51] These statements were followed up by former Community Development and Social Service Minister Michael Kaingu who was concerned that donors were channelling funds through NGOs and not through the state apparatus, thereby undermining the authority of the state; and by former Works and Supply Minister Mike Mulongoti, who claimed that donors withheld funds because they wanted a regime change.[52] The outbursts did not stop with the change of government in Zambia in September 2011, when Michael Sata, of the Patriotic Front, took power. In May 2012 Sata criticised EU diplomats for interfering in internal affairs in Zambia. He was later backed by key leaders of some of the smaller opposition parties in the country.[53]

It is not only key ministers who see a possibility to vent their frustrations, but also civil servants in the ministries that traditionally have been closest to the traditional partners: 'At one point in time we had to agree with everything the donors said. Now we can disagree. The donors still act in a very coordinated manner but of late we have often disagreed with their policies. Historically, we were very dependent on the donors but over the years this dependency has been reduced.'[54] Civil servants thus have experienced a reduced role for aid from traditional partners in the budget and now have more control over their own policies. Simultaneously they appreciate the development finance from the NTSAs, which does not come 'with strings attached'. In the words of a high-ranking civil servant in the Ministry of Commerce:

> [The NTSAs] are pretty much who they always were and so is our relation to them. They just scaled up. It is still very much like Tazara days – just bigger. They provide loans to the treasury and the treasury then decides how to use the money. There are no Chinese expats here telling the treasury what to do. The Chinese have no project office coordinating the interventions. That is why we like that kind of support so much. It enables us to recognise own priorities.[55]

The outbursts from Zambian politicians do not necessarily reflect only the creation of development space but also the political competition taking place just before the presidential elections. However, in a speech to Boston University in

April 2012, former president Rupiah Banda reflected on the changing geographies of power and the resulting creation of development space, saying:

> the rise of China's presence in Africa, and the management of these East–West tensions, became an important issue for our government. When we were facing the challenge of financing, constructing and rehabilitating our infrastructure in the various sectors, it became clear that we needed to seek financing quickly, and could not delay our plans to develop the country. The rise of new financial powerhouses in Asia, as you all know, is producing a geopolitical shift…In some cases, we had successful partnerships with the West…However, in other cases, increasingly, our needs were matched by the Chinese. They offered the financing we needed and the technical knowhow, and so it followed that we should negotiate with them on certain projects.[56]

Importantly these signs of enlarged development space have continued since Michael Sata won the presidential elections. They include the decision to de-privatise the telecommunication provider Zamtel, a decision to take over Zambia Railways from a private company, a proposition to double mining royalties, the Bank of Zambia's ban on dollar-denominated transactions, and the public takeover of the Chinese-owned Collum mine.

Privatisation has been high on the agenda of donors for more than two decades and, even though the Zambian government managed to postpone the privatisation of the mines for some years, only a few companies have remained state-owned. One of the few remaining was Zamtel which, after heated discussions, was valuated and sold in late 2010. Just after the presidential elections, President Sata commissioned an inquiry into the privatisation process. The inquiry found that Zamtel was undervalued and it states: 'The Zamtel sale was a clear case of economic sabotage which pervaded and compromised key GRZ [Government of the Republic of Zambia] institutions to the extent that GRZ decisions and policy were being managed by a foreign consultant'.[57] Based on this conclusion, Zamtel was de-privatised. Similarly the Zambian government decided in late 2012 to take over Zambia Railways from its South African owner, thereby cancelling the agreement on privatisation.[58] The de-privatisation process does not seem to be stopping there. According to the Economist Intelligence Unit (EIU), 'The president, Michael Sata, has asked the Director of Public Prosecutions to look into older privatisations, including those of the Roan Antelope Mining Corporation, Kagem Mining, the Hotel Intercontinental in Livingstone and Lima Bank'.[59]

The Zambian government is not only flexing its growing muscles *vis-à-vis* its traditional development partners, it is also seeking to make foreign companies operating in Zambia work towards the country's overall development plans. To this end the government has recently introduced new laws which seek to increase the developmental benefit of the presence of multinationals in the country. They include a change in the tax regime, which entails a doubling of the mining royalties and a banning of dollar-denominated transactions to steer resource revenues through local banks, thereby minimising large-scale tax avoidance.[60] Likewise the Bank of Zambia Amendment Bill 2013 is now being discussed in Parliament. If passed, this bill will enable the Bank to better monitor and regulate foreign exchange flows as well as imports and exports.

Moreover, the Zambian government seems more eager to crack down on companies that do not abide by the new laws. The Zambian state recently took over the Chinese-owned Cullum mine because of 'gross abrogation of mining and environmental laws', of the failure to pay mineral royalties and of the killing of 12 miners.[61]

Conclusion

This article has set out to further our understanding of how and to what extent the rejuvenation of NTSAS' interests in Africa affects the Zambian government's ability to set, implement and fund its own development policies, ie to increase its 'development space'. It has shown that, although the financial flows comparable to aid from these actors are still small, they are growing rapidly. They are supplemented by much larger non-concessional flows that may also be developmental. And they come at a time when aid from traditional partners is becoming relatively less important. Therefore the rejuvenation of NTSAS' interest in Zambia has strengthened the sovereign frontier for the Zambian government, enabling it to draft its own development plans, finance key parts of the plan that previously could not be financed, and vent its dissatisfaction with the traditional partners. By furthering our understanding of how NTSAS have influenced the ability of Zambian political elites to exert power over domestic politics, the paper substantiates the conclusions brought forward in the African agency literature, which highlights how a variety of African actors is seeking to use the growing economic and political interest in their countries to leverage and structure the relationship with 'traditional' and 'non-traditional' development partners.

I have argued that not only is development financing from the NTSAS additional, its focus is also different. In other words, if we accept that what matters in terms of creation of development space is not aid per se but the availability of money for 'homegrown' development projects, then NTSAS' engagement is clearly fostering this process by making large-scale non-concessional borrowing available. The NTSAS broaden the view of development experiences. Their development experiences point towards a tailored development model that combines purposive state intervention with market-based economic growth and integration into world markets. While this type of development model is not yet explicitly prioritised in Zambia's development plans, the existence of competing visions and models may provide further impetus for new ideas in the long term. I have also shown that this money is intended to finance large-scale infrastructure projects – an area which was to a large extent neglected by the traditional partners. Finally, I have argued that NTSAS' direct impact on development space via development finance and competing development models has been reinforced by indirect impacts such as booming commodity prices leading to increases in internal revenue generation, economic growth, and access to international non-concessional finance.

All these interrelated processes affect the sovereign frontier and thus create 'development space'. However, a number of factors seem be slowing this process down. Most importantly Zambia has yet to develop a strategy *vis-à-vis* the NTSAS. Thus the Zambian government may easily end up pursuing random development projects proposed and funded by NTSAS such as China and India

(Brazil's aid is largely demand-driven) instead of homegrown projects. In this way Zambia may end up in a situation where the origin of dependence has moved – from the traditional partners to the NTSAs – and where 'real' development space is an illusion, as it is still being dictated by actors outside Zambia.[62] Moreover, it is debatable whether new funding possibilities and new ideas will change policies in the short to medium term – since Zambian politicians and civil servants may obstruct the potential for paradigmatic changes in visions, policies and ways of implementing policies.[63] Thus, at most we should expect incremental changes like the one described in the formulation of the Sixth National Development Plan above. It is also worth bearing in mind that the interface between the NTSAs and representatives of the Zambian government is relatively small – as the NTSAs prefer to deal directly with the State House rather than line ministries and decentralised entities. Consequently new ways of doing things and new ideas are not easily transferred to the people who work with these issues on a day-to-day basis. Notwithstanding these limitations, the article has also shown that the creation of development space was not limited to the Banda regime but has continued under the current Sata-led government.

In conclusion, the NTSAs have provided the Zambian government with more money to finance its plans and new ideas to feed into future visions. But change has been slow, incremental and episodic. In order to dramatically strengthen the sovereign frontier, the Zambian government needs to enhance its ability to define and implement policies of national relevance to social and economic development.

Aknowledgements

An earlier version of this paper was presented at the EADI/DSA general conference in York, September 2011. I am grateful to the participants at this conference, as well as to Stefano Ponte, members of the Development and Globalisation research group, Roskilde University, and an anonymous reviewer for their valuable comments. The support of the Consultative Research Committee for Development Research (Project 932) in funding this research is gratefully acknowledged.

Notes on Contributor

Peter Kragelund is associate professor in the Department of Society and Globalisation, Roskilde University. His main interests concern changes in the global economy and how these affect developing countries. In particular, his research has examined the relationship between foreign investments, development cooperation and local politics in Zambia. His work has been published in *Development and Change*, *Development Policy Review*, the *European Journal of Development Research*, *Journal of Modern African Studies* and *Review of African Political Economy*.

Notes

1. The term NTSA is preferred here over the more catchy 'emerging donors/actors' as none of the actors is new to development. Nonetheless, their role in Africa's development has been minimal in the past three decades compared to that of Africa's 'traditional' development partners – most of which are organised in the DAC. Hence the term 'non-traditional'. The last part of the term, namely 'state actors', signals their difference from the growing number of private actors engaged in development.

2. The term 'development finance' covers what is comparable to official development assistance (ODA), as well as other flows that may not be classified as ODA, either because they are not concessional (enough) or because their purpose is not first and foremost developmental. Flows of this type, which are characteristic of the NTSAs' engagement in Africa, may, however, be provided at highly competitive terms and may contribute to development.
3. Dreher et al., "Are 'New' Donors Different?'; Farooki and Kaplinsky, *The Impact of China on Global Commodity Prices*; Kragelund, "Back to Basics?"; and Reisen and Ndoye, *Prudent versus Imprudent Lending to Africa.*
4. Fraser, "Zambia," 299.
5. This research is part of a larger research project on the political economy of NTSAs in Zambia. For this particular subproject a total of 34 interviews was conducted with representatives of the NTSAs in Zambia (6), traditional bilateral partners (7), traditional multilateral partners (3), key ministries (8), members of the Zambian civil society and academia (8), and former special advisors to the Zambian president (2). Interviewees were chosen based on their perceived knowledge of the subject and their importance in key sectors of the Zambian economy.
6. Huse and Muyakwa, *China in Africa*, 40.
7. Buite, "Country Ownership."
8. Kragelund, "The Revival of Non-traditional State Actors' Interests."
9. Harrison, "Debt, Development and Intervention in Africa"; and Jackson and Rosberg, "Sovereignty and Underdevelopment."
10. Brown, "Sovereignty Matters."
11. Harrison, *The World Bank and Africa.*
12. Mohan and Lampert, "Negotiating China." See also Whitfield and Buur, this issue.
13. Corkin, *Uncovering African Agency.*
14. Feyissa, "Aid Negotiation"; and Grimm, *Aid Dependency.*
15. EIU, *Country Report Zambia: September 2010*; "Chinese Visit"; and "RB Commissions".
16. MOFNP, *Aid Policy*; and MOFNP, *Development Cooperation Report.*
17. Rakner, *Foreign Aid*, 9.
18. See also Bräutigam, "Aid 'with Chinese Characteristics'." The main point here is that, although most of the official finance from China is not to be regarded as ODA, it may indeed be developmental.
19. MOFNP, *Development Cooperation.*
20. In principle, only the Minister of Finance has the power to determine the conditions of a loan, but "this provision has been violated by ministry officials and diplomatic missions who have contracted loans...without authorization from the ministry of Finance and National Planning which only learns about this at point when the payment is due". Mwansa et al., *Responsible Borrowing*, 7.
21. Chileshe, *Chinese Debt, Aid and Trade*; "China gives Zambia K3.4 Billion"; "China promises Unconditional Aid"; "China gives Zambia $39 Million"; and "Chinese Projects Take-off."
22. Interview, MOFNP official, Lusaka, May 9, 2011.
23. Bräutigam, "Africa's Eastern Promise."
24. Interview, multilateral donor, Lusaka, August 17, 2010.
25. Interview, multilateral donor, Lusaka, August 19, 2010.
26. Interview, bilateral donor, Lusaka, August 19, 2010.
27. Interview, multilateral donor, Lusaka, August 17, 2010.
28. Cf. Bräutigam, "Aid 'with Chinese Characteristics'."
29. This is India's most important aid programme. It is based on a slots system to allocate aid. These slots are allocated to India's collaborating partners and reflect the economic and/or political importance India attributes to a given country. In total India channels some US$10 million per year via this programme, but African countries, including Zambia, only receive a small share of this. Cf. Kragelund, "Back to Basics?"
30. Interview, India High Commission, Lusaka, August 19, 2010.
31. ExIm Bank, "Export–Import Bank."
32. Bräutigam, "Aid 'with Chinese Characteristics'."
33. ExIm Bank, "Export–Import Bank."
34. "India set to Inject $5 bn"; and "Zambia Benefits."
35. Interview, Brazilian embassy, Lusaka, May 13, 2011.
36. Interview, MOFNP, Lusaka, May 3, 2011.
37. Interviews, bilateral donors, Lusaka, August 10, 2010, May 11, 2011.
38. Silwamba and Chilemba, "President Lula."
39. Adam and Simpasa, "The Economics of the Copper Price Boom."
40. Mining companies in Zambia paid taxes worth more than $2.5 billion in the first decade of this millennium. These taxes comprise company tax, PAYE, mineral royalties, export duties and windfall tax. Although the figure seems high, in 2010 company tax from all sectors of the Zambian economy plus mineral royalties from the mines made up only 14% of total tax revenues. On average the contribution of the mining sector to total revenues was 7%–8% in the first decade of this millennium. Haglund,

Zambia Mining Sector; Mwambwa et al., *A Fool's Paradise?*; and Mills and Herbst, *Africa's Third Liberation*.

41. Adam and Simpasa, "The Economics of the Copper Price Boom"; and Bova, "Copper Boom and Bust in Zambia."
42. IMF, *IMF Country Report Zambia*.
43. Saasa and Carlsson, *Aid and Poverty Reduction*.
44. Huse and Muyakwa, *China in Africa*, 31.
45. Fraser, "Zambia," 306.
46. *Ibid*., 318.
47. Interview, MOFNP, May 9, 2011.
48. Interview, MOFNP, Lusaka, May 3, 2011.
49. Chilemba, "Nobody asked Donors to Help Zambia."
50. Chellah, "Rupiah owes Donors."
51. Wangwe, "We have been Independent since 1964."
52. Kuyela, "Channel Funds to State"; and Zulu, "Donors are Seeking Regime Change."
53. Mulenga et al., "Sata is Right."
54. Interview, MOFNP, Lusaka, May 3, 2011.
55. Interview, Ministry of Commerce, Trade & Industry, Lusaka, May 4, 2011.
56. Banda, "Inaugural Address."
57. Zulu, *Report*, 4.
58. EIU, *Country Report Zambia: October 2012*.
59. EIU, *Country Report Zambia: February 2012*, 13.
60. England, "Zambia to Double Mine Royalties"; and Whitehead, "Zambia."
61. Chawe, "Zambia Seizes Controversial Chinese-owned Mine."
62. I thank the anonymous referee for drawing my attention to this important fact.
63. Interview, former special presidential advisor, Lusaka, May 10, 2011.

Bibliography

Adam, Christopher S., and Anthony M. Simpasa. "The Economics of the Copper Price Boom in Zambia." In *Zambia, Mining, and Neoliberalism: Boom and Bust on the Globalized Copperbelt*, edited by Alastair Fraser, and Miles Larmer, 59–90. New York: Palgrave Macmillan, 2010.

Banda, R. "Inaugural Address by President-in-Residence Rupiah Banda to Boston University," April 2, 2012. http://robertamsterdam.com/zambia/2012/04/04/inaugural-address-by-president-in-residence-rupiah-banda-to-boston-university/.

Bova, Elva. "Copper Boom and Bust in Zambia: The Commodity–Currency Link." *Journal of Development Studies* 48, no. 6 (2012): 768–782.

Bräutigam, Deborah. "Africa's Eastern Promise: What the West can Learn from Chinese Investment in Africa." *Foreign Affairs*, January 5, 2010.

Bräutigam, Deborah. "Aid 'with Chinese Characteristics': Chinese Foreign Aid and Development Finance meet the OECD-DAC Aid Regime." *Journal of International Development* 23 (2011): 752–764.

Brown, William. "Sovereignty Matters: Africa, Donors, and the Aid Relationship." *African Affairs* 112, no. 447 (2013): 262–282.

Buite, Willem H. "Country Ownership: A Term Whose Time has Gone." In *Conditionality Revisited: Concepts, Experiences and Lessons*, edited by Stefan G. Koeberle, Harold Bedoya, Peter Silarszky and Gero Verheye, 27–32. Washington, DC: World Bank, 2005.

Chawe, Michael. "Zambia Seizes Controversial Chinese-owned Mine." *Africa Review*, February 21, 2013. http://www.africareview.com/News/Zambia-seizes-controversial-Chinese-owned-mine/-/979180/1700242/-/joitl4z/-/index.html.

Chellah, George. "Rupiah owes Donors, Zambians an Apology – HH." *The Post*, June 30, 2010.

Chilemba, Patson. "Nobody asked Donors to help Zambia, says Rupiah." *The Post*, June 26, 2010.

Chileshe, Chilufya. *Chinese Debt, Aid and Trade: Opportunity or Threat for Zambia?* Johannesburg: South African institute of International Affairs, 2010.

"China gives Zambia K3.4 Billion Grant." *Times of Zambia*, February 10, 2006.

"China gives Zambia $39 Million for Roads." *Times of Zambia*, April 27, 2007.

"China promises Unconditional Aid." *Times of Zambia*, July 13, 2006.

"Chinese Projects Take-off Enlivens Government." *Times of Zambia*, February 26, 2008.

"Chinese Visit Pays Off for Zambia." *Lusakatimes.com*, March 11, 2010. http://www.lusakatimes.com/2010/03/11/chinese-visit-pays-off-for-zambia/.

Corkin, Lucy. *Uncovering African Agency: Angola's Management of China's Credit Lines*. Farnham: Ashgate, 2013.

Dreher, Axel, Peter Nunnenkamp, and Rainer Thiele. "Are 'New' Donors Different? Comparing the Allocation of Bilateral Aid Between non DAC and DAC Donor Countries." *World Development* 39, no. 11 (2011): 1950–1968.

Economist Intelligence Unit (EIU). *Country Report Zambia: September 2010*. London: EIU, 2010.
EIU. *Country Report Zambia: February 2012*. London: EIU, 2012.
EIU. *Country Report Zambia: October 2012*. London: EIU, 2012.
England, Andrew. "Zambia to Double Mine Royalties." *Financial Times*, November 11, 2011.
ExIm Bank. "Export–Import Bank of India." Accessed June 15, 2012. http://www.eximbankindia.com/index.asp.
Farooki, Masuma, and Raphael Kaplinsky. *The Impact of China on Global Commodity Prices: The Global Reshaping of the Resource Sector*. New York: Routledge, 2012.
Feyissa, Dereje. "Aid Negotiation: The Uneasy 'Partnership' between EPRDF and the Donors." *Journal of Eastern African Studies* 5, no. 4 (2012): 788–817.
Fraser, Alastair. "Zambia: Back to the Future?" In *The Politics of Aid: African Strategies for Dealing with Donors*, edited by Lindsay Whitfield, 299–328. Oxford: Oxford University Press, 2008.
Grimm, Sven. "Aid Dependency as a Limitation to National Development Policy? the Case of Rwanda." In African Agency in International Politics, edited by. William Brown, and Sophie Harman, 81–96. London: Routledge, 2013.
Haglund, Dan. *Zambia Mining Sector Fiscal Benchmarking and Assessment*. Oxford: Oxford Policy Management, 2013.
Harrison, Graham. *The World Bank and Africa: The Construction of Governance States*. London: Routledge, 2004.
Harrison, Graham. "Debt, Development and Intervention in Africa: The Contours of a Sovereign Frontier." *Journal of Intervention and Statebuilding* 1, no. 2 (2007): 189–209.
Huse, Martine Dahle, and Stephen L. Muyakwa. *China in Africa: Lending, Policy Space and Governance*. Oslo: Norwegian Campaign for Debt Cancellation and Norwegian Council for Africa, 2008.
IMF. *IMF Country Report*. Washington, DC: IMF, 2010.
"India set to Inject $5bn into Zambian Economy." *Times of Zambia*, January 27, 2009.
Jackson, Robert H., and Carl. G. Rosberg. "Sovereignty and Underdevelopment: Juridical Statehood in the African Crisis." *Journal of Modern African Studies* 24, no. 1 (1986): 1–31.
Kragelund, Peter. "Back to Basics? The Rejuvenation of Non-traditional Donors' Development Cooperation with Africa." *Development and Change* 42, no. 2 (2011): 585–607.
Kragelund, Peter. "The Revival of Non-traditional State Actors' Interests in Africa: Does it Matter for Policy Autonomy?" *Development Policy Review* 30, no. 6 (2012): 703–718.
Kuyela, Teddy. "Channel Funds to State, Donors Told." *Zambia Daily Mail*, October 13, 2010.
Mills, Greg, and Jeffrey Herbst. *Africa's Third Liberation: The New Search for Prosperity and Jobs*. Johannesburg: Penguin Books, 2012.
Ministry of Finance and National Planning (MOFNP). *Aid Policy and Strategy for Zambia*. Lusaka: MOFNP, 2007.
MOFNP. *Development Cooperation Report 2009*. Lusaka: MOFNP, 2010.
Mohan, Giles, and Ben Lampert. "Negotiating China: Reinserting African Agency into China–Africa Relations." *African Affairs* 112, no. 446 (2012): 92–110.
Mulenga, Allan, Lovely Kayombo, and Bright Mukwasa. "Sata is Right on EU Diplomats – Magande." *The Post*, May 14, 2012.
Mwambwa, Savio, Aaron Griffiths, and Andreas Kahler. *A Fool's Paradise? Zambia's Mining Tax Regime*. Lusaka: Centre for Trade Policy & Development, 2010.
Mwansa, Sydney, Goeffrey Chongo, and Chama Bowa. *Responsible Borrowing/Lending post Debt Cancellation: The Case of Zambia*. Lusaka: Jesuit Centre for Theological Reflection, 2011.
Rakner, Lise. *Foreign Aid and Democratic Consolidation in Zambia*. Helsinki: UNU-Wider, 2012.
"RB commissions $2bn Kafue Gorge Lower Hydro-electric Power Station." *Lusakatimes.com*, July 11, 2011. http://www.lusakatimes.com/2011/07/21/rb-commissions-2bn-kafue-gorge-hydroelectric-power-station/.
Reisen, Helmut, and Sokhna Ndoye. *Prudent versus Imprudent Lending to Africa: From Debt Relief to Emerging Lenders*. Paris: OECD Development Centre, 2008.
Saasa, Oliver, and Jerker Carlsson. *Aid and Poverty Reduction in Zambia*. Uppsala: Nordiska Afrikainstitutet, 2002.
Silwamba, Chibaula, and Patson Chilemba. "President Lula shares Brazil's Success Story." *The Post*, July 9, 2010.
Wangwe, Misheck. "We have been Independent since 1964, Kunda tells Donors." *The Post*, June 28, 2010.
Whitehead, Eleanor. "Zambia: Taking Aim at Tax Avoiders." *Financial Times*, June 21, 2013.
"Zambia benefits from $3bn Indian Investments." *Times of Zambia*, May 13, 2010.
Zulu, George. "Donors are seeking Regime Change in Zambia – Mulongoti." *The Post*, August 9, 2010.
Zulu, Sebastian. *Report to H.E. the President of the Republic of Zambia Mr. Michael Chilufya Sata of the Commission of Inquiry into the Sale of Zamtel chaired by hon. Sebastion Zulu S.C. Minister of Justice*. Commission of Inquiry into the Sale of Zamtel, 2011. http://www.scribd.com/doc/78559670/Zamtel-Commission-Report-Government-of-the-Republic-of-Zambia.

Diasporas as development partners for peace? The alliance between the Darfuri diaspora and the Save Darfur Coalition

Alexandra Cosima Budabin

University of Dayton, USA

There is increasing interest today in the relationship between diaspora groups and international development. As a stand-in for the domestic organisation in Keck and Sikkink's model of a 'transnational advocacy network', diasporas serve as important sources of legitimacy and first-hand knowledge to support the 'information politics' of host country NGOs; in turn, diasporas gain access to policy making around development and conflict resolution. But these alliances present a complicated picture of power and agency with unevenness across actors. Using field research on the US-based NGO Save Darfur Coalition and its partnership with the Darfuri diaspora, I argue that a host country NGO must balance its relationships across numerous stakeholders, including the diaspora, as well as short and long-term development needs. In addition, the strength of the alliance across actors may be influenced by the status of the diaspora and the home and host country contexts.

Introduction

In 2009 I attended a panel discussion, called 'The Darfur Debate', at Columbia University between Professor Mahmood Mamdani, who had written a book on Darfur, and long-time Darfur advocate John Prendergast. The panellists duelled over the causes of the Darfur conflict, the role of the USA and the international community, and the impact of advocacy efforts. During the question and answer period, numerous Sudanese in the audience came forward to express their dissatisfaction with the proceedings. One woman caustically stated, 'I'd like to tell the organisers of such meetings in the future: if you're organising anything about Sudan and Darfur in particular, please don't have three white men sitting there and talking about our issues. Don't. Don't. Because we're here. And some of us have been involved in moving the issue around Darfur since it started'.[1]

The proceedings of 'The Darfur Debate' made visible the marginalised status of the Darfuri and Sudanese diaspora groups as compared to the US-based NGOs addressing the fate of their homeland. As news of the Darfur conflict reached the outside world, advocacy groups and religious organisations in the USA mobilised under the umbrella of the Save Darfur Coalition (SDC), a non-governmental organisation, to shape US policy towards Sudan around humanitarian aid, peacekeeping, diplomatic efforts and censuring the government of Sudan. Initially the SDC's engagement with the Sudanese diaspora in the USA was limited, in spite of the existence of an organised and politically active South Sudanese diaspora. Meanwhile, the more recently arrived Darfuri diaspora had begun their own efforts to organise themselves in the USA to assist in peace and development efforts in their homeland. Over time the SDC improved its outreach and integrated Darfuri diaspora members as board members, staff, presenters and eyewitnesses to enable their participation in political lobbying in the USA. Yet, five years later, the Sudanese diaspora members were still resentful of any event that failed to include their voices. Debates around Darfur's fate were being conducted without the input of Darfuris or other Sudanese.

There is increasing interest today in the relationship between diasporas and other actors in international development. In possession of transnational linkages to their home country, diasporas are inclined to pledge assistance and remit various types of support from afar, goals that may be shared by some development actors in the host country such as NGOs. In certain situations less-resourced diasporas will seek to work with host country NGOs and their networks to coordinate strategies around advocacy efforts to support development interventions. As a stand-in for domestic groups in a 'transnational advocacy network' (TAN), diasporas raise the network's legitimacy by furnishing local knowledge and contacts, while remaining geographically convenient and cross-culturally conversant. But alliances within TANs exhibit an uneven distribution of power and agency across actors. Even though they represent the victim group, less-resourced diaspora groups have a weaker capacity to influence and shape policy 'asks' or the organisational strategy of a network. The NGOs play the part of the 'agent', the more powerful actor who 'acts' on behalf of the diaspora group. In this article I deepen our understanding of new alliances for development through an analysis of an advocacy NGO's attempts to integrate a young diaspora group into a TAN initiated in a host country concerning development issues around conflict and reconstruction in the diaspora's homeland.

The article is a case study of the relationship between the Save Darfur Coalition, the lead NGO for a transnational network, and the recently arrived Darfuri diaspora based in the USA. The TAN model offers a fresh lens for understanding the dynamics across alliances forged between a disparate cast of actors in their efforts to shape national and international policy making around human rights and development issues. In particular, the status of stakeholders such as a diaspora group, representing the 'domestic group' within such networks, deserves additional scrutiny.

The original conception of NGOs neglected diaspora groups as development partners, as well as the intricate dynamics across actors in the networks.[2] Subsequent studies have paid closer attention to questions surrounding legitimacy and representation in such networks.[3] In exploring transnational linkages, diaspora literatures around development have focused on home associations, remittances, coalition building and direct political lobbying in the host country.[4] Within the field of conflict resolution scholarship has primarily focused on diaspora participation in international processes or securing external political, economic or military support for the homeland.[5] Classic case studies of diasporas in conflict resolution have looked at well established groups with extensive resources and influence in domestic lobbying and international diplomacy.[6] Here, instead, I focus on the characteristics of a TAN case study, and then theorise from this about the capacity for a young diaspora group to influence policy making in the host country in order to shape interventions around conflict resolution and post-conflict reconstruction. By means of the TAN model and the role of 'information politics', I explore the possibilities and limits of considering diasporas as actors within TANs as representing new development alliances.

My data are drawn from three years of field research conducted primarily in the USA between 2008 and 2010, and which included participant observation and 50 semi-structured interviews. This article is based on interviews with board members, executive directors and outreach staff of the SDC and with members of the Sudanese diaspora in the USA. I supplement this with public campaign materials from the SDC, its main partner organisations, and newspaper articles. According to the 2010 census, the Sudanese population in the USA has around 40,000 members, of whom Darfuris number in the thousands. While many activists from the South of Sudan have been organising themselves since the 1990s, both in the USA and internationally, the Darfuris in the USA were slower to mobilise until the outbreak of violence in their region in 2003. Their fledging organisations were soon surpassed by host country NGOs, which formed a large and influential transnational advocacy network. While it might also have been desirable to have collected material from a wider representation of the Darfuri diaspora in the USA, outside the SDC network, this was not within the scope of this research project. Therefore this article mainly reflects the building of the alliance between the SDC and Darfuris from the point of view of the primary sources on the SDC (a centralised body with a professional staff) and extensive secondary sources.

To demonstrate how TANs may reflect the uneven power dynamics across actors, and how this limits the ability for diasporas to build alliances for international development in the host country, the article will proceed as follows. The first section will highlight relevant themes from the literature around diasporas, development and conflict resolution. I present the structure of transnational advocacy networks and outline a schema for examining the host and home country contexts of network partners, as well as dynamics across these partners. The second section reviews background information on the Sudanese diaspora, its politics and the outbreak of violence in Darfur. The third section tracks the SDC's attempts to integrate the Sudanese diaspora in the USA. The final section draws conclusions about new alliances for development by analysing the intricacies and challenges of bringing a young diaspora group into a TAN based in the host country.

The case of the SDC demonstrates the dynamics of integrating younger and less established diaspora groups into a TAN which are complicated because of their heterogeneous make-up, links to controversial political and military groups in the home country, lack of political skills needed in the host country, and limited financial resources. In the dynamic between the dominant Northern-based NGOs and their struggling Southern counterparts, there is a heightened awareness of the need to remain representative of and accountable to the true 'stakeholders' – the victims and domestic organisations in the home country.[7] Yet NGOs immersed in TANs must balance these stakeholder relationships with political expediency. I argue that, while diaspora groups serve an important legitimating role in the area of 'information politics' by acting as witnesses, credible sources of information and valuable links to home country groups, the NGOs dominate the partnership – directing the advocacy efforts, tailoring the campaigns to the host country political context, seeking out influential connections and furnishing support for the diaspora group. I maintain that there are negative consequences of these uneven alliances for the TAN's policy 'asks', which must balance short- and long-term development goals.

Diasporas as development actors within transnational advocacy networks

Definitions of diaspora groups vary widely, since the concept originally referred to the narrative of the Jews who were exiled from their homeland in the first century. Other prominent victimised groups include the Turkish Armenians, the Kurds and Tibetans who share 'a collective trauma, a banishment, where one dreamed of home but lived in exile'.[8] These days the concept of diaspora has expanded to encompass not just exiles or refugees but also economic and political migrants who create transnational linkages, as 'ethnic minority groups of migrant origins residing and acting in host countries but maintaining strong sentimental and material links with their countries of origins – their homelands'.[9]

Diasporas have attracted extensive consideration for their potential contribution as international development actors producing economic growth in the homeland. A rapid increase in international migration from 195 million in 2005 to 214 million in 2010 is just one cause.[10] The World Bank estimated that official economic remittances to developing countries rose to $372 billion in 2011, triple the amount of official development assistance.[11] This 'migration–development nexus' has impelled host country governments to regard diasporas as development actors who can contribute to aid effectiveness as sources of 'ideas about political, social and cultural change'.[12] Alone in supporting projects initiated in the home country, diaspora organisations operate 'often under difficult conditions and without external backup'.[13] Younger diaspora groups may attempt to mobilise on their own but with tepid results; for example, Kleist tracked the fate of Somali diaspora organisations in Europe that failed to coordinate beyond an initial conference.[14]

Diaspora groups may seek donors and assistance from national development agencies in the host country. To more effectively endorse development interventions from the host country, diaspora groups can adopt agendas and engage politically: at the local level diasporas create hometown associations to channel political and economic support;[15] nationally, diaspora groups form interest groups to lobby 'institutions of their host states to advocate causes for their home states';[16] at the transnational level diasporas lobby international governmental organisations such as the United Nations, the Organisation for Security and Cooperation in Europe (OSCE), and the European Council. But not every diaspora group will achieve the same level of influence: scholars speculate that determining factors include 'size of the community, the duration of their stay, their legal status, their level of education, their wealth', along with the 'national interest of their host country and homeland'.[17]

This article is concerned with diaspora groups as actors of development in the area of conflict resolution. Of course, conflict and development are closely linked and analyses of some key development indicators unsurprisingly reveal a relationship between conflict, fragility and poor development outcomes.[18] To date diasporas have earned a predominantly negative reputation in the international community for their activities in fuelling and sustaining conflict through arms and money transfers.[19] Nevertheless, diasporas 'can be *both* peace-wreckers and peace-makers' as Smith and Stares note, based on research from a variety of case studies.[20] Through linkages at the local level diasporas send remittances and other support to aid in post-conflict reconstruction and will contribute to political processes in the home country.[21] At the national and transnational levels diasporas will seek to engage in lobbying in the host country and, in international arenas, to weigh in on debates around the potential benefits of humanitarian assistance, which offers short-term solutions in the area of relief, or development aid, which takes a long-term approach for rebuilding the country and addressing underlying grievances. But, similarly to other local actors affected by conflict, diaspora groups face high hurdles to reaching these arenas and asserting their interests.[22] As Smith points out, 'diasporas without access to power of some sort, whether direct or surrogate, do not intervene in conflicts'.[23]

Advancing agendas and gaining attention for ongoing conflicts in both national and international policy-making arenas will also require strategic partnerships. Better established diaspora groups (eg Jewish and Armenian groups in the USA) have been more successful in their host country lobbying efforts, gaining political access without having to rely on coalition building. Shain finds that these groups, with their longer histories as diasporas, can be considered independent actors in conflict resolution processes.[24] Less established diaspora groups with limited financing and lower political visibility might aim for 'co-opting of NGOs at both the national and international level'.[25] But, as the case of the Save Darfur Coalition and its relationship with the Darfuri diaspora demonstrates, such 'co-opting' is not straightforward; diasporas and NGOs may build partnerships based on different interests and goals for development and conflict resolution.

Transnational advocacy networks

Focusing on the collective action challenges faced by an NGO as it integrates a diaspora group into a TAN offers a means of understanding and explaining organisational and advocacy strategies. Keck and Sikkink explore the impact of global advocacy campaigns by theorising around the formation and influence of TANS – actors with the goal of 'chang[ing] the behavior of states and international organizations'.[26] A TAN engages in global advocacy campaigns through protests, rallies, petitions, letter writing and lobbying. Coalescing broad support around a strong message is essential for attracting media attention and pushing a decision maker to respond to the policy 'asks'.

As originally conceived, the TAN 'boomerang' is a set of linkages sparked by domestic organisations that 'bypass their state and directly search out international allies to try to bring pressure on their states from outside'.[27] These international allies might include international and domestic NGO research and advocacy organisations, local social movements, foundations, media, churches, regional and international governmental organisations, and sympathetic governments. Nevertheless, there are situations where the domestic organisations do not exist or are suppressed by the state or other society actors; thus victim groups may not be able to forge effective links for transnational activism. In these cases diasporas may replace the position of the domestic organisation in order to represent a home country's issue.

These alliances within a TAN aim to be mutually beneficial: 'for less powerful third world actors, networks provide access, leverage, and information (and often money) they could not expect to have on their own; for northern groups, they make credible the assertion that they are struggling with, and not only for, their southern partners'.[28] However, 'such relationships can produce considerable tensions'.[29] Northern-based advocacy NGOs and a diaspora group may share the same larger objectives of shaping the behaviour of more powerful actors, but their interests will diverge in compelling ways, particularly in the pursuit of long- and short-term goals that underlie development and conflict resolution debates.

In the absence of strong links to the domestic groups in the host country, diaspora groups offer an important bridge by providing both local knowledge and the emotional pull of an injured party, making important contributions to what Keck and Sikkink call 'information politics', whereby TANs 'gain influence by serving as alternate sources of information' for advocacy NGOs operating externally.[30] As Wade explains, advocacy NGOs have, 'as a category, come to command more trust among the public in industrialised countries than governments, companies and the media'.[31] The active and visible presence of a diaspora, as a stakeholder, serves as an important source of legitimacy by validating the nature of the claims made.

Diaspora groups also offer a geographically convenient link to the nature of the human rights violations and conflict issues. There is also an emotional component to the accounts of local stakeholders: 'Information flows in advocacy networks provide not only facts but testimony – stories told by people whose lives have been affected'.[32] By providing witness testimony, diaspora groups humanise the facts of a situation, enabling advocacy NGOs to package the information in ways that showcase evidence, build public support and gain political influence.

For a diaspora group seeking access to more powerful actors in the host country and in the international arena, the potential to influence development interventions may depend on its ability to form an alliance with a TAN. One challenge for building strong partnerships lies in the make-up of the diaspora, which is 'rarely a homogenous community'. A consequence is that the NGO will have to grapple with 'conflicting political agendas in the homeland [that] may spill over into communities living abroad' and impede political influence in the host country.[33] In addition to a plurality of visions for the homeland, these agendas may include support and linkages to controversial military forces during conflict.

Diasporas seeking to partner with TANs in the area of development may also clash over temporal perspectives for the home country. Diaspora groups will adopt long-term views, while seeking to address short-term crises. But for advocacy around human rights violations or humanitarian issues the TAN will aim to present a succinct 'causal story' of the issue or situation at hand; nuancing an issue in terms of root causes will not be favourable for the needs of political advocacy and mass mobilisation. For example, Autessere has found that intervention narratives rife in TANs around 'conflict minerals' in the Congo drown out any consideration of the many other forms of local conflict.[34] Parsed accounts of development issues may play better for 'information politics' purposes but they mask the complex interaction of on the ground realities.

Finally, there will be structural concerns, particularly with a young diaspora group. Establishing a partnership may depend on an NGO's ability to locate and identify members of the diaspora. Moreover, the host country context will also place certain demands on diaspora members in terms of necessary language and political skills for advocacy activities like rallies and letter writing. Whether the TAN helps build skills within the diaspora group to foster autonomy and coordinate their preferences will depend on the dynamics of their collaboration. The following case study will show some of the conditions through which NGOs are aided and constrained in their partnerships with diaspora groups as part of a TAN.

The Sudanese diaspora in the USA and earlier activism

As a national diaspora group Sudanese have left their country as a result of political, economic and social pressures. In part, this can be characterised as an involuntary migration, a mass displacement caused by the various civil and regional conflicts that have plagued the country since its independence in 1956.[35] Over half a million Sudanese are considered asylum seekers or refugees; the main countries of asylum for Sudanese have historically been Egypt, Ethiopia, Uganda, Kenya and Chad, while smaller groups have taken refuge in the USA, UK, France and Italy.[36]

Outside Sudan the diaspora reflects the regional, racial, religious and ethnic diversity of a country categorised by hundreds of languages, dozens of ethnic groups and geographical distinctions. As one Sudanese scholar described it: 'how someone is identified frequently depends upon the social and cultural context of a given situation'.[37] Major societal cleavages run along the constructed dichotomies of Arab–African or Muslim–Christian, but there are numerous inter-ethnic clashes within and across regions. Various organisations on behalf of the Sudanese diasporas are titled by region, religious or ethnic group.

Earlier conflict in the western Sudanese region of Darfur between 1996 and 1998 produced dedicated activists in the diaspora with high hopes for advocacy.

One refugee from Darfur, Mohamed Adam Yahya, fled to Egypt and became chairman of an organisation called the Representatives of the Massaleit Community in Exile (RCME). Mr Yahya described the role of the diaspora in broadcasting the situation in Darfur: 'We are able, by our messages [...] by our literature and that kind of information, we are able to enable the outside to bring pressure over the government of Sudan'.[38] An open letter written by RCME entitled 'The Hidden Slaughter and Ethnic Cleansing in Western Sudan' reached the UN Secretary General and other human rights organisations. But this early activism failed to end harassment and persecution by the government of Sudan.

In the USA concern for the North–South conflict in Sudan had become an increasing feature of the political landscape. Emphasis on the religious angle of this conflict activated many in the Christian community. During the 1990s the Southern Sudanese diaspora, now numbering around 20,000 members, successfully cultivated the public response, made connections to key religious organisations, and achieved elite insider status to exert influence in Washington, DC.[39] The US government was sufficiently moved to take action: in 1999 the Congress condemned the government of Sudan for committing genocide in various parts of the country. In 2000 newly elected President George W Bush signalled early on that Sudan's humanitarian crises and ensuing cycle of conflicts would be a top priority for his administration and appointed a Special Envoy for Sudan. Following the attacks of 9/11 Sudan became a strategically important country and potential ally in the Arab world. To solidify cooperation with Khartoum, President Bush focused energy and resources on supporting the North–South peace process, initiated in 1989. In this period the USA also accepted 6500 Sudanese as refugees.[40] The example of the South Sudan campaign suggested that a combination of elite advocacy and mass support could produce beneficial US pressure on the government of Sudan.

More recently arrived, members of the Darfuri diaspora were fragmented in the USA before 2003, according to Dr Suliman Baldo, a Sudanese academic who worked as the Africa Director for the International Center for Transitional Justice in New York. Darfuris were clustered in a handful of cities and states; chain migration from Sudan had led to high concentrations of people from the same area or town.[41] Informal forms of organisation and support were mainly social or cultural. Dr Baldo explained, 'There wasn't much political activity'.[42] But this began to shift in 2002, when some members of the Darfuri diaspora formed their own transnational organisation, Darfur Peace and Development, based in Washington, DC and Darfur.

During the spring of 2003 reports began to surface with descriptions of a new pattern of violence in Darfur.[43] Rebel groups, often drawn from various ethnic groups, were beginning to attack government forces out of frustration over regional marginalisation and underdevelopment. In response government planes and a counter-insurgency movement sponsored by the government destroyed villages and killed Darfur's inhabitants. Amid the fighting nearly two million Darfuris became Internally Displaced Persons, while 150,000 refugees poured over the border to Eastern Chad. However, international attention was trained on the ongoing North–South peace process. In the USA the outbreak of violence spurred the diaspora to better coordinate action. Baldo emphasised that 'when the rebellion broke out, there was a sense of identification immediately'.

The diaspora organisation RCME spoke to the UN news and issued a press release focusing on Massaleit victims.[44] However, for the most part the Darfuri diaspora would not reach a broader audience for another year, and not without more powerful allies.

In March 2004 a UN Human Rights Coordinator for Sudan compared the Darfur situation to Rwanda's genocide in 1994.[45] Following this declaration mainstream news outlets like the *New York Time* began reporting on Darfur. Activated by the spectre of genocide and a potential repeat of US inaction in the face of Rwanda, different groups in the country began responding. The Committee on Conscience within the US Holocaust Memorial Museum (USHMM), which held a mandate to raise awareness in the USA and exert pressure on the government in order to address genocide or crimes against humanity, began issuing press releases on the threat of genocide. In June the USHMM convened a panel on 'Bearing Witness for Darfur', which included US Congress members, a representative of the Darfuri community-in-exile and a Holocaust survivor. The following month the USHMM issued a 'genocide emergency' for Darfur; this coincided with a US Senate and House of Representatives joint resolution that also described the armed conflict in Darfur as genocide.

Operating independently from these US organisations, the Darfuri diaspora was becoming mobilised. In June 2004 I attended a rally during a speech by the then UN Secretary-General, Kofi Annan, at Harvard University, where Darfur was referenced alongside other conflicts and atrocities in Sudan. The Darfur Peace and Development organisation participated alongside Southern Sudanese diaspora and anti-slavery advocacy organisations.[46] But the impetus for a broader coalition came from US organisations and advocacy efforts would soon concentrate solely on Darfur.

Save Darfur Coalition

The SDC was the outcome of a meeting hosted by the USHMM and the American World Jewish Service on 14 July 2004 called the 'Darfur Emergency Summit'. Initial concern among Holocaust remembrance and Jewish organisations was spurred by perennial calls to 'Never forget' the Holocaust, which also prompted anti-genocide action with the motto 'Never again'. On the day of the meeting over 50 leaders from a diverse array of religious, humanitarian and human rights organisations showed up. The assembled group released a Unity Statement and Call to Action elaborating the SDC's goals 'to raise public awareness and to mobilize North Americans and members of the international community' in response to the conflict in Darfur.[47] Of the dozens of organisations signing the Call to Action, only four appeared to be envoys of the Sudanese and Darfuri diaspora: the South Sudanese Community in America, Sudan Peace Advocates Network (SPAN), Darfur Peace and Development, and RMCE. The main responsibility for organising the SDC fell to an American, David Rubenstein, who had experience working with non-profit groups in the USA. His background made him the more US-savvy candidate for coordinating and building the coalition.

Independently of the SDC the Darfuri diaspora continued to actively insert itself into policy discussions and providing accounts to US media. The Darfur

Peace and Development's programme director, Omer Ismael, spoke to a couple of media outlets about the crisis in Darfur over the summer.[48] Just two weeks after the Darfur Emergency Summit, the *New York Times* reported on a new group called the Darfur Rehabilitation Project, founded by a Darfuri named Yahya Osman.[49] However, both these organisations would receive scant coverage, while the SDC would dominate the headlines. Nevertheless, Darfuris did assist in the preparation of reports that contributed to US Secretary of State Colin Powell's September testimony delivered to the Senate Committee on Foreign Relations, calling the situation in Darfur genocide.[50] Mohamed Yahya transformed the RCME into the Damanga Coalition for Freedom and Democracy but only began issuing press releases in 2005. For the Darfuri diaspora to reach a wider audience of both the public and decision makers the strategic course of action would be to partner with more powerful players in the host country.

The SDC was also seeking to link up with powerful actors and soon came to coordinate a TAN of over 100 NGOs, in the USA and abroad. In particular, established US-based organisations were considered critical partners – the expectation being that, with enough attention from the public, US decision makers would be moved to respond. Within two years SDC had opened offices in Washington, DC, built a staff of over 30 people, and was operating with a budget in the tens of millions of dollars, which was spent on advertisements, lobbying and campaigns. The cause of Darfur generated substantial student activism on campuses; this was in part thanks to the star presence of Hollywood celebrities like Don Cheadle and George Clooney.

As a mobilisation vehicle SDC amassed a membership of a million activists and built a substantial donor base, quickly becoming the largest US social movement since the anti-apartheid campaigns against South Africa. Rallies held in Washington and New York drew tens of thousands of activists, with contemporaneous events held around the USA and the world. The combination of elite advocacy along with its mass mobilisation earned the SDC enviable access to Congress, the White House and the US Department of State. Alongside its international partners the SDC also lobbied the United Nations, the EU and the International Criminal Court. These campaigns demonstrated the reach of the SDC as a TAN, raising awareness of Darfur and shaping international policy.[51]

This rapid growth was the result of a combination of factors: previous activism around South Sudan, a legion of bipartisan Sudan allies in Congress, the 10th anniversary of the Rwandan genocide, and the US designation of the armed conflict in Darfur as genocide.[52] Established US-based organisations had extensive outreach resources already in place, along with large memberships. For example, a coveted meeting held with President Bush at the White House in 2006 was arranged by a former Southern Sudanese advocate. Compared with other partners in the Coalition, the Darfur diaspora was just not as important in the US context in gaining access and generating public support.

Attempts at outreach

Despite the SDC's success in mobilisation, the partnership between the Darfuri diaspora and the SDC was slow to develop and did not appear to be a priority. First, there was the issue of finding and connecting to a diaspora spread across a dozen states in the USA. But this lack of engagement was not the result of Darfuri reluctance to get involved. Baldo described how, '[Darfuri] communities then started going to events organised by the US movement in solidarity with the victims in Darfur and to bring in a way the voices of the victims in events organised in parishes and on campuses.' Throughout 2004 and 2005, according to Niemat Ahmadi, Darfuri Liaison Officer for the SDC, the coalition did make efforts to bring Darfuris to protests and meetings with UN country-missions.[53] During the autumn of 2005 Dr Gloria White-Hammond, who had been active in the Southern Sudan advocacy efforts, joined the SDC Executive Board.[54] As one who knew instinctively that a successful mobilisation around Darfur *needed* to include Darfuris, Dr White-Hammond commented: 'The mantra was that any successful social movement to change the status of a marginalised people is led by those people. So where are they? It was really frustrating'.[55] As the SDC Executive Director at the time, Mr Rubenstein, described, 'We just didn't spend a lot of time reaching out to them at first'.[56] It should be noted that, based on conversations with SDC staff members, it seems there was also little energy expended in reaching out to grassroots groups in the home country of Darfur at this time.

Beside the challenges of locating a dispersed diaspora, diversity *within* the Darfur diaspora revealed that they could not be approached as a bounded and unified entity. Rubenstein recalled:

> There was as much conflict in a room of twenty people of the Sudanese diaspora as there was in any other meeting that I've been to. They just had different opinions about things and they had strong values. These are people who had a lot on the line, they had relatives back where they came from and wanted to do what they thought was best for them. A lot of them had political points of view that were different from one another.[57]

While not specifying these divergent points of view, the landscape of identity politics in Sudan provides some clues to the discord. First, there were different regional conflicts in Sudan. The SDC Outreach Coordinator recalled coordinating challenges as a result of 'internal Sudanese tensions between Darfurians and Southern Sudanese'.[58] The Southern Sudanese had attracted the support of numerous Christian organisations and their presence at the original 'Darfur Emergency Summit' signalled that these Southern Sudanese advocates were expressing solidarity with the Darfuris, who were mainly Muslim. But, as Darfur quickly dominated US public discussions, the issues surrounding Southern Sudan were becoming subsumed. The focus on Darfur rankled other Sudanese diaspora members. White-Hammond recalled: 'The South Sudanese…would come to these rallies and feel like "why are they only talking about Darfur, what about us?"'. Rubenstein observed 'the two [diaspora groups] were in conflict with one another to some degree'. As he put it, 'whenever we would talk about Darfur, people would talk about the Christians and the evangelicals. I had to obviously make clear that it wasn't about that. That was a different place in the same country.'

Additionally the SDC held reservations about some of the transnational linkages, which included supporting various rebel groups, for example by providing satellite phones so rebels could speak to media and human rights organisations. A former Field Organiser for a SDC partner organization, who coordinated outreach for rallies and speaking events and arranged the inclusion of Darfuris and Sudanese as speakers, described the challenge of managing these loyalties: 'While most of the major Sudanese activists in the United States are motivated by heartfelt concerns about human rights abuses in Darfur, many of these Darfuri activists have affinity toward or ties with one of the political parties or rebel groups'.[59] He described a hesitancy (among some US human rights organisations) to give a forum or political voice to everyone in the Sudanese diaspora, and the necessity of vetting speakers.

While the SDC raised the profile of the Darfuri rebel campaigns by publicising the issues in Darfur based on the reports from the diaspora members, they were hesitant to offer a show of outright support for specific rebel groups.[60] Human rights organisations had documented rebel attacks on civilians and disruption of humanitarian relief efforts, complicating the advocacy efforts of the rebels.[61] The risk, according to the Field Organiser, was that a speaker with controversial ties would have a 'negative impact on the reputation and image and legitimacy of the movement'. Rubenstein recalled trying to balance efforts to include the diaspora with the diversity of loyalties: 'we tried to get advice and wisdom and guidance from people who lived there. On the other hand, quite a few of the people we were dealing with had pretty strong ties to rebels. And our goal was not about to take sides on one side or the other.' Overall the SDC was not in a position to nuance the political pluralism and controversial loyalties within the Darfuri and across Sudanese diaspora.

As the SDC produced its own educational and awareness materials about Darfur, accurately representing the diaspora's various ethnic cleavages and pluralist visions did not serve the TAN's 'information politics'. To streamline messaging for t-shirts, subway advertisements and rallies, the SDC adopted general short-term positions on the humanitarian conditions, rather than endorsing the particular political platforms of Darfur's armed groups and engaging with the long-term development dimensions of Sudan's conflicts. According to staff members, the exigencies of human rights advocacy dictated simplified and uncontroversial representations. Rubenstein argued, 'I think overall we did a good job of presenting it evenly and fairly and helpfully. In ways that are clear enough to understand but not so specific as to confuse people or lose their attention. And it was very hard to include the opinions of lots and lots of people with different backgrounds in trying to tell our story.' The SDC's 'information politics' reveal that the advocacy NGO managed the campaign around educating the public about Darfur and made decisions to represent the conflict in a certain way for greater political effectiveness.

Legitimacy, advocacy skills and policy asks

Outside forces spurred the SDC to become more attuned to issues of representation and inclusion when the low profile of the Darfuri diaspora attracted negative media attention. When the proposed speaking list for a huge rally held in Washington in April 2006 was released, an article recounted how 'Sudanese immigrants objected that the original list of speakers included eight Western Christians, seven Jews, four politicians and assorted celebrities – but no

Muslims and no one from Darfur'.[62] This was quickly corrected: two Darfuris were added to the roster, although top billing for the event went to the Hollywood actor George Clooney. Such changes came fast: a protest held in New York five months later included representatives from 12 national Darfuri organisations. The fact that there were now a dozen Darfuri organisations signals their growing strength and visibility, but also their fragmentation. Again, top billing went to a non-Sudanese speaker, former US secretary of state Madeleine Albright. Here we see how powerful US players were more politically expedient to the movement than unknown Darfuri diaspora members.

For the first three years of the SDC's existence, the Sudanese diaspora was not represented on the main strategic planning body of the SDC, an Executive Board made up of members from its partner organisations such as the American World Jewish Service and National Association of Evangelicals. This Board made the decisions around distributing funds, coordinating events and crafting policy 'asks'. Many of these board members were leaders or NGOs and elite advocates, with access to major donors, membership lists and political actors.[63] The absence of Darfuris on the board doubtless reflects their low status in US politics; however, this absence resulted in a lack of diaspora input in the planning of SDC activities and the proposed interventions.

In mid-2007 the SDC underwent a shake-up amid criticisms of the Executive Board's strategy. After launching a massive advertising campaign that called for a more aggressive approach to the situation in Darfur, humanitarian agencies complained that the proposed course of action endangered relief efforts. The president of a coalition of aid groups stated in a letter to the SDC: 'I am deeply concerned by the inability of Save Darfur to be informed by the realities on the ground'.[64] In response the Board reorganised itself and added two Darfuri members and a Southern Sudanese member.

Another important institutional step came with the appointment of a native of North Darfur, Niemat Ahmadi, to the position of Darfuri Liaison Officer, in which she managed the relationship between the SDC and the Darfuri diaspora. Ms Ahmadi provided the media with lists of Darfuris to speak with and offered quotes from Darfuris in the USA and abroad. Facing criticism over a lack of connection to the situation in Darfur, the SDC was raising the profile of diaspora members and actively seeking their input.

Outside its elite advocacy efforts and marketing campaigns the SDC was also leading a large social movement, hosting numerous public events to raise awareness. Nonetheless, the SDC hesitated to put the diaspora front and centre because of the host country context – US audiences who favoured familiar faces from celebrity and political circles. When asked about the diaspora's participation in advocacy efforts, Rubenstein praised the work of one diaspora activist 'who tries really hard and really cares but is not going to be very influential on Americans in part because he doesn't have the American skills, doesn't have the American connections. That's not how people respond in this country.' The Field Organiser also observed, 'not everyone is comfortable speaking. Not everyone is a good speaker, an articulate speaker in English, is able to be illustrative in the way that they talk.'

In response to this deficit in presentation skills and to aid in diaspora coordination, the SDC hosted a two-day meeting of Darfuri activists in 2006. The event highlighted the need for 'an umbrella organization that addresses the holistic issues such as peace process, advocacy, civil society and movements unification among common denominators if not under one leadership', according to its first president, Ibrahim Hamid.[65] With the help of the SDC and International Refugee Initiative, the Darfur Leaders Network (DLN) was established in 2007 as an independent non-profit organisation 'of leaders from Darfuri civil society organizations of the diaspora located in the United States'.[66] Explaining its sponsorship of the DLN in its *2008 Annual Report*, the SDC wrote that it 'continuously works to amplify the voices of Darfuris, which are often drowned out' and that the DLN enabled the diaspora 'to advocate on Darfur with a united voice…these platforms allow Sudanese to articulate a way forward for their country'.[67]

However, the DLN faced its own hurdles to outreach and cohesion. In an interview Ibrahim Hamid noted that the Darfuri diaspora across the USA 'is new and dispersed', with its potential membership 'working hard in low paying jobs to make their ends meet'. In-person meetings were difficult to organise; the president also acknowledged that, 'within Darfuri community there are many differences in term of ethnic or political backgrounds. Therefore, it is hard sometimes to create synergy and harmony among them to build good working relationships.' These challenges echo those faced by the SDC, suggesting the inevitable difficulties of coordinating with a recently arrived diaspora with various social cleavages.

But the DLN did distance itself from the SDC by adopting more long-term positions on Darfur-related advocacy. The president described the development of a position paper in 2007 'that addresses the root causes to the conflict such as the devolution of power (power sharing, wealth sharing), restitution, land, etc'. The DLN then dispatched delegates to get support for the paper from members of the Darfuri diaspora in the UK, France and Belgium. Significantly this position paper went beyond the policy 'asks' of the SDC to concentrate more closely on issues of underdevelopment and post-conflict reconstruction.

Five years after its founding the SDC appeared to have more contact with the Darfuri diaspora. In its *2008 Annual Report*, it devoted a section to the 'Darfur Diaspora' under the heading 'Amplifying Voices'.[68] Ahmadi described how the DLN's position papers laid out Darfuri demands and also influenced SDC organisational strategy. But, rather than grapple with the more controversial aspects of the political situation, the SDC continued to focus on civilian protection and humanitarian relief. As then executive director Jerry Fowler notes, 'It's not necessarily our role to take any particular position on how [the issues of Sudan] should be resolved other than on the basis that extreme violence not be used against civilians'.[69] The 'information politics' of the SDC may have made more visible the presence of the Darfuri diaspora but did not nuance the policy 'asks' to reflect long-term development discourses.

A major policy shift did occur when SDC began to address Darfur as part and parcel of the turbulent situation in Sudan. White-Hammond recounted: 'Let's just say eventually we figured it out. One of the things that I knew was really important was acknowledging that it had to be all of Sudan. And you had to acknowledge that Darfur wasn't the first genocide.' The SDC policy 'asks' began to reflect this reality: postcards sent to US President Barack Obama in 2009 requested his ""unstinting resolve" to end the genocide in Darfur' while also asking for the achievement of 'Sustainable peace for all Sudan'.[70] A new campaign was formed under the banner 'Sudan Now', which lasted until December 2011; today the organisation is known as 'United to End Genocide'. The diaspora itself must have deepened its solidarity across regional divisions; the SDC Outreach Coordinator noted, 'Some of the most powerful stuff that I've seen has been Southern Sudanese coming and speaking out for Darfurians and vice versa'.

Conclusion

This article has used the model of a TAN to discuss diaspora groups as partners for development acting in alliance with NGOs. I have outlined the debates around diasporas and development, with attention to home and host country contexts, as well as the role played by a domestic organisation, or diaspora group, in contributing to the 'information politics' dimension of a TAN. These factors lay out the necessary contours to explain the nature of the relationship between the SDC and the Darfuri diaspora. I have presented evidence from semi-structured interviews with members of the Darfuri diaspora in the USA and SDC representatives, which revealed a dynamic partnership that over time became a stronger alliance. I have argued that a host country NGO must balance its relationships across numerous stakeholders, including the diaspora, as well as short- and long-term development needs. In addition, the strength of the alliance across actors may be influenced by the status of the diaspora and the home and host country contexts.

Darfuri diaspora members, without the resources and organising skills of more established diasporas, needed assistance in gaining political access. In building a network of different stakeholders, the SDC faced the initial tasks of mobilising public support and seeking powerful allies; these objectives did not hinge on diaspora involvement. Compared with other NGOs and political actors, the Darfuri diaspora was a weak player in the US political context, decentralised and fragmented. Suspect links to rebel groups in the home country also became a source of liability to the SDC. The SDC attempted a major transfer of resources in helping the diaspora build their own Darfuri Leaders Network but the SDC remained the lead organisation for the TAN, making room for diaspora inclusion and participation, but through the mouthpiece of a liaison officer. The SDC's resulting policy 'asks' for the most part avoided the long-term political, social and economic causes of the Darfur conflict in favour of addressing short-term humanitarian concerns.

It is clear that diaspora groups can be development partners in efforts to address civil conflict and post-conflict reconstruction efforts. Latching on to a TAN may involve a necessary learning curve but, in the end, diaspora groups will gain in resources, access and familiarity with the political context of the host country. Indeed, no Darfuri I spoke to complained about the relationship with the SDC; its contentious nature was only raised by SDC staff members. To Sudanese diasporas elsewhere in the world the creation of the Save Darfur Coalition demonstrated the effective engagement of the Darfuri diaspora in the USA.[71] Meanwhile, as a US-based TAN, the SDC did not suffer from the absence of diaspora voices; it amassed a mass membership, inspired fervent activism and gained access to political spheres like Congress and the White House. But holding a 'Darfur Debate' without a Darfuri on the panel is an insult to the commitment of the diaspora to assist in and shape the response to their cause in the homeland.

Notes on Contributor

Alexandra Cosima Budabin is a Peter McGrath Human Rights Research Fellow at the University of Dayton, OH. She holds a PhD from the New School of Social Research. Her work focuses on non-state actors in human rights and conflict resolution.

Notes

1. "The Darfur Debate," Columbia University School of International and Public Affairs and Institute for African Studies, 2009. http://www.youtube.com/watch?v=yGOpfH_5_pY.
2. Keck and Sikkink, *Activists beyond Borders*.
3. See Hudson, "NGOs' Transnational Advocacy Networks."
4. See Bebbington and Kothari, "Transnational Development Networks"; and Mercer et al., "Unsettling Connections."
5. See Smith, "Diasporas in International Conflict."
6. See Shain, "The Role of Diasporas."
7. Simmons, "Learning to Live with NGOs."
8. Cohen, *Global Diasporas*, ix.
9. Sheffer, "A New Field of Study," 3.
10. UN Department of Economic and Social Affairs, *International Migration and Development*.
11. World Bank, *Migration and Remittances*.
12. Kleist, "Mobilising 'The Diaspora'," 307.
13. Kleist, *Diaspora Contributions to Development and Reconstruction*, 2.
14. Kleist, "Mobilising 'The Diaspora'."
15. Mercer et al., "Unsettling Connections."
16. Koinova, "Diasporas and International Politics," 149.
17. Østergaard-Nielsen, "Diasporas in World Politics," 229.
18. Gates et al., "Development Consequences of Armed Conflict."
19. Collier and Hoeffler, *Greed and Grievances in Civil War*.
20. Smith and Stares, "Preface," viii. Emphasis added.
21. Al-Ali et al., "Refugees and Transnationalism."
22. See Mac Ginty and Richmond, "The Local Turn in Peace Building."
23. Smith, "Diasporas in International Conflict," 5.
24. Shain, "The Role of Diasporas."
25. Østergaard-Nielsen, "Diasporas in World Politics," 225.
26. Keck and Sikkink, *Activists beyond Borders*, 2.
27. Ibid., 12.
28. Ibid., 12–13.
29. Ibid., 13.
30. Ibid., 18–22.
31. Wade, "Accountability Gone Wrong," 26.
32. Keck and Sikkink, *Activists beyond Borders*, 19.
33. Østergaard-Nielsen, "Diasporas in World Politics," 227.
34. Autesserre, "Dangerous Tales," 10–12.
35. See Johnson, *The Root Causes of Sudan's Civil Wars*; and Iyob and Khadiagala, *Sudan*.
36. UNHCR, "Sudan".
37. Assal, "Somalis and Sudanese in Norway," 177.
38. Yahya, interview with author, March 16, 2009.
39. See Hertke, *Freeing God's Children*.
40. Rytina, *Annual Flow Report*.
41. At this time there were no refugees from the 2003 Darfur conflict. Any refugees among the Sudanese in the USA had received asylum based on other conflicts and evidence of persecution.
42. Baldo, interview with author, February 4, 2009.

43. Flint and de Waal, *Darfur*; Prunier, *Darfur*; and Natsios, *Sudan, South Sudan & Darfur*.
44. IRINnews, reported in Prunier, *Darfur*, 126. One such press release can be found at http://members3.boardhost.com/makongu/msg/183.html.
45. IRINnews, "Sudan."
46. "Anti-Slavery Advocates protest Annan's Inaction", *The Harvard Crimson*. http://www.thecrimson.com/article/2004/6/10/anti-slavery-advocates-protest-annans-inaction-as/. (accessed 4 January 2014).
47. Save Darfur Coalition, "Diverse Coalition issues Unity Statement and Call to Action on Sudan," 2004. http://archive.uua.org/news/2004/040805.html.
48. Cole, "Debate over Meaning of 'Genocide' delays Sudan Solution."
49. Kugel, "BROOKLYN UP CLOSE."
50. Steele, "Officials: Violence in Darfur Continues."
51. While significant Darfur-related campaigns took place in France and the UK, the US- based SDC would prove to be the wealthiest and longest-running organisation.
52. See Hamilton and Hazlett, "'Not on Our Watch': The Emergence of the American Movement for Darfur."
53. Ahmadi, interview with author, April 20, 2010.
54. Dr White Hammond, a medical doctor and minister, had visited South Sudan and founded an organisation for women called Sisters' Keepers.
55. White-Hammond, interview with author, November 14, 2008.
56. Rubenstein, interview with author, February 12, 2010.
57. Ibid.
58. Save Darfur Coalition outreach staff member, interview with author, November 4, 2008.
59. field organiser, personal communication, October 10, 2010.
60. Jumbert and Lanz, "Globalised Rebellion," 204.
61. See Hoile, *The Darfur Rebels*.
62. Cooperman, "Groups plan Rally on Mall."
63. Hamilton and Hazlett, "'Not on Our Watch'," 351.
64. Strom and Polgreen, "Darfur Advocacy Group undergoes a Shake-Up."
65. Quoted in Michelle, "Darfur Leaders' Network."
66. Darfur Leaders Network, "About." http://darfurleadersnetwork.org. (accessed 18 June 2010)
67. Save Darfur Coalition, *2008 Annual Report*.
68. Ibid.
69. Save Darfur Coalition, Postcard from "Be a Voice for Darfur" campaign, 2008. http://www.AddYourVoice.org.
70. Assal, "Refugees from and to Sudan," 9–10.

Bibliography

Al-Ali, N., R. Black, and K. Koser. "Refugees and Transnationalism: The Experience of Bosnians and Eritreans in Europe." *Journal of Ethnic and Migration Studies* 27, no. 4 (2001): 615–634.

Assal, M. A. M. "Somalis and Sudanese in Norway: Religion, Politics, Clan/Ethnicity in the Diaspora." In *Diaspora Within and Without Africa: Homogeneity, Heterogeneity, Variation*, edited by Leif Manger, and Munzoul Assal. Uppsala: Nordic Africa Institute, 2006: 165–196.

Assal, Munzoul A. M. "Refugees from and to Sudan." American University in Cairo, 23–25 October.

Autesserre, Severine. "Dangerous Tales: Dominant Narratives on the Congo and their Unintended Consequences." *African Affairs* 111, no. 443 (2012): 202–222.

Bebbington, A., and U. Kothari. "Transnational Development Networks." *Environment and Planning A* 38, no. 5 (2006): 849–866.

Cohen, R. *Global Diasporas: An Introduction*. Seattle: University of Washington Press, 1997.

Cole, Jacquelyn. "Debate over Meaning of 'Genocide' delays Sudan Solution, Experts Argue." *Kansas City infoZine*. http://www.infozine.com/news/stories/op/storiesView/sid/3037/ (accessed 8 January 2014).

Collier, P., and A. Hoeffler. *Greed and Grievances in Civil War*. Policy Research Working Paper. Washington, DC: World Bank, 2001.

Cooperman, Alan. "Groups plan Rally on Mall to protest Darfur Violence, Bush Administration is urged to Intervene in Sudan." *Washington Post*, April 27, 2006. http://www.washingtonpost.com/wp-dyn/content/article/2006/04/26/AR2006042602182.html.

Flint, Julie, and Alex de Waal. *Darfur: A Short History of a Long War*. London: Zed, 2005.

Gates, S., H. Hegre, H. v. M. Nygård, and H. v. Strand. "Development Consequences of Armed Conflict." *World Development* 40, no. 9 (2012): 1713–1722.

Hamilton, Rebecca, and Chad Hazlett. "'Not on Our Watch': The Emergence of the American Movement for Darfur." In *War in Darfur and the Search for Peace*, edited by Alex de Waal. Cambridge, MA: Global Equity Initiative, Harvard University, 2007.

Hertke, A. *Freeing God's Children: The Unlikely Alliance for Global Human Rights*. Lanham, MD: Rowman & Littlefield, 2004.

Hoile, David. *The Darfur Rebels, War Crimes and Human Rights Abuses*. European Sudanese Public Affairs Council, 2005. http://www.espac.org/darfur/darfur-rebels-war-crime.asp#18.

Hudson, Alan. "NGOs' Transnational Advocacy Networks: From 'Legitimacy' to 'Political Responsibility'?" *Global Networks* 1, no. 4 (2001): 331–352.

IRINnews. "Sudan: Gov't Stresses Commitment to Just and Peaceful Solution to Darfur Conflict." 2004. http://www.irinnews.org/fr/Report/49251/SUDAN-Gov-t-stresses-commitment-to-just-and-peaceful-solution-to-Darfur-conflict.

Iyob, Ruth, and G. M. Khadiagala. *Sudan: The Elusive Quest for Peace*. Boulder, CO: Lynne Rienner, 2006.

Johnson, D. H. *The Root Causes of Sudan's Civil Wars*. Bloomington: Indiana University Press, 2003.

Jumbert, Maria Gabrielsen, and David Lanz. "Globalised Rebellion: The Darfur Insurgents and the World." *Journal of African Studies* 51, no. 2 (2013): 193–217.

Keck, Margaret E., and Kathryn Sikkink. *Activists beyond Borders: Advocacy Networks in International Politics*. Ithaca, NY: Cornell University Press, 1998.

Kleist, Nauja. *Diaspora Contributions to Development and Reconstruction in Fragile Situations*. DIIS Policy Brief. Copenhagen: DIIS, July 2012.

Kleist, Nuaja. "Mobilising 'The Diaspora': Somali Transnational Political Engagement." *Journal of Ethnic and Migration Studies* 34, no. 2 (2008): 307–323.

Koinova, Maria. "Diasporas and International Politics: Utilising the Universalistic Creed of Liberalism for Particularistic and Nationalist Purposes." In *Diaspora and Transnationalism: Concepts, Theories and Methods*, edited by R. Baubock, and T. Faist, 149–165. Amsterdam: Amsterdam University Press, 2010.

Kugel, Seth. 'BROOKLYN UP CLOSE: Sudanese Immigrants see the Strife in Darfur, and feel the Pain at Home." *New York Times*, August 1, 2004. http://www.nytimes.com/2004/08/01/nyregion/brooklyn-up-close-sudanese-immigrants-see-strife-darfur-feel-pain-home.html.

Mac Ginty, Roger, and Oliver P. Richmond. "The Local Turn in Peace Building: A Critical Agenda for Peace." *Third World Quarterly* 34, no. 5 (2013): 763–783.

Mercer, C., B. Page, and M. Evans. "Unsettling Connections: Transnational Networks, Development and African Home Associations." *Global Networks* 9, no. 2 (2009): 141–161.

Michelle. "Darfur Leaders' Network: Diaspora Organizing for Peace." Change.org, http://humanrights.change.org/blog/view/darfur_leaders_network_diaspora_organizing_for_peace. (accessed 19 April 2010).

Natsios, Andrew S., and South Sudan. *Sudan & Darfur: What Everyone Needs to Know*. Oxford: Oxford University Press, 2012.

Østergaard-Nielsen, Eva. "Diasporas in World Politics." In *Non-State Actors in World Politics*, edited by Daphne Josselin, and William Wallace, 218–234. Basingstoke: Palgrave, 2001.

Prunier, Gerard. *Darfur: The Ambiguous Genocide*. Ithaca, NY: Cornell University Press, 2007.

Rytina, Nancy F. *Annual Flow Report: Refugee Applicants and Admissions to the United States, 2004*. Department of Homeland Security Office of Immigration Statistics, September 2005.

Save Darfur Coalition. *2008 Annual Report*, 2008. http://www.savedarfur.org/pages/annual_report.

Shain, Yossi. "The Role of Diasporas in Conflict Perpetuation or Resolution." *SAIS Review* 22, no. 2 (2002): 115–144.

Sheffer, G. "A New Field of Study: Modern Diasporas in International Politics." In *Modern Diasporas in International Politics*, edited by G. Sheffer. London: Croom Helm, 1986: 1–15.

Simmons, P. J. "Learning to Live with NGOS." *Foreign Policy*, Fall (1998): 82–96.

Smith, H. "Diasporas in International Conflict." In *Diasporas in Conflict: Peace-makers or Peace-wreckers?*, edited by H. Smith, and P. Stares. Tokyo: United Nations University Press, 2007.

Smith, H., and P. Stares. "Preface." In *Diasporas in Conflict: Peace-makers or Peace-wreckers?*, edited by H. Smith, and P. Stares. Tokyo: United Nations University Press, 2007.

Steele, Stephen. "Officials: Violence in Darfur Continues after US Genocide Call." Catholic News Service, September 14, 2004. http://www.catholicnews.com/data/stories/cns/0405043.htm.

Strom, Stephanie, and Lydia Polgreen. "Darfur Advocacy Group undergoes a Shake-Up." *New York Times*, June 2, 2007. http://www.nytimes.com/2007/06/02/world/africa/02darfur.html.

UN Department of Economic and Social Affairs. *International Migration and Development*. 2011. http://www.un.org/en/development/desa/newsletter/2011/march/feature.shtml.

UNHCR. "Sudan" *2012 unhcr Statistical Snapshot*. 2012. http://www.unhcr.org/pages/49e483b76.html#.

Wade, Robert. "Accountability Gone Wrong: The World Bank, NGOs, and the US Government in a Fight over China." *New Political Economy* 14, no. 1 (2009): 25–48.

World Bank. *Migration and Remittances*. Washington, DC: World Bank, 2012. http://go.worldbank.org/RR8SDPEHO0.

New development alternatives or business as usual with a new face? The transformative potential of new actors and alliances in development

Nicola Banks and David Hulme

Brooks World Poverty Institute, University of Manchester, UK

The state, market and civil society constitute the three main institutional domains of the 'development' landscape. Perceptions of these three actors have evolved over time alongside conceptualisations of what constitutes and best promotes 'development'. The array of contributions in this special issue points towards a worrying implication for the transformative potential of development activities and interventions. While the new diversity in actors and alliances brings new opportunities for development, we see the majority placing the responsibility for development in the hands of the state and market. Furthermore, the hollowing out of civil society – apparent from the lack of priority given to it in the Global South and the promotion of development as 'responsible consumerism' in the North – represents a missed opportunity for consolidating the progress made in the commitment to poverty reduction since the UN Millennium Declaration. Reaching greater transformative potential would require focusing as much on inclusive social development as on inclusive economic development. Doing so would tackle the big questions of power and inequality that remain among the root causes of poverty today.

Introduction

Richey and Ponte started off this special issue highlighting the fact that the new development actors and alliances are not so much 'new' as 'newly studied' by international development scholars. They highlighted several themes emerging from the presence of these diverse actors, including their creation of a new role for business in development; the constitution of consumers as development actors; the changing roles of state actors, elites and transnational networks; the role of celebrities as mediators of development; and debates around communication, images and representations in international development. Our aim here is to consolidate these foundations and reflections, and to draw upon the empirical case studies presented to reflect further on what these new actors and alliances mean for the conceptualisation of 'development' and the transformational potential of their development activities and interventions. In doing so, we consider the context in which these actors and alliances are emerging and evolving, and the scale and additionality of their activities in the broader 'development' sector.

The institutional landscape of development can be crudely characterised along the three pillars of state, market and civil society. Conceptualisations of what constitutes and best promotes 'development' have evolved and continue to evolve alongside changing perceptions of the relative roles of these three pillars. We situate our overview and synthesis of the new actors and alliances presented in this issue within these three institutional dimensions, which increasingly function at the global as well as national levels. Throughout our analysis we place an explicit focus on poverty reduction as a development outcome, reflecting not only our interests and expertise, but also the emerging centrality of poverty in contemporary conceptualisations of 'development'.

The rise of poverty in development thought

Concepts and priorities encompassed in 'development' evolve over time, shaped both by increasing knowledge and theorisation across disciplines and by how these theories are picked up by key stakeholders that drive the development agenda.[1] Poverty may have been a major factor driving the international development agenda since the 1950s but, with early development models focusing on the causes of underdevelopment and the need for economic growth, poverty reduction as the leading development objective is a relatively recent phenomenon.[2] By shining the development spotlight on economic growth, modernisation and, later, neoliberal thinking placed poverty in a subsidiary position, on the premise that subsequent reforms and changes would trickle down into broader goals of poverty reduction: a strategy since widely criticised for its neglect of poverty and human development.[3] The late 1990s and the UN Millennium Declaration marked a turning point for poverty, feeding into the subsequent adoption of the Millennium Development Goals (MDGs), which brought poverty to the forefront of international development.[4] While representing a global consensus on development policies and targets – even in the absence of a common understanding of what constitutes development or on the strategies necessary for achieving it – the MDGs are not radical, nor overly ambitious, having set aside contested concepts in favour of reaching agreement on shared goals and milestones.[5]

Tensions underlying the two main contemporary schools of development thought remain. From a neoliberal growth perspective the MDGs have shifted attention to social policy and may slow down the growth on which poverty reduction depends. From this perspective unleashing growth through markets must remain the top priority.[6] Meanwhile, structuralists on the far left maintain that progress made in prioritising poverty in the MDGs has been insufficient, given its conceptualisation of poverty as a lack of goods and services, its failure to recognise the need for the redistributive agendas necessary for tackling inequality, and its acceptance that global capitalism must remain the engine of growth and poverty reduction.[7]

With discussions on a post-2015 agenda underway, this special issue is a timely contribution to take stock of emerging actors and alliances and what these entail for poverty and human development in the future development agenda. To what extent can these actors and alliances be seen as a return to neoliberal ideas promoting economic growth (and thereby a *reversal* of advances made in bringing poverty to the forefront of the development agenda)? To what extent can they *advance* the poverty agenda by offering a transformative potential, focusing not only on material improvements but also social and political ones? These are some of the questions we seek to answer in the following sections. We discuss contributions to this issue by sector, judging how their emergence is changing or consolidating, and strengthening or weakening the perceived importance of the roles of the state, market and civil society in development. In doing so, we hope to see whether the evidence points to any convergence of the two main intellectual sides – neoliberal and structuralist – on the goals of development, and what this means for poverty.

'Bringing the state back in'? Increasing state sovereignty in developmental policies

Neoliberal growth models categorised the state as part of the problem of underdevelopment, arguing for a reduction in its size, influence and 'interference' as a precondition for growth take-off and acceleration. The state-led rapid growth successes of the Asian Tigers brought the state's role back into the spotlight, with these 'developmental states' seen to achieve broad-based legitimacy as a result of the broader societal impacts that growth created.[8] Regardless of an increasingly significant role for non-state and private actors in development, the state remains a key actor for its role in mobilising the resources necessary for the discharge of its public functions,[9] and in shaping social, economic and political processes and institutions.[10] This has led to calls that any post-MDG agenda should emphasise the importance and role of a capacitated state as the main driver of development.[11]

However, the scope for national governments to influence their development agenda has been limited by a lack of resources and the side-lining of national ownership that has occurred through an over-emphasis on the role of foreign aid in strategies and processes for poverty reduction. Donor–state 'partnerships' mask power relationships that remain balanced away from recipient governments. Furthermore, the aid which they receive is tied to certain conditionalities that seek to address externally identified governance problems such as unstable and undemocratic political systems, pervasive corruption, human and civil rights abuses, and state breakdowns or failures.[12]

Three papers in this collection address the role of new development actors and alliances in expanding the space and capacity of states to determine development outcomes. As we engage with here, Kragelund explores the space for increased state sovereignty through the increased influence of non-traditional donors such as China, India and Brazil, while Whitfield and Buur, and McGoey (as we discuss in the next section), explore the expansion of the developmental roles and capacities of states through partnerships with ruling elites and philanthrocapitalists, respectively.

In his paper Kragelund explores how new sources of development finance may be expanding sovereignty and national control over the development process in the context of Zambia. Africa houses more countries that rely on foreign aid for a significant share of income than any other continent, with aid conditional on recipient countries pursuing policies and governance reforms that donors identify as necessary for promoting growth and reducing poverty.[13] Given the difficulties this dependency creates for recipient governments to secure control over negotiations and outcomes of conditionalities, states pursue different strategies to enhance their sovereign rights, including, as Kragelund shows, searching for unconditional assistance from non-traditional donors.

While the majority of discussions on emerging powers focus on China, India and Brazil, a much broader range of countries has growing influence on the world economy and politics. The N-11 countries of Egypt, Bangladesh, Indonesia, Iran, South Korea, Mexico, Nigeria, Pakistan, Philippines, Turkey and Vietnam have potential agenda-setting power for the future, alongside no intention of conforming to or subordinating themselves to the current 'Concert of Great Powers' agreed between a small number of countries.[14] More than 30 donor countries operate outside the Development Assistance Committee (DAC), but there is not yet sufficient evidence to decisively tell us whether the increasing emergence of non-DAC donors does and will offer alternative forms of development finance that means conditionalities can be avoided.[15] Kragelund's evidence emphasises that it is not only increased resources, but also the perceived importance of additional finance flows that generates greater state sovereignty. Non-financial resources also play a role, as in the ability of countries like Brazil to showcase an alternative pathway to development that achieves growth and poverty reduction while shunning neoliberal models.

While the increasing emergence of these non-traditional donors is commonly discussed as *the* factor that will trigger a change in power relations between African states and 'traditional' donors, Kragelund argues that it is difficult to see these resources as substitutes, both in the scale and forms of assistance. Whether measured as grants, loans or technical cooperation, the activities of non-traditional donors remain small relative to traditional donors, and the nature of finance flows themselves means that they are inherently different offerings from traditional aid, rather than a replacement.[16] As Kragelund highlights, these differences mean that these new forms of assistance do not follow guidelines regarding definitions and disclosures of aid volumes and engage directly with State House (rather than being processed through the Ministry of Finance), which is not obliged to disclose information on the scope and magnitude of grants to ministries. Bypassing ministries and the civil service weakens the development of institutions that have been identified as key to successful state-donor negotiations, including professional civil services, capable state and planning institutions, and centralised aid management systems.[17] It is unsurprising that these new forms of development assistance create tension between traditional and non-traditional development partners, with traditional donors seeing these changes as 'propping up' the institutional weaknesses and distortions they seek to challenge, or as 'undoing' the changes they are trying to institutionalise in terms of discipline in financial management and accountability. The influence of these new actors on the broader development agenda, including poverty, is also unclear. While development assistance from DAC countries has focused increasingly on poverty since the 1990s, development assistance from non-DAC donors is not influenced by recipient country poverty levels (as measured by GDP per capita), but more on the preferences of national leaders.[18]

Positive developmental outcomes may not be assured under financing arrangements from non-traditional donors, but this is by no means an argument against greater state autonomy and national ownership in development policies. Instead, it highlights the need to advocate that greater state autonomy be met with institutions and processes that ensure good governance. While traditional donors have pursued this by encouraging discipline in financial management, accountability and other aspects of governance, missing from this perspective is the role and importance of a vibrant civil society in holding government to account and legitimising their choice of developmental strategies, as we will return to in our concluding section.

New alliances for enhancing developmental states

Recent work has demonstrated not only that 'institutions matter', but that institutions are absolutely fundamental to successful social and economic development outcomes.[19] The state, its politics and national political systems play an important role in shaping the institutions that drive economic growth, acting as a tool for highlighting their credible commitment to engage in production without expropriating rents.[20] Whitfield and Buur's and McGoey's articles present analyses of two alliances that influence these processes, namely alliances between ruling elites and domestic productive sectors, and between governments and philanthrocapitalists. Again, these alliances are not 'new' in absolute terms. State–business relations and industrial policy have long been recognised as a key component of the developmental state story,[21] and while we have witnessed a major scale-up and diversification in global giving, foundations such as Rockefeller and Ford have been operating for nearly a century to promote human development and social well-being across the globe. Their contributions, however, bring insight into the new configurations that these alliances are taking, and their potential to enhance the developmental roles of states.

Whitfield and Buur analyse the cocoa and sugar industries in Ghana and Mozambique to explore the conditions under which alliances between ruling elites and domestic productive sectors can be 'developmental'. Such analysis is an important step forward in understanding the political determinants of economic growth. This is crucial in overcoming the ongoing emphasis on the determinants of long-run average economic growth rates, which comes at a cost of overlooking the political dynamics of economic growth and a limited understanding of within-country growth patterns.[22] As Whitfield and Buur explain, political survival is the main motivation for ruling elites, underlining the policies they choose to implement, the alliances they choose to enter, the sectors and industries they choose to support, and their interactions with productive capitalists and state bureaucrats. Crucially Whitfield and Buur show that close relationships can, under certain conditions, lead to positive outcomes in terms of economic growth. They show that alliances between strong ruling elites and domestic productive sectors were able to drive the rehabilitation of the declining sugar industry in Mozambique and have been central to the success of Ghana's cocoa sector. This happened through taking advantage of mutual interests within these alliances, bureaucratic 'pockets of efficiency' arising from well managed factional interests, and state–capitalist relationships that offered productive incentives.

Those alliances which focus on economic growth and sectoral invigoration actually signal a shift away from pro-poor growth towards another version of 'trickle-down' economics that justifies inequalities on the basis of growth. While the case studies in Whitfield and Buur illustrate how alliances can shape government policy and actions for the developmental 'good', there is no assurance that all alliances will share these common characteristics and outcomes. Indeed, these same characteristics could be used for the 'bad' by a predatory interest group. Close ties between business and government are often exclusionary and discriminatory and, most commonly, it is labour and civil society that are weak and excluded in the process.[23] There is little discussion in Whitfield and Buur's article of whether and how the benefits to growth will be distributed to low-income groups. Yet, as decades of experience have shown, growth is not automatically or necessarily inclusive,[24] necessitating the redistribution of its benefits for pro-poor growth to occur and for development to be inclusive. Moving forward would require not only identifying groups that can promote and advance economic development, but also identifying the processes and groups that are likely to facilitate more inclusive political and social institutions and backing the processes that embrace these.

Whitfield and Buur outline a theory for how alliances can contribute to the creation of inclusive economic institutions, but we also need to recognise that, without additional inclusive *social* institutions that allow broader citizen participation and greater accountability and responsiveness of elected officials, improved economic outcomes are not likely to be joined with improved social outcomes.[25] Understanding the political, institutional and political economy conditions that lead to developmental states and elite commitment to *inclusive* growth and development is an important gap in our existing knowledge.[26]

In her analysis of the 'philanthrocapitalist turn', McGoey argues that changes in scale and modus operandi in the field of philanthropy offer an additional alliance through which governments can expand their developmental role. She demonstrates that, contrary to the decline of the state's role in development that some infer from the rise of philanthrocapitalism, state support is integral to this process, both as a key source of funding for fledgling and established businesses and, somewhat ironically, as a justification for philanthropic movements on the basis of inept and waning government policies. This latter justification, of course, allows little scope for any form of partnership in such 'alliances', and would instead seem some confirmation of beliefs that philanthropy plays an important role in making up for state and market failure. The case studies of increased financial support that she highlights – namely the UK's Department for International Development's (DFID) financial support to Vodafone's M-Pesa scheme in Kenya – are from developed countries, illustrating new forms of development assistance from the North made possible by the philanthropic turn, rather than any increased power, commitment or developmental capacity of the state in recipient countries.

More worrying for the developmental capacity of states, perhaps, are the dangers posed to accountability in national and global arenas by the excessive voice and political influence of unelected and unaccountable stakeholders in national and international development agendas. As McGoey highlights, the Gates Foundation has reshaped the global health research and agenda-setting landscape, and it is these policy-making and agenda-setting powers that constitute the most controversial aspect of philanthrocapitalism.[27] We must try to understand the repercussions of a situation in which charitable foundations have a greater sway in health policy than health ministries in some developing countries, setting agendas by their global priorities and values rather than in-country needs, and thereby displacing the roles of state and civil society in designing, implementing and contesting policies and programmes. With global foundations lacking accountability and responsiveness to stakeholders in recipient countries, this also leaves no role for civil society to hold them to account for their developmental policies and outcomes.

A role for civil society would require greater representation and participation of those whom agendas, policies and programmes seek to benefit, whether implemented by the state, NGOs, or philanthrocapitalist foundations. A role for civil society would also encourage and enforce greater accountability in their implementation. However, this form of downward accountability is weak amongst philanthrocapitalists and public–private partnerships, particularly when international in scope.[28] Philanthropists, and especially philanthrocapitalists, favour upwards accountability to themselves. McGoey's paper also highlights another way in which the philanthrocapitalist turn is changing the development landscape, through the rise of business-oriented philanthropy and the use of the market to tackle social problems, as we discuss in the next section.

Markets for development?

Major global development institutions such as the UN have endorsed a policy of proactively engaging business in development since the 1990s.[29] Papers by McGoey and by Blowfield and Dolan both discuss actors and alliances that are promoting development through market-based solutions. McGoey explores how public–private partnerships allow philanthrocapitalists to champion market-based solutions to health and development in order to remedy market failures in the provision of basic services or treatments. Blowfield and Dolan explore possibilities and probabilities of different forms of business as a development agent.

In the early twenty-first century the field of philanthropy changed dramatically in scale and modus operandi. A new generation of philanthrocapitalists has opened charitable foundations underpinned by business management and organisational techniques that have transformed philanthropy into a lucrative industry in itself and brought 'for-profit' management techniques into the 'not-for-profit' sector. Both these channels aim to find solutions to social problems through business and the market via 'creative capitalism', which encompasses, among others, corporate social responsibility, triple bottom line accounting, and 'bottom of the pyramid' interventions, arguing that their solutions will be more sustainable because the market is a superior mechanism for generating and sustaining large-scale social and economic change.[30] This has led to a large increase in the engagement of the private sector in development programmes through public–private partnerships (PPPs) and new financing mechanisms.

While, theoretically, the diverse initiatives encompassed within 'bottom billion capitalism' put poverty at the forefront of objectives, capitalist structures, processes and beliefs remain at the core of these development 'solutions', so it is difficult to view them as a genuine development alternative. What is different about these approaches, Blowfield and Dowlan explain, is that, while based on the foundations of neoliberal values of competition, efficiency and self-governance, they are also premised on an ideology of inclusion, seeking to democratise access to markets and to extend opportunities for finance capital, income and affordable goods and services to those who have been excluded from these or included on unfavourable terms.

We have argued elsewhere about the difficulties even NGOs face in prioritising downwards accountability to beneficiaries and recipients.[31] If NGOs have battled with accountability to the poor, can we expect these other actors, whose interests and priorities are less naturally aligned with excluded groups, to have greater success? Similarly to problems of accountability in the philanthocapitalist turn, developmental accountability is rare in business initiatives for development. Blowfield and Dolan advocate an alternative model that is built around and judged upon what it achieves for its primary beneficiaries – the poor – who to date have been forced to conform to the requirements of business and have been incidental to acting out the role of development agent. Another concern they illustrate is that it is hard to measure the social benefits and limitations of these projects until well after investment. Microfinance now offers profitable returns to investors after years of funding and subsidies, but this is accompanied by the growing realisation of the social problems that accompany microfinance as a for-profit service and the fact that there is limited evidence to identify its positive impact on poverty reduction.[32]

The creativity that capitalism encourages has meant that the unleashing of market forces has led different actors to evolve in new ways, extending their roles to become legitimate development actors. A level of pragmatism has also been reached in this broad acceptance of their role as new development actors: they have huge voice, lobbying power and political influence, and developing countries have no alternative but to work with them, and certainly not against them. We would argue that one inherent paradigm shift is that these actors and alliances have all emerged in opposition to the broad acceptance that inequality is a good – or at least justifiable – thing. There is growing recognition, amid an unprecedented concentration of incomes in the hands of the rich across the globe, that inequality can be 'inefficient' for growth – particularly in the most unequal countries – and reflects market and government failures (such as cronyism and corruption) that also reduce growth.[33] The concept of poverty, however, is hushed in papers discussing the roles of the state, the market and state–market alliances as development actors, relegating, in line with neoliberal theories and models, poverty reduction to a secondary outcome that occurs after initial objectives of economic growth and wealth creation are met.

For 'development' to generate successful economic *and* social outcomes requires a paradigm shift away from 'development' as an economic process that extends access to goods and services to otherwise marginalised groups, and towards an economic *and* social process that also facilitates redistributions of power, representation and accountability, and more inclusive social, economic and political institutions. This highlights the importance of a vibrant civil society with the capacity to contest neoliberal dominance and push for a stronger structuralist development agenda that seeks to transform societal relations and address issues of power and inequality. The evidence on emerging development actors and alliances in the civil society domain presented here, however, does not offer significant hope that such change is taking place. As the next section discusses, there is evidence neither of efforts to strengthen civil society at the local or national level in developing countries, nor of a strengthened global civil society that engages with these core issues. Instead, the articles presented in this collection suggest that global civic action is becoming increasingly based around charity and socially responsible consumption.

The hollowing out of local and global civil society?

Outside the market and the state, civil society is the arena in which people and associations mobilise around common concerns, to challenge and uphold ideological hegemony and the existing social order. It is not the participating civil society organisations (CSOs) themselves, but the space in which they are formed and participate in dialogue and negotiations to advance their interests, that constitutes 'civil society'.[34] Following the state-driven and market-led ideologies of earlier times, 'strengthening civil society' became an explicit policy objective in the 'good governance'-focused development agenda of the 1990s. While civil society actors are incredibly diverse – ranging from community or grassroots associations, to volunteer movements, social movements, cooperatives, labour unions, professional groups, religious organisations, advocacy and development NGOs, formal non-profits, social enterprises, foundations, church groups and think-tanks, among others – the new development actors we see emerging here within civil society are restricted to the global, not local or national, realm. Earlier we discussed the increased scale and influence of philanthropists as they become major players on the development scene. The other roles allocated to civil society by the development actors presented here are also at the global level, including global citizens as 'concerned consumers' (see articles by Ponte and Richey; Kothari) or global advocates for justice and poverty reduction in the developing world (see papers by Brockington; Budabin). We ask what this implies for civil society in terms of loss of diversity and transformative potential, when civic action and engagement with real world issues becomes charity-based around socially responsible consumption.

The new philanthrocapitalist turn has not only brought new resources to the international development arena. New actors have, armed with vast capital and networking capabilities, been able to bring new ways of thinking and disseminating information and ideas to a broad audience using heavy branding, new technologies and celebrity advocates.[35] Under a capitalist system marketing and advertising have become legitimate *and* essential activities. Kothari's paper on the Empire Marketing Board illustrates an early example of how business interests combined public needs, interests and values in order to sell more goods, raising consumer consciousness through the use of popular and visual representations of development issues in their branding and marketing strategy.

While development imagery has been a long – and sometimes controversial – means of generating charitable support, Ponte and Richey highlight the difference between selling ideas of development and using imaginaries of development to sell products to Northern consumers. In both papers the authors show the process through which marketing campaigns old and new place the role and responsibility for social and economic development in the hands of British or Western consumers. Kothari details the superiority of the British invoked by Empire Marketing Board advertisements. Likewise Ponte and Richey explore how companies can use development imagery and the commodification of development to cultivate a sentiment of 'heroism' in which consumers feel responsible for successful development outcomes in the global South. Also problematic in these strategies is the fact that development causes must be presented in compelling yet simple ways, which swallows the complexity of these issues. In doing this, Ponte and Richey argue, 'development' becomes a world in which buying shoes or collecting vouchers become 'solutions' to poverty and underdevelopment. Although initiatives that extend immunisations, distribute malaria bed nets or educate children in developing countries can unarguably be defined as 'development goods', these strategies and priorities still meet market-based ends. None of the causes marketed or the products sold seeks to address the complex structural difficulties of poverty and underdevelopment that a genuine development alternative would promote. Placing responsibility for solutions in the West, these campaigns take responsibility and capability away from the people and places that the campaigns seek to represent and, in doing so, undermine civil society. Furthermore, Kothari notes, these strategies do not just 'sell' the product, they also sell the *cause* and justify the need for ongoing interventions or charitable consumerism from the West. This goes some way to illustrating why civil society groups have always been suspicious of the role of business in development:[36] not only on the premise that businesses are 'pushing in' but because, in the process, civil society is being 'pushed out' of the development arena.

One popular strategy of such 'Brand Aid' initiatives is to consolidate these messages by using celebrities to provide compelling stories to capture public interest and to legitimise development 'causes'. Brockington examines how, by using celebrities in their advocacy and activities, NGOs are changing the way that the public views development issues. He reveals the complex political economy that emerges from these relationships and some worrying trends that they threaten. Not only does this strategy further consolidate the trend of development through consumerism, more worryingly it also threatens a loss of diversity in the development causes promoted and the magnification of struggles faced by smaller or less powerful NGOs lacking the financial or organisational capacity to attract popular celebrity advocates, who are expensive in time and money and require a strong reputation to attract their interest. Brockington discusses the tendency for celebrity engagement in non-contentious issues and the oversimplification of the messages they convey, as well as the creation of a professional and competitive 'celebrity industry' within the development sector that requires and consumes significant resources: most large charities have a dedicated celebrity liaison post and, while celebrities do not receive fees for their involvement, large resources are consumed in research and communication with them, in publicity and in travel costs.

In her case study of diasporas as a development partner Budabin highlights another danger of the development 'package' sold by NGOs to Western consumers of the humanitarian cause logic, namely its danger of displacing those at the heart of its intended advocacy and activities. Central to tensions in the USA between the South Sudanese diasporas and advocacy networks promoting the plight of Darfurian refugees were differences between the short-term strategies of the network – requiring clear, simple and compelling messages on *behalf of* those they represent – and the long-term development needs and priorities of the diaspora and their populations in their home countries, which are often subject to complex social, economic and political agendas. As she details, the Save Darfur Coalition (SDC) had humanitarian goals of preventing extreme violence against civilians, but stayed clear of the political complexities and antagonisms across different groups that were central to the conflict. This meant it engaged neither with the root causes of the conflict, nor with issues of post-conflict reconstruction and development. While the diaspora could provide the coalition with first-hand testimonies to substantiate its campaign, the political and social cleavages represented in the diaspora, as well as in Darfur, made their fuller inclusion and participation in SDC activities difficult. Again, one cannot argue against the 'developmental good' of SDC's humanitarian aims, which even reached the White House. However, these tensions meant that, ultimately, SDC's activities struggled to align with the needs and interests of the diaspora and displaced populations in Darfur. Requiring durable solutions for peace and development in their homeland, these groups face, above all, political and social issues of power imbalances and inequalities that require a non-violent civil society space in which they can be contested and negotiated at the local level.

Conclusion: the transformative potential of new actors and alliances in development

While we have limited our exploration of the broad set of issues arising from the articles in this collection to the pillars of state, market and civil society, we see important implications emerging from our synthesis. Above all, we argue that the focus of new actors and alliances on strengthening state and market development forces risks the displacement of civil society, its role in holding the state to account and, ultimately, the transformative potential of development. In effect, we see the return to a neoliberal development approach that relegates poverty reduction to an indirect outcome of development activities rather than an explicit objective.

It would, of course, be simplistic to argue that any or all of these actors or alliances offer purely a developmental 'good' or 'bad'. The new insights presented by this diverse collection of papers emphasises that new actors and alliances have the potential to strengthen, weaken or bring new roles to the state, the market and civil society. The articles show that our understanding of their roles and contributions must be deeper and more nuanced, allowing us to identify the factors and processes assisting these actors and alliances to contribute or enhance the developmental good and, in doing so, to avoid their tendency to contribute to rising inequality by putting markets and states first. Finding ways to harness this new diversity so as to reduce, rather than exacerbate, inequalities is a key challenge for the future in a post-MDG world.[37]

One of the limitations of the contributions to this collection is that they do not adequately reflect systematically upon the relative scale and influence of the new developmental actors. We see, for example, the potential of non-traditional donors, whose entrance is slowly and incrementally building state sovereignty in developmental policy – but, importantly, not state capacity or good governance alongside. We also see that philanthrocapitalists such as the Gates Foundation are increasingly shaping development priorities at the global and local levels. At the same time it is important not to overestimate the potential of both as a development alternative, given the scale of their funding *vis-à-vis* traditional donors. While the articles do not explore the additionality that these actors and their activities bring to 'development', or whether they can deliver and implement their development agendas more efficiently than traditional actors, they do give us new insight into their impact and influence on the global development agenda. Looking across these new actors and alliances along the three pillars, a shift away from civil society and back to the state and the market is visible, with private interests moving beyond business to capture space in the development process.

The philanthrocapitalist turn highlights starkly the fact that new actors and alliances in the development sector do not bring any deep structural transformations. Philanthrocapitalists exist only because of their (past and present) capacity to maximise profit in their other activities, regardless of their social, health or environmental impacts. With business viewing poverty as a product of market failure, in their role as potential development actors they recognise only those problems for which the market can produce a solution. This also means that discussions of 'exclusion' tend to be of services that can be extended to poor populations, not of the inequalities in power and voice that keep poor populations systematically socially and politically excluded. Whether the development system will be able to confront issues of poverty and inequality when it caters increasingly to the priorities set by the global elite – which for the large part coincide with the interests of business – remains questionable, despite significant progress made among the global power elite in commitment to poverty.[38]

Crucially we see no new actors or alliances that seek to empower and expand space for domestic civil society or that seek to build or strengthen state–civil society relationships. The new actors' transformative potential, therefore, is vastly limited, because they neither prioritise civil society, nor challenge existing systems, markets and power distributions. National civil society is being bypassed and replaced by a re-imagination of global civil society, in which the market has found ways to link compassion and consumerism, giving the impression that we, as consumers, can facilitate development and poverty reduction through purchasing power. The articles collected here also point towards a worrying trend in the conceptualisation of a polarised global civil society. At one end we have a small number of philanthrocapitalists, celebrities and elites with power and influence but little accountability. At the other end we see a disconnection of a global civil society in the West in which repackaging, branding and marketing of development teaches us not that we have to be a global citizen, but that our priority must be to be a socially responsible consumer. This hollowing out of civil society means that our good deed becomes socially responsible purchasing, risking the elimination of the richness and exchange of ideas, and of volunteering and political engagement with global issues.

Development policy – among development actors and alliances both old and new – must, therefore, differentiate between poverty and inequality and incorporate an understanding of power and discrimination into their understanding of poverty.[39] Only through this can the current emphasis on inclusive economic institutions be met with an equal focus on inclusive *social* institutions. Where institutions derive their legitimacy from is a critical determinant of behaviour, and their strategies and outcomes will vary hugely depending on whether their legitimacy is aligned with the needs and interests of business (as among the actors and alliances presented here) or of marginalised social groups.[40] This leaves us with the central questions of how existing institutions can become more socially inclusive, and of the role of new actors and alliances in strengthening this process. Social and economic institutions often represent opposing interests. While partnerships, self-regulation, voluntarism and welfarism are key to institutional approaches to business and development, societal approaches, for example, draw upon confrontation and resistance, societal control and regulation, the mobilisation of social power and collective agency and local autonomy.[41] These two roads will not automatically align over time; redirecting them towards a greater social development agenda is impossible without creating and supporting space for domestic civil society actors to place checks, balances and demands on state and market forces. While no one mechanism can guarantee economic *and* social developmental outcomes, without a vibrant civil society there is no means through which groups can press for more equitable and inclusive distribution and redistributions.

We can argue, therefore, that the new development actors and alliances discussed in this special issue offer a 'business as usual with a new face' approach rather than a genuine development alternative. They are founded on neoliberal principles that overlook the crucial role of civil society in development. Viewing the problem of 'development' as one of state or market failure, the actors and alliances presented here seek to address and fix these failures. Both the market and the state, however, produce – and rely upon – severe structural inequalities in social relations, power and distribution. Their market-based solutions do not and will not address the root structural causes of poverty and inequality. While the state will remain central to economic growth and social outcomes, achievements in both realms require good governance and a more empowered and effective domestic civil society. With domestic civil society bypassed or ignored by these new actors and alliances, the question we are left with, therefore, is whether any of these new actors and alliances will take up this increasingly important challenge.

Notes on Contributors

Nicola Banks is an ESRC Future Research Leader at the Brooks World Poverty Institute and Institute for Development Policy and Management, University of Manchester. Her research interests include urban poverty and inequality, with a particular focus on young people's experiences of urban poverty.

David Hulme is Executive Director of the Brooks World Poverty Institute, University of Manchester and Chief Executive Officer of the Effective States for Inclusive Development Research Centre. With over 30 years' experience in world-leading research on poverty and development, he has authored and co-authored a number of recent books and papers on global poverty and governance.

Notes

1. Fakuda-Parr and Hulme, "International Norm Dynamics."
2. Hulme, "Poverty in Development Thought."
3. Hulme, *Global Poverty*; Fakuda-Parr and Hulme, "International Norm Dynamics"; and Hulme, "Poverty in Development Thought."
4. Hulme, "Poverty in Development Thought."
5. Thakur, "From the Millennium Development Goals"; and Hulme, "Poverty in Development Thought."
6. Fakuda-Parr and Hulme, "International Norm Dynamics."
7. Hulme, "Poverty in Development Thought."
8. Routley, "Developmental States."
9. Debiel et al., "Global Governance under Pressure."
10. Evans et al., *Bringing the State Back In*; and Leftwich, *States of Development.*
11. Thakur, "From the Millennium Development Goals."
12. Fraser and Whitfield, "The Politics of Aid"; and Hulme and Wilkinson, "Introduction."
13. Fraser and Whitfield, "The Politics of Aid"; and Dreher et al., "Are New Donors Different?"
14. Debiel et al., "Global Governance under Pressure."
15. Dreher et al., "Are New Donors Different?"
16. Bräutigam, "Aid 'with Chinese Characteristics'"; and Dreher et al., "Are New Donors Different?"
17. Fraser and Whitfield, "The Politics of Aid."
18. Dreher et al., "Are New Donors Different?"
19. Acemoglu and Robinson, *Why Nations Fail.*
20. Sen, "The Political Dynamics of Economic Growth."
21. Routley, "Developmental States."
22. Sen, "The Political Dynamics of Economic Growth."
23. Routley, "Developmental States."
24. Leftwich, *Developmental States, Effective States and Poverty Reduction.*
25. Acemoglu and Robinson, *Why Nations Fail*; and Sen, "The Political Dynamics of Economic Growth."
26. The 'Effective States for Inclusive Development' (ESID) research programme at the University of Manchester is seeking to generate knowledge to fill these information gaps.
27. Rogers, "Why Philanthro-policymaking Matters."
28. Bure and Walt, "Global Public–Private Partnerships"; and Edwards, "Gates, Google and the Ending of Global Poverty."
29. Mukherjee-Reed, "Business, Development and Inequality."
30. Edwards, "Gates, Google and the Ending of Global Poverty."
31. Banks and Hulme, "The Role of NGOs and Civil Society."
32. Roodman, *Due Diligence.*
33. Beddoes, "For Richer, For Poorer."
34. Banks and Hulme, "The Role of NGOs and Civil Society."
35. Rogers, "Why Philanthro-policymaking Matters."
36. Mukherjee-Reed, "Business, Development and Inequality."
37. Debiel et al., "Global Governance under Pressure."
38. Bull, "The Global Elite."
39. Dani and de Haan, "Social Policy in a Development Context."
40. Mukherjee-Reed, "Business, Development and Inequality."
41. Ibid.

Bibliography

Acemoglu, D., and J. Robinson. *Why Nations Fail: The Origins of Power, Prosperity and Poverty*. London: Pine Books, 2012.

Banks, N., and D. Hulme. *The Role of ngos and Civil Society in Development and Poverty Reduction*. BWPI Working Paper 171. Manchester: Brooks World Poverty Institute (BWPI), 2012.

Beddoes, Z. M. "For Richer, For Poorer: Special Report on World Economy." *The Economist* October 13, 2012.

Bräutigam, D. "Aid 'with Chinese Characteristics': Chinese Foreign Aid and Development Finance Meet the OECD-DAC Aid Regime." *Journal of International Development* 23 (2011): 752–764.

Bull B. "The Global Elite, Public–Private Partnerships, and Multilateral Governance." In *Global Governance, Poverty and Inequality*, edited by R. Clapp and R. Wilkinson, 209–233. Abingdon: Routledge, 2010.

Bure, K., and G. Walt. "Global Public–Private Partnerships: Part II – What are the Health Issues for Global Governance?" *Bulletin of the World Health Organization* 78, No. 5 (2000): 699–709.

Dani, A., and A. de Haan. "Social Policy in a Development Context: Structural Inequalities and Inclusive Institutions." In *Inclusive States: Social Policy and Structural Inequalities*, edited by A. A. Dani and A. de Haan, 3–37. Washington, DC: World Bank, 2008.

Debiel, T., M. Roth, and C. Ulbert. "Global Governance under Pressure: Trends and Outlook." In *Global Trends 2013: Peace, Development, Environment*, edited by T. Debiel, J. Hippler, M. Roth and C. Ulbert, 9–20. Bonn/Duisberg: Development and Peace Foundation/Institute for Development and Peace, 2012.

Dreher, A., P. Nunnenkamp, and R. Thiele. "Are 'New' Donors Different? Comparing the Allocation of Bilateral Aid between Non-DAC and DAC Donor Countries." *World Development* 39, no. 11 (2011): 1950–1968.

Edwards, M. "Gates, Google, and the Ending of Global Poverty: Philanthrocapitalism and International Development." *Brown Journal of Economic Affairs* 15, no. 2 (2009): 35–42.

Evans, P., D. Rueschemeyer, and T. Skocpol. *Bringing the State Back In*. Cambridge: Cambridge University Press, 1985.

Fraser, A., and L. Whitfield. The Politics of Aid: African Strategies for Dealing with Donors. Global Economic Governance Programme Working Paper 2008-42. Oxford: University College Oxford, 2008.

Fukuda-Parr, S., and D. Hulme. "International Norm Dynamics and the 'End of Poverty': Understanding the Millennium Development Goals." *Global Governance* 17, no. 1 (2011): 17–36.

Hulme, D. *Global Poverty: How Global Governance is Failing the Poor*. London: Routledge, 2010.

Hulme, D. "Poverty in Development Thought: Symptoms or Causes…Synthesis or Uneasy Compromise?". In *Development: Ideas and Experiences*, edited by B. Currie-Elder, R. Kanbur, D. Malone and R. Medhora, forthcoming. Oxford: Oxford University Press, 2014.

Hulme, D., and R. Wilkinson. "Introduction: Moving from MDGs to GDGs – Development Imperatives beyond 2015." In *The Millennium Development Goals and Beyond: Global Development after 2015*, edited by R. Wilkinson and D. Hulme, 1–15. London: Routledge, 2012.

Leftwich, A. *Developmental States, Effective States and Poverty Reduction: The Primacy of Politics*. Geneva: UNRISD Project on Poverty Reduction and Policy Regimes, 2008.

Leftwich, A. *States of Development: On the Primacy of Politics in Development*. Cambridge: Polity Press, 2000.

Mukherjee Reed, A. "Business, Development, and Inequality." In *Global Governance, Poverty and Inequality*, edited by J. Clapp and R. Wilkinson, 235–262. Abingdon: Routledge, 2010.

Rogers, R. "Why Philanthro-Policymaking Matters." *Society* 48, no. 5 (2011): 376–381.

Roodman, D. *Due Diligence: An Impertinent Inquiry into Microfinance*. Washington, DC: Center for Global Development, 2012.

Routley, L. *Developmental States: A Review of the Literature*. ESID Working Paper 3. Manchester: Effective States for Inclusive Development programme, 2012.

Sen, K. "The Political Dynamics of Economic Growth." *World Development* 47 (2012): 71–86.

Thakur, R. "From the Millennium Development Goals to Global Development Goals." In *The Millennium Development Goals and Beyond: Global Development after 2015*, edited by R. Wilkinson and D. Hulme, 54–83. London: Routledge, 2012.

Index

Note: Page numbers in **bold** type refer to **figures**
Page numbers in *italic* type refer to *tables*
Page numbers followed by 'n' refer to notes

For Product Safety Concerns and Information please contact our EU representative GPSR@taylorandfrancis.com Taylor & Francis Verlag GmbH, Kaufingerstraße 24, 80331 München, Germany